Keto Air Fryer Cookbook for Beginners

800 Easy, Healthy & Low Carb Air Frying Recipes to Heal Your Body & Help You Lose Weight on the Ketogenic Diet

Britne Daren

Bronce Mancinea

© Copyright 2020 Britne Daren and Bronce Mancinea - All Rights Reserved.

In no way is it legal to reproduce, duplicate, or transmit any part of this document by either electronic means or in printed format. Recording of this publication is strictly prohibited, and any storage of this material is not allowed unless with written permission from the publisher. All rights reserved.

The information provided herein is stated to be truthful and consistent, in that any liability, regarding inattention or otherwise, by any usage or abuse of any policies, processes, or directions contained within is the solitary and complete responsibility of the recipient reader. Under no circumstances will any legal liability or blame be held against the publisher for any reparation, damages, or monetary loss due to the information herein, either directly or indirectly.

Respective authors own all copyrights not held by the publisher.

Legal Notice:

This book is copyright protected. This is only for personal use. You cannot amend, distribute, sell, use, quote or paraphrase any part of the content within this book without the consent of the author or copyright owner. Legal action will be pursued if this is breached.

Disclaimer Notice:

Please note the information contained within this document is for educational and entertainment purposes only. Every attempt has been made to provide accurate, up-to-date and reliable, complete information. No warranties of any kind are expressed or implied. Readers acknowledge that the author is not engaging in the rendering of legal, financial, medical or professional advice.

By reading this document, the reader agrees that under no circumstances are we responsible for any losses, direct or indirect, which are incurred as a result of the use of information contained within this document, including, but not limited to, errors, omissions, or inaccuracies.

Table of Contents

Introduction 9
Chapter 1: Why Keto Diet? 10
   The Science Behind the Keto Diet 10
Chapter 2: Instant Vortex Air Fryer Basics 11
   What is Instant Vortex Plus Air Fryer? 11
   How Instant Vortex Plus Air Fryer Works?
   11
   Features of Instant Vortex Plus Air Fryer
   11
   Benefits of Using Vortex Air Fryer 12
   Care and Cleaning 13
Chapter 3: Breakfast & Brunch Recipes ... 14
   Breakfast Turkey Sausage 14
   Cheese Egg Quiche 14
   Savory Breakfast Casserole 14
   Egg Chorizo Casserole 15
   Zucchini Spinach Egg Casserole 15
   Sausage Egg Omelet 16
   Ham Cheese Casserole 16
   Cheese Ham Egg Muffins 16
   Crustless Cheese Egg Quiche 17
   Perfect Baked Omelet 17
   Veggie Egg Casserole 17
   Broccoli Casserole 18
   Cauliflower Muffins 18
   Zucchini Bread 19
   Delicious Zucchini Frittata 19
   Egg Bites 20
   Cheesy Zucchini Quiche 20
   Spinach Sausage Egg Muffins 20
   Tomato Kale Egg Muffins 21
   Cheese Pepper Egg Bake 21
   Healthy Breakfast Donuts 21
   Almond Broccoli Muffins 22
   Simple & Easy Breakfast Quiche 22
   Italian Breakfast Frittata 23
   Parmesan Zucchini Frittata 23
   Fresh Herb Egg Cups 23
   Bake Cheese Omelet 24
   Feta Pepper Egg Muffins 24
   Sun-dried Tomatoes Egg Cups 24
   Vanilla Raspberry Muffins 25
   Mushroom Kale Egg Cups 25
   Breakfast Bake Egg 26
   Sun-dried Tomatoes Kale Egg Cups 26
   Easy Chicken Egg Cups 26
   Roasted Pepper Egg Cups 27
   Easy Breakfast Sausage 27
   Spinach Bacon Egg Bake 27
   Zucchini Breakfast Casserole 28
   Egg Casserole 28
   Basil Cheese Zucchini Quiche 29
   Spinach Egg Bake 29
   Asparagus Quiche 30
   Spinach Pepper Breakfast Egg Cups ... 30
   Moist Pumpkin Muffins 30
   Cheddar Cheese Ham Quiche 31
   Healthy Zucchini Gratin 31
   Coconut Jalapeno Muffins 32
   Artichoke Quiche 32
   Breakfast Vegetable Quiche 32
   Tomato Feta Frittata 33
Chapter 4: Poultry Recipes 34
   Healthy Chicken Tenders 34
   Sweet & Tangy Chicken 34
   Parmesan Chicken Breast 35
   Garlic Herb Turkey Breast 35
   Simple & Juicy Chicken Breasts 35
   Cauliflower Chicken Casserole 36
   Flavorful Greek Chicken 36
   Simple Baked Chicken Breast 37
   Baked Chicken Thighs 37
   Tasty Chicken Wings 37
   Italian Turkey Tenderloin 38
   Pesto Parmesan Chicken 38
   Lemon Chicken Breasts 38
   Spicy Chicken Wings 39
   Meatballs 39
   Hot Chicken Wings 39
   Fajita Chicken 40

Meatballs	40
Herb Wings	40
Rosemary Garlic Chicken	41
Easy Cajun Chicken Breasts	41
Veggie Turkey Breast	41
Flavorful Asian Chicken Thighs	42
Mustard Chicken Drumsticks	42
Meatballs	43
Burger Patties	43
Chicken Burgers	43
Italian Chicken	44
Tasty Chicken Tenders	44
Air Fry Chicken Drumsticks	44
Jerk Chicken	45
Garlic Ranch Chicken Wings	45
Chicken Fritters	45
Tandoori Chicken	46
Chicken Nuggets	46
Ranch Chicken Wings	47
Garlic Butter Wings	47
Chicken Vegetable Burger Patties	47
Meatballs	48
Jalapeno Meatballs	48
Chicken Skewers	49
Meatballs	49
Tasty Chicken Tenders	49
Baked Feta Dill Chicken	50
Thyme Sage Turkey Breast	50
Meatballs	50
Pecan Mustard Chicken Tenders	51
Flavorful Spiced Chicken	51
Easy Lemon Chicken	52
Persian Kabab	52
Whole Chicken	52
Asian Chicken Wings	53
Cheese Fajita Chicken	53
Spicy Chicken Wings	53
Cheesy Chicken Casserole	54
Chicken Sun-dried Tomatoes & Mushrooms	54
Meatloaf	55
BBQ Meatloaf	55

Chicken Pepper Zucchini Casserole	55
Delicious Chicken Fajita Casserole	56
Chapter 5: Meat Recipes	**57**
Pecan Dijon Pork Chops	57
Simple & Juicy Steak	57
Marinated Ribeye Steaks	57
Pork Chop Fries	58
Pork Kebabs	58
Meatballs	59
Feta Cheese Meatballs	59
Asian Meatballs	59
Spicy Pork Patties	60
Herb Pork Chops	60
Spicy Parmesan Pork Chops	60
Moist Pork Chops	61
Air Fried Pork Bites	61
Meatballs	61
Beef Kebabs	62
Steak Tips	62
Rosemary Beef Tips	63
Ranch Patties	63
Sirloin Steak	63
Easy Beef Kebabs	64
Steak & Mushrooms	64
Meatballs	64
Air Fryer Beef Fajitas	65
Flavorful Burger Patties	65
Meatballs	65
Juicy Pork Tenderloin	66
Meatloaf	66
Baked Beef & Broccoli	67
Lemon Pepper Pork	67
Meatballs	67
Meatloaf	68
Spiced Pork Tenderloin	68
Stuffed Pork Chops	69
Spicy Pork Chops	69
Meatballs	69
Air Fryer Lamb Chops	70
Lemon Herb Lamb Chops	70
Breaded Pork Chops	70
Cajun Herb Pork Chops	71

Creole Seasoned Pork Chops	71
Thai Pork Chops	72
Coconut Pork Chops	72
Savory Dash Seasoned Pork Chops	72
Jerk Pork Cubes	73
Spicy Asian Lamb	73
Meatballs	73
Smokey Steaks	74
Meatloaf	74
Chipotle Steak	74
Simple Beef Kabab	75
Meatballs	75
Baked Lamb Chops	76
Spicy Pork Tenderloin	76
Lemon Garlic Sirloin Steak	76
Meatloaf	77
Meatloaf	77
Garlic Thyme Lamb Chops	78
Flavorful Air Fryer Kabab	78
Meatballs	78
Delicious Herb Beef Patties	79
Baked Lamb Patties	79
Roasted Sirloin Steak	79
Greek Beef Casserole	80
Basil Cheese Lamb Patties	80
Mini Meatloaf	81
Air Fryer Stew Meat	81
Flavorful Beef Satay	81
Stuffed Bell Peppers	82
Steak Fajitas	82
Ranch Pork Chops	83
Buttery Steak Bites	83
Taco Stuffed Peppers	83
Meatballs	84
Greek Meatballs	84
Breaded Pork Chops	84
Pecan Crusted Pork Chops	85
Garlicky Pork Chops	85
Meatballs	85
Asian Pork Steak	86
Dijon Pork Chops	86

Chapter 6: Vegetable Recipes 87

Crisp & Crunchy Asparagus	87
Balsamic Brussels Sprouts	87
Healthy Roasted Vegetables	87
Parmesan Zucchini Noodles	88
Rosemary Basil Mushrooms	88
Baked Brussels Sprouts	89
Old Bay Cauliflower Florets	89
Rosemary Mushrooms	89
Air Fry Bell Peppers	90
Asian Green Beans	90
Mushrooms Cauliflower Roast	90
Roasted Cauliflower Cherry Tomatoes	91
Healthy Roasted Broccoli	91
Air Fry Baby Carrots	91
Crispy Brussels Sprouts	92
Broccoli Fritters	92
Baked Artichoke Hearts	92
Roasted Veggies	93
Lemon Garlic Cauliflower	93
Delicious Ratatouille	93
Air Fry Parmesan Tomatoes	94
Spiced Green Beans	94
Roasted Squash	94
Parmesan Baked Zucchini	95
Parmesan Eggplant Zucchini	95
Cheese Broccoli Stuffed Pepper	96
Creamy Spinach	96
Beans with Mushrooms	97
Broccoli Nuggets	97
Tasty Baked Cauliflower	97
Cauliflower Tomato Rice	98
Squash Noodles	98
Cheesy Zucchini Noodles	99
Roasted Carrots	99
Cheese Baked Broccoli	99
Cheddar Cheese Broccoli	100
Stuffed Bell Peppers	100
Baked Artichoke Spinach	101
Delicious Zucchini Casserole	101
Cheesy Baked Zoodle	102
Parmesan Squash Casserole	102
Roasted Cauliflower and Broccoli	102

- Pecan Green Bean Casserole 103
- Delicious Spaghetti Squash 103
- Brussels Sprouts and Broccoli 104
- Cauliflower Casserole 104
- Basil Eggplant Casserole 104
- Air Fry Green Beans 105
- Spicy Okra 105
- Lemon Green Beans 105
- Air Fry Asparagus 106
- Mixed Vegetables 106
- Crisp Brussels Sprouts 106
- Jicama & Green Beans 107
- Tasty Cauliflower Rice 107
- Squash & Zucchini 108
- Spinach Squares 108
- Air Fried Cabbage 108
- Vegetable Kebabs 109

Chapter 7: Seafood Recipes 110
- Old Bay Shrimp 110
- Crunchy Fish Sticks 110
- Garlic Butter Fish Fillets 110
- Parmesan Shrimp 111
- Flavorful Tuna Steaks 111
- Baked Tilapia 111
- Baked Parmesan Tilapia 112
- Pecan Crusted Fish Fillets 112
- Bagel Crust Fish Fillets 113
- Moist & Juicy Baked Cod 113
- Baked Salmon Patties 113
- Easy Air Fryer Scallops 114
- Pesto Scallops 114
- Mayo Cheese Crust Salmon 115
- Juicy Baked Halibut 115
- Delicious Crab Cakes 115
- Simple Salmon Patties 116
- Easy Tuna Patties 116
- Baked Mahi Mahi 117
- Baked Basa 117
- Parmesan Cod 117
- Old Bay Baked Cod 118
- Baked Mayo Cod 118
- Blackened Tilapia 119
- Lemon Pepper Tilapia 119
- Garlic Butter Baked Shrimp 119
- Cajun Salmon Cakes 120
- Cajun Catfish Fillets 120
- Old Bay Shrimp 121
- Lemon Garlic Shrimp 121
- Healthy Lemon Pepper Shrimp 121
- Cod with Vegetables 122
- Baked Mahi-Mahi 122
- Healthy Swordfish Fillets 122
- Flavorful Prawns 123
- Air Fry Fish Patties 123
- Air Fry Blackened Shrimp 124
- Delicious Shrimp Fajitas 124
- Jumbo Shrimp 124
- Tasty Crab Patties 125
- Lemon Pepper White Fish 125
- Cajun Scallops 125
- Italian Tilapia Fillets 126
- Greek Baked Salmon 126
- Greek Style Fish Fillets 126
- White Fish Fillet with Roasted Pepper 127
- Roasted Fish Fillets 127
- Rosemary Basil Salmon 127
- Shrimp with Cherry Tomatoes 128
- Tomato Basil Fish Fillets 128
- Cod with Asparagus 129
- Baked Salmon & Carrots 129
- Pesto Fish Fillets 129
- Baked Shrimp Scampi 130
- Mediterranean Salmon 130
- Tangy Salmon 130
- Salsa Fish Fillets 131
- Cheese Herb Salmon 131
- Easy Bacon Shrimp 132
- Crispy Coconut Shrimp 132

Chapter 8: Snacks & Appetizers 133
- Green Bean Fries 133
- Quick & Delicious Biscuits 133
- Easy Sausage Balls 133
- Tasty Zucchini Chips 134

Healthy Onion Rings 134
Perfect Cauliflower Tots 135
Crispy Parmesan Asparagus Fries 135
Crispy Air Fried Pickles 136
Crab Stuffed Jalapenos 136
Asiago Asparagus Fries 136
Chicken Stuffed Poblanos 137
Crispy Air Fried Zucchini 137
Thai Meatballs 138
Cheese Balls 138
Cheese Herb Zucchini 138
Meatballs 139
Chicken Meatballs 139
Delicious Spinach Dip 140
Garlic Dip 140
Cauliflower Hummus 140
Crispy Tofu 141
Spicy Mixed Nuts 141
Air Fried Walnuts 141
Tasty Cauliflower Bites 142
Meatballs 142
Parmesan Brussels Sprouts 142
Crab Dip 143
Stuffed Chicken Jalapenos 143
Broccoli Cheese Balls 144
Spinach Sausage Balls 144
Pepperoni Chips 144
Crispy Zucchini Fries 145
Simple Parmesan Zucchini Bites 145
Cheesy Jalapeno Poppers 146
Yummy Chicken Dip 146
Roasted Cashew 146
Roasted Cauliflower Florets 147
Tasty Zucchini Chips 147
Healthy Carrots Chips 147
Lamb Patties 148
Herb Olives 148
Buffalo Chicken Dip 148
Healthy Mixed Nuts 149
Ricotta Dip 149
Chicken Cheese Dip 150
Spicy Artichoke Dip 150

Crispy Cauliflower Florets 150
Fresh Herb Mushrooms 151
Goat Cheese Dip 151
Zucchini Dill Dip 151
Meatballs 152
Mexican Cheese Dip 152
Cheddar Cheese Garlic Dip 152
Air Fry Pecans 153
Air Fry Taro Fries 153
Stuffed Mushrooms 153
Crispy Zucchini Chips 154
Roasted Nuts 154
Cinnamon Apple Chips 155
Cheese Pesto Jalapeno Poppers 155

Chapter 9: Dehydrated Recipes 156
Spicy Cauliflower Popcorn 156
Carrot Cake Cookies 156
Easy Kiwi Chips 156
Sun-Dried Tomatoes 157
Crunchy Broccoli Chips 157
Easy Apple Chips 157
Cabbage Chips 158
Green Bean Chips 158
Healthy Cucumber Chips 158
Snap Pea Chips 159
Beet Chips 159
Crunchy Kale Chips 159
Tasty Tomato Chips 160
Dehydrated Okra 160
Strawberry Chips 160
Lemon Slices 160
Smoky Eggplant Chips 161
Eggplant Jerky 161
Pear Chips 162
Curried Apple Chips 162
Broccoli Bites 162
Delicious Cauliflower Popcorn 163
Chili Lime Cauliflower Popcorn 163
Healthy Dehydrated Almonds 163
Radish Chips 164
Orange Slices 164
Dehydrated Bell Peppers 164

Dried Raspberries 164
Brussels Sprout Chips 165
Dehydrated Carrot Slices 165
Dried Apricots 165
Coconut Peanut Butter Balls 165
Parmesan Tomato Chips 166
Spicy Rosemary Almonds 166
Dehydrated Raspberries 166
Lemon Avocado Chips 167
Squash Chips 167
Smokey Tofu Jerky 167
Lemon Chicken Jerky 168
Parmesan Zucchini Chips 168

Chapter 10: Desserts Recipes 169
Protein Donut Balls 169
Delicious Brownie Cupcake 169
Vanilla Cranberry Muffins 169
Blueberry Almond Muffins 170
Lemon Cupcakes 170
Almond Lemon Bars 171
Egg Custard 171
Coconut Pumpkin Custard 171
Vanilla Peanut Butter Cookies 172
Pumpkin Cookies 172
Almond Pecan Cookies 173
Vanilla Coconut Cake 173
Choco Almond Cake 173
Butter Cake 174

Walnut Carrot Cake 174
Chocolate Brownies 175
Walnut Muffins 175
Cinnamon Strawberry Muffins 176
Cream Cheese Cupcakes 176
Quick Brownie 176
Tasty Pumpkin Muffins 177
Cappuccino Cupcakes 177
Lemon Blueberry Muffins 177
Almond Butter Brownies 178
Choco Butter Brownie 178
Almond Cake 179
Ricotta Cake 179
Almond Brownie Bombs 179
Cinnamon Nut Muffins 180
Easy Berry Muffins 180
Chocolate Cheese Brownies 181
Chocolate Macaroon 181
Easy Chocolate Cake 182
Cheesecake Muffins 182
Choco Protein Brownie 182
Vanilla Butter Cookies 183
Sliced Apples 183
Orange Muffins 183
Raspberry Cobbler 184
Brownie Bites 184

Chapter 11: 30-Day Meal Plan 185
Conclusion 187

Introduction

The advanced technology makes you're cooking smart with their smart functions. In this book, I have introduced you with a healthy and nutritious diet plan is a combination of healthy air fryer cooking methods. The book contains information about the keto diet with healthier keto recipes. Keto is basically a low carb high fat diet that allows a moderate amount of protein intake during the diet. Most of the researches are done over keto diet and finally, it proves that keto diet is not only staying you fit and healthy but also useful to cure certain medical conditions like Parkinson's, Alzheimer's, type-2 diabetes, high blood pressure, epilepsy, some cancers, and heart-related diseases.

The book contains different types of healthy keto recipes from breakfast to desserts. All the recipes are made into instant vortex plus 6 in 1 air fryer. An instant vortex air fryer is equipped with advanced technology and comes with 6 built-in smart functions like Air fry, bake, broil. Roast, reheat and dehydrate, etc. Using these functions, you can easily cook your food without worrying temperature and time setting. The main advantage of using instant vortex plus air fryer is that it requires very little oil to fry your favorite French fries. It makes your fried food crisp from outside and tender from inside. You can make fried chicken, doughnuts, shrimps, potato chips, French fries, and more.

The recipes written in this book are unique and selected from globally inspired dishes. All the recipes are written into an easily understandable form with its exact cooking and preparation time. You can find exact nutritional values under each recipe; this will help you to keep the track of how many calories you have consumed every day. Daily calorie count will help to stay your body into the state of ketosis. The 30 days meal plan helps you to achieve your goal. There are various types of books available on this topic, thanks for choosing my book. I hope you have enjoyed your favorite recipes from this book and get success in your keto journey.

Chapter 1: Why Keto Diet?

Keto diet is one of the most effective diet plans compare to other diets. It gives long term health benefits and also helps to cure various medical conditions like Alzheimer's, Parkinson's, metabolic syndromes, high blood pressure, epilepsy conditions, and obesity. Keto diet is basically a low carb and high fat diet forces your body to burn fats for energy instead of glucose. Due to keto diet results, most of the peoples like movie stars, sportspersons, women's and health-conscious peoples follow a keto diet plan to maintain their body weight and stamina.

The keto diet comes with various health benefits such as rapid weight loss. This is one of the major benefits noticed during the keto diet and it gives long term weight loss benefits. When you are on a keto diet your body used ketones for energy instead of glucose. These ketones are one of the best energy sources for our brain it full fills 70 percent of our brain energy needs and also improves our brain functions. The keto diet also helps to improve the level of HDL (good cholesterol) and LDL (bad cholesterol). It also helps to increase blood circulation by 75 percent and heart efficiency by 30 percent. Due to anti-aging properties, it also helps to improve your life span.

The Science Behind the Keto Diet

The main focus of the keto diet is to push you're your body into the state of ketosis. In this stage, your body uses ketones as fuel instead of glucose. Basically, our body uses glucose (carb) as a primary source of energy. Our body converts extra glucose into the form of glycogen. When the glycogen level is increased it is converted into body fats and stored them into liver and muscle. Keto diet is one of the low carb diets, due to low carb consumption our body pushes itself into the state of ketosis. In ketosis state, our body breaks down fats for energy. During this process, fatty acids are released from stored fats and our liver converted it into ketones. To stay our body into ketosis just cut down the carbohydrates from the daily diet. Once our body has no source of carb then it automatically shifts into ketosis because our brain needs glucose(carb) or ketones for daily energy needs.

Chapter 2: Instant Vortex Air Fryer Basics

What is Instant Vortex Plus Air Fryer?

Instant pot vortex plus air fryer is one of the latest and advanced cooking appliances that require very less or no oil to air fryer your food without compromising taste and texture this will make instant vortex plus air fryer is a unique appliance. Instant pot vortex air fryer is a multifunctional 6 in 1 cooking appliance that comes with 6 built-in smart programs. It works as a multi-cooker appliance that performs various operations like it air fry you're crispy French fries, roasts your favorite chicken or meat, broils your fish or meat, bakes a delicious cake, and cookies, dehydrates fruit slices and you can also reheat your food.

Instant vortex plus air fryer is used to cook your food with hot air circulation technology. It blows very hot air into the vortex air fryer food chamber to cook your food fast and evenly from all sides. It is large enough to fry 2 pounds of French fries or you can roast 4 pounds of chicken at a time. Using instant vortex air fryer, you can enjoy your favorite deep-fried food at home within less time.

How Instant Vortex Plus Air Fryer Works?

Instant vortex plus air fryer is a versatile cooking appliance consumes 1500 watt and produces maximum heat of 400° F. The vortex air fryer plus cooks your food by circulating very hot air into food basket to cook your food evenly from all sides. You can fry a bowl of French fries by just adding 1 tbsp of oil and your vortex air fryer makes your French fries crisp from outside and tender from inside.

Instant vortex air fryer plus comes with a big digital touch panel display which shows you cooking time and temperature. Vortex air fryer cooking basket is easily detachable from the main unit. You just need to remove the food basket from the main unit and add food into the basket and place it into its original position. Select the appropriate program and press the start button. If food requires turning or flipping then vortex air fryer beeps for ten seconds and after that, it starts remaining cooking process automatically.

Features of Instant Vortex Plus Air Fryer

Instant vortex air fryer plus are easy to operate and comes with six smart functions

1. Display Panel

The instant vortex air fryer comes with a digital display panel that shows the current cooking time and cooking temperature. It also shows the error messages remainders like if your air fryer is on standby mode then display reads OFF.

2. Smart Programs

Smart programs are preset functions where you never need to worry about time and temperature both are preset. You can also customize these settings as per your recipe needs. These 6 smart functions are

- Air Fry: This function allows you to fry your food within very less oil or no oil. You can fry crispy French fries, chicken nuggets, cauliflower wings, and more with this function. It makes your food crisp from outside and tender from inside.
- Bake: If you are cake and cookies lover then this function is for you. Bake your favorite cake and cookies within very less time.
- Roast: To roast your favorite chicken, meat, and vegetables you can use this function.
- Broil: This function is used with your burger or melting cheese on the top of nachos, French onion, and more.

- **Reheat:** This function helps to reheat your leftover food or frozen food within very less time.
- **Dehydrate:** This function is used to dry your favorite fruit slices, jerky, veggies, and more.

3. Other functions
   - **Time:** This function is used to set appropriate time to require for your recipe.
   - **Temp:** This function is used to adjust the appropriate temperature settings.
   - **Start:** This function allows starting the cooking program.
   - **Cancel:** This function is used to pause or cancel the current cooking process.

4. Dial

The dial is given to adjust the time and temperature settings while cooking food. You can just rotate the dial to choose appropriate cooking time and temperature. When you press the dial it also wakes up the display panel.

Benefits of Using Vortex Air Fryer

The vortex air fryer comes with various benefits some of them are as follows

1. Save cooking time

Amazing cooking gadget for those people who have a busy schedule. Your vortex air fryer runs on hot air circulation technology. It blows very hot air (400° F) into the cooking chamber. This will help to cook your food within very less time.

2. Less oil and fats require cooking

Compare to other traditional deep-frying cooking methods vortex air fryer consumes less or no oil to cook your favourite dishes. Instead of the deep-frying method, your air fryer requires just 15 % of oil to cook your food. The vortex air fryer cuts down the fats, calories from your food without compromising the taste and texture of your food.

3. Multi-Tasking

Your vortex air fryer is one of the multitasking cooking appliances that perform the operations of air frying, broiling, baking, reheating, roasting, and dehydrating in a single appliance. You never need to buy a separate appliance to perform these tasks, your vortex air fryer is capable to handle all the tasks.

4. Smart Functions

Vortex air fryer is 6 in 1 cooking appliance preloaded with 6 smart functions. These smart functions include Air fry, Bake, Roast, Reheat, Broil and Dehydrate. While using these functions you never need to worry about time and temperature setting all are preset. You can also customize your settings as per your recipe needs.

5. Healthy Cooking method

When we deep-fried food most of the essential vitamins and nutrients are destroyed during this process and bad fats are added into your food. Your vortex air fryer requires just 15 % of oil to cook your food by circulating hot air around the food basket to cook your food evenly. This will help to protect vitamins and nutrients without adding bad fats. You can enjoy your food with a healthy cooking method.

6. Safe to use

Compare to traditional deep-frying method vortex air fryer is safe to use because it is close to all side so there is no risk of splatter hot oil over your skin.

Care and Cleaning

Always remember to clean your instant vortex plus air fryer after each use

1. Before starting the cleaning, process unplug your air fryer and let it cool at room temperature.
2. Avoid using scouring pads, powders, and hashing chemical detergents they may damage the coating of the instant pot.
3. Remove the food basket from the main unit. Use cloth or sponge and solution of warm water you can also use dish soap to clean the air fryer basket. Do not put your air fryer basket into the dishwasher.
4. Remove the cooking tray and clean it with the help of a warm water solution. The cooking tray is dishwasher safe so you can clean it into the dishwasher. Do not use metal cleaning utensils because the cooking tray has a non-stick coating.
5. While cleaning the cooking chamber use vinegar and baking soda mixture to clean the food residue and grease. Take a damp cloth and clean the cooking chamber.
6. Take a clean damp cloth to clean the exterior body of the air fryer wipe dry.
7. After clean and dry all pats, place the cooking tray into the air fryer basket and put the basket into its original position. Now your instant vortex air fryer is ready for next use.

Chapter 3: Breakfast & Brunch Recipes

Breakfast Turkey Sausage

Preparation Time: 10 minutes; Cooking Time: 10 minutes; Serve: 8
Ingredients:
- 2 lbs ground turkey
- 1 tsp dried thyme
- 1 tsp paprika
- 2 tsp garlic powder
- 2 tsp dry sage
- 2 tsp fennel seeds
- 1 tsp sea salt

Directions:
1. Add ground meat and remaining ingredients into the mixing bowl and mix until well combined.
2. Take 2-3 tablespoon of meat mixture and flatten into patties.
3. Place the cooking tray in the air fryer basket.
4. Select Air Fry mode.
5. Set time to 10 minutes and temperature 370 F then press START.
6. The air fryer display will prompt you to ADD FOOD once the temperature is reached then place sausage patties in the air fryer basket.
7. Serve and enjoy.

Nutritional Value (Amount per Serving):
Calories 227; Fat 12.6 g; Carbohydrates 1.1 g; Sugar 0.2 g; Protein 31.3 g; Cholesterol 116 mg

Cheese Egg Quiche

Preparation Time: 10 minutes; Cooking Time: 45 minutes; Serve: 6
Ingredients:
- 8 eggs
- 6 oz cheddar cheese, shredded
- 5 tbsp butter, melted
- 6 oz cream cheese

Directions:
1. Add eggs, cheese, butter, and cream cheese into the mixing bowl and blend using a hand mixer until well combined.
2. Pour egg mixture into the greased pie dish. Cover dish with foil.
3. Select Bake mode.
4. Set time to 45 minutes and temperature 325 F then press START.
5. The air fryer display will prompt you to ADD FOOD once the temperature is reached then place the pie dish in the air fryer basket.
6. Serve and enjoy.

Nutritional Value (Amount per Serving):
Calories 382; Fat 34.7 g; Carbohydrates 1.6 g; Sugar 0.7 g; Protein 16.7 g; Cholesterol 305 mg

Savory Breakfast Casserole

Preparation Time: 10 minutes; Cooking Time: 45 minutes; Serve: 8
Ingredients:
- 12 eggs
- 1 tbsp hot sauce
- 3/4 cup heavy whipping cream
- 2 cups cheddar cheese, shredded
- 12 oz breakfast sausage
- Pepper
- Salt

Directions:
1. Heat large pan over medium-high heat.
2. Add sausage in a pan and cook for 5-7 minutes or until meat is no longer pink.
3. Add cooked sausage in a 9*13-inch baking dish.

4. In a large bowl, whisk eggs with hot sauce, cream, cheese, pepper, and salt.
5. Pour egg mixture over sausage in baking dish. Cover dish with foil.
6. Select Bake mode.
7. Set time to 40 minutes and temperature 350 F then press START.
8. The air fryer display will prompt you to ADD FOOD once the temperature is reached then place the baking dish in the air fryer basket.
9. Serve and enjoy.

Nutritional Value (Amount per Serving):
Calories 391; Fat 32.2 g; Carbohydrates 1.2 g; Sugar 0.7 g; Protein 23.8 g; Cholesterol 326 mg

Egg Chorizo Casserole

Preparation Time: 10 minutes; Cooking Time: 55 minutes; Serve: 6

Ingredients:
- 8 eggs
- 1 cup cheddar cheese, shredded
- 1 bell pepper, diced
- 4 oz can green chiles, drained and chopped
- 3/4 cup heavy cream
- 1/2 lb ground chorizo sausage
- 1/4 tsp pepper
- 1/2 tsp salt

Directions:
1. Cook chorizo in a pan over medium-high heat for 8 minutes or until browned.
2. In a bowl, whisk eggs with cream, pepper, and salt. Stir in cooked chorizo, cheese, bell pepper, and green chiles.
3. Pour egg mixture into the greased baking dish. Cover dish with foil.
4. Select Bake mode.
5. Set time to 40 minutes and temperature 350 F then press START.
6. The air fryer display will prompt you to ADD FOOD once the temperature is reached then place the baking dish in the air fryer basket.
7. Serve and enjoy.

Nutritional Value (Amount per Serving):
Calories 356; Fat 29.6 g; Carbohydrates 5.5 g; Sugar 2.7 g; Protein 17.5 g; Cholesterol 282 mg

Zucchini Spinach Egg Casserole

Preparation Time: 10 minutes; Cooking Time: 30 minutes; Serve: 8

Ingredients:
- 10 eggs
- 1/4 cup goat cheese, crumbled
- 4 cherry tomatoes, cut in half
- 1/3 cup cheddar cheese, grated
- 1/3 cup ham, chopped
- 1 small zucchini, sliced
- 1/2 cup spinach
- 2/3 cup heavy cream
- Pepper
- Salt

Directions:
1. In a bowl, whisk eggs with cream, pepper, and salt. Stir in cheddar cheese, ham, zucchini, and spinach.
2. Pour egg mixture into the greased baking dish. Top with goat cheese and cherry tomatoes. Cover dish with foil.
3. Select Bake mode.
4. Set time to 30 minutes and temperature 350 F then press START.
5. The air fryer display will prompt you to ADD FOOD once the temperature is reached then place the baking dish in the air fryer basket.
6. Serve and enjoy.

Nutritional Value (Amount per Serving):

Calories 209; Fat 15.7 g; Carbohydrates 4.2 g; Sugar 2.5 g; Protein 13.6 g; Cholesterol 240 mg

Sausage Egg Omelet

Preparation Time: 10 minutes; Cooking Time: 30 minutes; Serve: 12

Ingredients:
- 7 eggs
- 1 lb breakfast sausage
- 1 tsp mustard
- 3/4 cup heavy whipping cream
- 1/4 onion, chopped
- 2 cups cheddar cheese, shredded
- 1/2 bell pepper, chopped
- 1/4 tsp pepper
- 1/2 tsp salt

Directions:
1. Add sausage into the pan and cook until brown, add onion and bell pepper and cook for 2 minutes.
2. In a bowl, whisk eggs with 1 1/2 cups cheddar cheese, cream, mustard, pepper, and salt. Stir in sausage mixture.
3. Pour egg mixture into the greased 9*13-inch baking dish. Top with remaining cheese. Cover dish with foil.
4. Select Bake mode.
5. Set time to 20 minutes and temperature 350 F then press START.
6. The air fryer display will prompt you to ADD FOOD once the temperature is reached then place the baking dish in the air fryer basket.
7. Serve and enjoy.

Nutritional Value (Amount per Serving):
Calories 271; Fat 22.4 g; Carbohydrates 1.4 g; Sugar 0.7 g; Protein 15.6 g; Cholesterol 157 mg

Ham Cheese Casserole

Preparation Time: 10 minutes; Cooking Time: 35 minutes; Serve: 12

Ingredients:
- 12 eggs
- 1/2 cup cheddar cheese, shredded
- 4 oz cream cheese, cubed
- 2 cups ham, diced
- 1 cup heavy cream
- 1/4 tsp pepper
- 1/4 tsp salt

Directions:
1. In a large bowl, whisk eggs with cream, pepper, and salt. Stir in cheddar cheese, cream cheese, and ham.
2. Pour egg mixture into the greased 9*13-inch baking dish. Cover dish with foil.
3. Select Bake mode.
4. Set time to 35 minutes and temperature 350 F then press START.
5. The air fryer display will prompt you to ADD FOOD once the temperature is reached then place the baking dish in the air fryer basket.
6. Serve and enjoy.

Nutritional Value (Amount per Serving):
Calories 186; Fat 14.9 g; Carbohydrates 1.8 g; Sugar 0.4 g; Protein 11.4 g; Cholesterol 206 mg

Cheese Ham Egg Muffins

Preparation Time: 10 minutes; Cooking Time: 20 minutes; Serve: 12

Ingredients:
- 12 eggs
- 1 3/4 cup cheddar cheese, shredded
- 2 cups ham, diced
- 1 tsp garlic, minced
- 1/2 pepper
- 1/2 tsp salt

Directions:
1. In a bowl, whisk eggs with garlic, pepper, and salt. Stir in cheddar cheese and ham.
2. Pour egg mixture into the silicone muffin molds.
3. Select Bake mode.
4. Set time to 20 minutes and temperature 375 F then press START.
5. The air fryer display will prompt you to ADD FOOD once the temperature is reached then place muffin molds in the air fryer basket.
6. Serve and enjoy.

Nutritional Value (Amount per Serving):
Calories 167; Fat 11.8 g; Carbohydrates 1.6 g; Sugar 0.4 g; Protein 13.4 g; Cholesterol 194 mg

Crustless Cheese Egg Quiche

Preparation Time: 10 minutes; Cooking Time: 45 minutes; Serve: 6

Ingredients:
- 12 eggs
- 12 tbsp butter, melted
- 4 oz cream cheese, softened
- 8 oz cheddar cheese, grated
- Pepper
- Salt

Directions:
1. In a bowl, whisk eggs with butter, cream cheese, half cheddar cheese, pepper, and salt.
2. Pour egg mixture into the greased 9.5-inch pie pan. Sprinkle remaining cheese on top. Cover dish with foil.
3. Select Bake mode.
4. Set time to 45 minutes and temperature 325 F then press START.
5. The air fryer display will prompt you to ADD FOOD once the temperature is reached then place the pie pan in the air fryer basket.
6. Serve and enjoy.

Nutritional Value (Amount per Serving):
Calories 548; Fat 50.9 g; Carbohydrates 1.7 g; Sugar 0.9 g; Protein 22.2 g; Cholesterol 449 mg

Perfect Baked Omelet

Preparation Time: 10 minutes; Cooking Time: 45 minutes; Serve: 6

Ingredients:
- 8 eggs
- 1 cup bell pepper, chopped
- 1/2 cup onion, chopped
- 1/2 cup cheddar cheese, shredded
- 6 oz cooked ham, diced
- 1 cup unsweetened almond milk
- 1/2 tsp salt

Directions:
1. In a bowl, whisk eggs with milk and salt. Stir in bell pepper, onion, cheese, and ham.
2. Pour egg mixture into the greased 8-inch baking dish.
3. Select Bake mode.
4. Set time to 45 minutes and temperature 350 F then press START.
5. The air fryer display will prompt you to ADD FOOD once the temperature is reached then place the baking dish in the air fryer basket.
6. Serve and enjoy.

Nutritional Value (Amount per Serving):
Calories 185; Fat 12 g; Carbohydrates 4.4 g; Sugar 1.9 g; Protein 14.9 g; Cholesterol 244 mg

Veggie Egg Casserole

Preparation Time: 10 minutes; Cooking Time: 30 minutes; Serve: 10

Ingredients:

- 12 eggs, lightly beaten
- 1 cup cheddar cheese, shredded
- 2 bell pepper, diced
- 1 tsp garlic, minced
- 1 cup onion, chopped
- 5 bacon slices, cooked and chopped
- 1 tbsp olive oil
- 1/4 tsp pepper
- 1/2 tsp sea salt

Directions:
1. Heat oil in a pan over medium heat.
2. Add garlic and onion in a pan and sauté until onion is softened.
3. In a bowl, whisk eggs with pepper and salt. Stir in cheddar cheese, bell pepper, bacon, garlic, and onion.
4. Pour egg mixture into the greased 9*13-inch baking dish. Cover dish with foil.
5. Select Bake mode.
6. Set time to 30 minutes and temperature 350 F then press START.
7. The air fryer display will prompt you to ADD FOOD once the temperature is reached then place the baking dish in the air fryer basket.
8. Serve and enjoy.

Nutritional Value (Amount per Serving):
Calories 197; Fat 14.4 g; Carbohydrates 3.7 g; Sugar 2.2 g; Protein 13.4 g; Cholesterol 219 mg

Broccoli Casserole

Preparation Time: 10 minutes; Cooking Time: 20 minutes; Serve: 4
Ingredients:
- 2 cups broccoli florets, chopped
- 1 cup cheddar cheese, grated
- 1/2 cup sour cream
- 1/2 cup heavy cream
- Pepper
- Salt

Directions:
1. In a bowl, whisk together heavy cream, sour cream, 1/2 cheddar cheese, pepper, and salt.
2. Add broccoli florets into the baking dish. Pour heavy cream mixture over broccoli. Top with remaining cheese.
3. Cover baking dish with foil.
4. Select Bake mode.
5. Set time to 20 minutes and temperature 350 F then press START.
6. The air fryer display will prompt you to ADD FOOD once the temperature is reached then place the baking dish in the air fryer basket.
7. Serve and enjoy.

Nutritional Value (Amount per Serving):
Calories 243; Fat 21.1 g; Carbohydrates 5.1 g; Sugar 1 g; Protein 9.5 g; Cholesterol 63 mg

Cauliflower Muffins

Preparation Time: 10 minutes; Cooking Time: 25 minutes; Serve: 12
Ingredients:
- 5 eggs
- 1 cup cheddar cheese, shredded
- 1/2 tsp garlic powder
- 1/2 cup onion, chopped
- 1/2 cup baby spinach
- 6 oz ham, diced
- 3 cups cauliflower rice, squeeze out excess liquid
- Pepper
- Salt

Directions:
1. In a bowl, whisk eggs with cheese, garlic powder, pepper, and salt. Stir in onion, spinach, ham, and cauliflower rice.
2. Pour egg mixture into the silicone muffin molds.

3. Select Bake mode.
4. Set time to 25 minutes and temperature 375 F then press START.
5. The air fryer display will prompt you to ADD FOOD once the temperature is reached then place muffin molds in the air fryer basket.
6. Serve and enjoy.

Nutritional Value (Amount per Serving):
Calories 104; Fat 6.6 g; Carbohydrates 3.1 g; Sugar 1.4 g; Protein 8.1 g; Cholesterol 86 mg

Zucchini Bread

Preparation Time: 10 minutes; Cooking Time: 60 minutes; Serve: 12
Ingredients:
- 2 eggs, lightly beaten
- 1 1/2 cups zucchini, grated
- 1/4 cup butter, melted
- 1 tsp baking soda
- 1/2 cup erythritol
- 1/2 tsp ground cinnamon
- 2 cups almond flour
- 1/2 tsp salt

Directions:
1. In a small bowl, whisk together eggs and butter.
2. In a mixing bowl, mix together almond flour, cinnamon, sweetener, baking soda, and salt.
3. Add zucchini and egg mixture and mix until well combined. Pour batter into the greased loaf pan.
4. Select Bake mode.
5. Set time to 60 minutes and temperature 350 F then press START.
6. The air fryer display will prompt you to ADD FOOD once the temperature is reached then place the loaf pan in the air fryer basket.
7. Slice and serve.

Nutritional Value (Amount per Serving):
Calories 74; Fat 6.9 g; Carbohydrates 1.6 g; Sugar 0.5 g; Protein 2.1 g; Cholesterol 37 mg

Delicious Zucchini Frittata

Preparation Time: 10 minutes; Cooking Time: 30 minutes; Serve: 4
Ingredients:
- 8 eggs
- 1 tbsp parsley, chopped
- 3 tbsp parmesan cheese, grated
- 2 small zucchinis, grated
- 1/2 cup pancetta, chopped
- 2 tbsp olive oil
- Pepper
- Salt

Directions:
1. Heat oil in a pan over medium heat. Add zucchini and pancetta into the pan and sauté for 8-10 minutes.
2. In a bowl, whisk eggs with parsley, cheese, pepper, and salt. Stir in sauteed zucchini and pancetta.
3. Pour egg mixture into the greased 8-inch baking dish.
4. Select Bake mode.
5. Set time to 20 minutes and temperature 350 F then press START.
6. The air fryer display will prompt you to ADD FOOD once the temperature is reached then place the baking dish in the air fryer basket.
7. Serve and enjoy.

Nutritional Value (Amount per Serving):
Calories 295; Fat 23.4 g; Carbohydrates 3.1 g; Sugar 1.7 g; Protein 19.1 g; Cholesterol 348 mg

Egg Bites

Preparation Time: 10 minutes; Cooking Time: 10 minutes; Serve: 4

Ingredients:
- 4 eggs
- 1/4 cup cheddar cheese, shredded
- 4 bacon slices, cooked and crumbled
- 1/2 bell pepper, diced
- 1/2 onion, diced
- 1 tbsp unsweetened almond milk
- Pepper
- Salt

Directions:
1. In a bowl, whisk eggs with cheese, milk, pepper, and salt. Stir in bacon, bell pepper, and onion.
2. Pour egg mixture into the 4 silicone muffin molds.
3. Select Air Fry mode.
4. Set time to 10 minutes and temperature 300 F then press START.
5. The air fryer display will prompt you to ADD FOOD once the temperature is reached then place muffin molds in the air fryer basket.
6. Serve and enjoy.

Nutritional Value (Amount per Serving):
Calories 205; Fat 14.8 g; Carbohydrates 3.2 g; Sugar 1.7 g; Protein 14.7 g; Cholesterol 192 mg

Cheesy Zucchini Quiche

Preparation Time: 10 minutes; Cooking Time: 60 minutes; Serve: 8

Ingredients:
- 6 eggs
- 2 medium zucchinis, shredded & Squeeze out excess liquid
- 2 tbsp fresh parsley, chopped
- 1/2 cup olive oil
- 1 cup cheddar cheese, shredded
- 1 cup almond flour
- 1/2 tsp dried basil
- 2 garlic cloves, minced
- 1 tbsp dry onion, minced
- 2 tbsp parmesan cheese, grated
- 1/2 tsp salt

Directions:
1. Add all ingredients into the large bowl and mix until well combined. Pour mixture into the greased 9-inch pie dish.
2. Cover pie dish with foil.
3. Select Bake mode.
4. Set time to 60 minutes and temperature 350 F then press START.
5. The air fryer display will prompt you to ADD FOOD once the temperature is reached then place the pie dish in the air fryer basket.
6. Slice and serve.

Nutritional Value (Amount per Serving):
Calories 246; Fat 22.7 g; Carbohydrates 3.3 g; Sugar 1.4 g; Protein 9.5 g; Cholesterol 139 mg

Spinach Sausage Egg Muffins

Preparation Time: 10 minutes; Cooking Time: 20 minutes; Serve: 6

Ingredients:
- 2 eggs
- 5 egg whites
- 3 lean breakfast turkey sausage
- 1/4 cup cheddar cheese, shredded
- 1/4 cup spinach, chopped
- 1/4 cup unsweetened almond milk
- Pepper
- Salt

Directions:
1. In a pan, brown the turkey sausage over medium-high heat until sausage is brown.
2. Cut sausage in small pieces and set aside.

3. In a bowl, whisk eggs, egg whites, milk, pepper, and salt. Stir in spinach.
4. Pour egg mixture into the silicone muffin molds. Divide sausage and cheese evenly between each muffin mold.
5. Select Bake mode.
6. Set time to 20 minutes and temperature 350 F then press START.
7. The air fryer display will prompt you to ADD FOOD once the temperature is reached then place muffin molds in the air fryer basket.
8. Serve and enjoy.

Nutritional Value (Amount per Serving):
Calories 103; Fat 5.8 g; Carbohydrates 0.5 g; Sugar 0.3 g; Protein 12.1 g; Cholesterol 85 mg

Tomato Kale Egg Muffins

Preparation Time: 10 minutes; Cooking Time: 25 minutes; Serve: 6
Ingredients:
- 5 eggs
- 3 tomatoes, chopped
- 2/3 cup unsweetened almond milk
- 1 green onion, chopped
- 1/2 cup kale, shredded
- 1/8 tsp pepper
- 1/4 tsp salt

Directions:
1. In a bowl, whisk eggs with milk, pepper, and salt. Stir in tomatoes, kale, and onion.
2. Pour egg mixture into the silicone muffin molds.
3. Select Bake mode.
4. Set time to 25 minutes and temperature 350 F then press START.
5. The air fryer display will prompt you to ADD FOOD once the temperature is reached then place muffin molds in the air fryer basket.
6. Serve and enjoy.

Nutritional Value (Amount per Serving):
Calories 72; Fat 4.2 g; Carbohydrates 3.7 g; Sugar 2 g; Protein 5.5 g; Cholesterol 136 mg

Cheese Pepper Egg Bake

Preparation Time: 10 minutes; Cooking Time: 30 minutes; Serve: 2
Ingredients:
- 3 eggs
- 1/2 cup cottage cheese
- 1 1/2 tbsp jalapeno, chopped
- 1/2 cup pepper jack cheese, shredded
- 1/8 tsp pepper
- 1/8 tsp sea salt

Directions:
1. In a bowl, whisk eggs with pepper and salt. Stir in jalapeno, pepper jack cheese, and cottage cheese.
2. Pour egg mixture into the greased 7-inch baking dish. Cover dish with foil.
3. Select Bake mode.
4. Set time to 30 minutes and temperature 350 F then press START.
5. The air fryer display will prompt you to ADD FOOD once the temperature is reached then place the baking dish in the air fryer basket.
6. Serve and enjoy.

Nutritional Value (Amount per Serving):
Calories 377; Fat 26.5 g; Carbohydrates 2.9 g; Sugar 0.9 g; Protein 30.8 g; Cholesterol 313 mg

Healthy Breakfast Donuts

Preparation Time: 10 minutes; Cooking Time: 20 minutes; Serve: 6
Ingredients:

- 4 eggs
- 1/2 tsp instant coffee
- 1/3 cup unsweetened almond milk
- 1 tbsp liquid stevia
- 3 tbsp cocoa powder
- 1/4 cup butter, melted
- 1/3 cup coconut flour
- 1/2 tsp baking soda
- 1/2 tsp baking powder

Directions:
1. Add all ingredients into the large bowl and mix until well combined.
2. Pour batter into the silicone donut molds.
3. Select Bake mode.
4. Set time to 20 minutes and temperature 350 F then press START.
5. The air fryer display will prompt you to ADD FOOD once the temperature is reached then place donut molds in the air fryer basket.
6. Serve and enjoy.

Nutritional Value (Amount per Serving):
Calories 145; Fat 12 g; Carbohydrates 5.6 g; Sugar 0.7 g; Protein 5.2 g; Cholesterol 129 mg

Almond Broccoli Muffins

Preparation Time: 10 minutes; Cooking Time: 30 minutes; Serve: 6
Ingredients:
- 2 eggs
- 1 cup broccoli florets, chopped
- 1 cup unsweetened almond milk
- 1 cup coconut flour
- 1 cup almond flour
- 1 tsp baking powder
- 2 tbsp nutritional yeast
- 1/2 tsp sea salt

Directions:
1. Add all ingredients into the large bowl and mix until well combined.
2. Pour batter into the silicone muffin molds.
3. Select Bake mode.
4. Set time to 30 minutes and temperature 350 F then press START.
5. The air fryer display will prompt you to ADD FOOD once the temperature is reached then place muffin molds in the air fryer basket.
6. Serve and enjoy.

Nutritional Value (Amount per Serving):
Calories 82; Fat 4.9 g; Carbohydrates 5.7 g; Sugar 0.7 g; Protein 5.3 g; Cholesterol 55 mg

Simple & Easy Breakfast Quiche

Preparation Time: 10 minutes; Cooking Time: 45 minutes; Serve: 6
Ingredients:
- 6 eggs
- 1 cup unsweetened almond milk
- 1 cup tomatoes, chopped
- 1 cup cheddar cheese, grated
- 1 tsp garlic powder
- Pepper
- Salt

Directions:
1. In a bowl, whisk eggs with cheese, milk, garlic powder, pepper, and salt. Stir in tomatoes.
2. Pour egg mixture into the greased pie dish. Cover dish with foil.
3. Select Bake mode.
4. Set time to 45 minutes and temperature 350 F then press START.
5. The air fryer display will prompt you to ADD FOOD once the temperature is reached then place the pie dish in the air fryer basket.
6. Serve and enjoy.

Nutritional Value (Amount per Serving):

Calories 152; Fat 11.3 g; Carbohydrates 2.4 g; Sugar 1.3 g; Protein 10.7 g; Cholesterol 183 mg

Italian Breakfast Frittata

Preparation Time: 10 minutes; Cooking Time: 30 minutes; Serve: 6

Ingredients:
- 6 eggs
- 3/4 cup mozzarella cheese, shredded
- 1/4 cup fresh basil, chopped
- 1/2 cup tomatoes, chopped
- 1 tsp Italian seasoning
- 2 tbsp water
- Pepper
- Salt

Directions:
1. In a bowl, whisk eggs with water, 1/2 cheese, Italian seasoning, pepper, and salt.
2. Stir in remaining cheese, basil, and tomatoes.
3. Pour egg mixture into the greased 8-inch pie dish. Cover dish with foil.
4. Select Bake mode.
5. Set time to 30 minutes and temperature 350 F then press START.
6. The air fryer display will prompt you to ADD FOOD once the temperature is reached then place the pie dish in the air fryer basket.
7. Serve and enjoy.

Nutritional Value (Amount per Serving):
Calories 78; Fat 5.3 g; Carbohydrates 1.2 g; Sugar 0.8 g; Protein 6.7 g; Cholesterol 166 mg

Parmesan Zucchini Frittata

Preparation Time: 10 minutes; Cooking Time: 30 minutes; Serve: 4

Ingredients:
- 8 eggs
- 2 zucchinis, chopped and cooked
- 1 tbsp fresh parsley, chopped
- 3 tbsp parmesan cheese, grated
- 1 tsp garlic powder
- Pepper
- Salt

Directions:
1. In a large bowl, whisk eggs with garlic powder, pepper, and salt. Stir in parsley, cheese, and zucchini.
2. Pour egg mixture into the greased baking dish. Cover dish with foil.
3. Select Bake mode.
4. Set time to 30 minutes and temperature 350 F then press START.
5. The air fryer display will prompt you to ADD FOOD once the temperature is reached then place the baking dish in the air fryer basket.
6. Serve and enjoy.

Nutritional Value (Amount per Serving):
Calories 158; Fat 9.9 g; Carbohydrates 4.7 g; Sugar 2.6 g; Protein 13.8 g; Cholesterol 330 mg

Fresh Herb Egg Cups

Preparation Time: 10 minutes; Cooking Time: 20 minutes; Serve: 6

Ingredients:
- 6 eggs
- 1 tbsp fresh parsley, chopped
- 1 tbsp chives, chopped
- 1 tbsp fresh basil, chopped
- 1 tbsp fresh cilantro, chopped
- 1/4 cup mozzarella cheese, grated
- 1 tbsp fresh dill, chopped
- Pepper
- Salt

Directions:
1. In a bowl, whisk eggs with pepper and salt. Add remaining ingredients and stir well.

2. Pour egg mixture into the silicone muffin molds.
3. Select Bake mode.
4. Set time to 20 minutes and temperature 350 F then press START.
5. The air fryer display will prompt you to ADD FOOD once the temperature is reached then place muffin molds in the air fryer basket.
6. Serve and enjoy.

Nutritional Value (Amount per Serving):
Calories 68; Fat 4.6 g; Carbohydrates 0.8 g; Sugar 0.4 g; Protein 6 g; Cholesterol 164 mg

Bake Cheese Omelet

Preparation Time: 10 minutes; Cooking Time: 25 minutes; Serve: 6

Ingredients:
- 8 eggs
- 1/4 cup cheddar cheese, shredded
- 2 tbsp green onions, chopped
- 1/4 tsp garlic powder
- 1/2 cup unsweetened almond milk
- 1/2 cup half and half
- Pepper
- Salt

Directions:
1. In a bowl, whisk eggs with milk, half and half, garlic powder, pepper, and salt. Stir in green onion and cheese.
2. Pour egg mixture into the greased 8-inch baking dish. Cover dish with foil.
3. Select Bake mode.
4. Set time to 25 minutes and temperature 350 F then press START.
5. The air fryer display will prompt you to ADD FOOD once the temperature is reached then place the baking dish in the air fryer basket.
6. Serve and enjoy.

Nutritional Value (Amount per Serving):
Calories 134; Fat 10 g; Carbohydrates 1.8 g; Sugar 0.6 g; Protein 9.3 g; Cholesterol 231 mg

Feta Pepper Egg Muffins

Preparation Time: 10 minutes; Cooking Time: 20 minutes; Serve: 12

Ingredients:
- 4 eggs
- 1/2 cup egg whites
- 1 tsp garlic powder
- 2 tbsp feta cheese, crumbled
- 2 tbsp green onion, chopped
- 4 fresh basil leaves, chopped
- 1/4 cup unsweetened coconut milk
- 1 red bell pepper, chopped
- Pepper
- Salt

Directions:
1. In a bowl, whisk eggs, egg whites, milk, garlic powder, pepper, and salt.
2. Stir in cheese, bell pepper, green onion, and basil.
3. Pour egg mixture into the silicone muffin molds.
4. Select Bake mode.
5. Set time to 20 minutes and temperature 350 F then press START.
6. The air fryer display will prompt you to ADD FOOD once the temperature is reached then place muffin molds in the air fryer basket.
7. Serve and enjoy.

Nutritional Value (Amount per Serving):
Calories 46; Fat 3 g; Carbohydrates 1.5 g; Sugar 1 g; Protein 3.5 g; Cholesterol 56 mg

Sun-dried Tomatoes Egg Cups

Preparation Time: 10 minutes; Cooking Time: 20 minutes; Serve: 12

Ingredients:
- 6 eggs
- 1 1/2 tbsp basil, chopped
- 2 tsp olive oil
- 1/2 cup feta cheese, crumbled
- 4 cherry tomatoes, chopped
- 4 sun-dried tomatoes, chopped
- Pepper
- Salt

Directions:
1. In a bowl, whisk eggs with pepper and salt. Add remaining ingredients and stir well.
2. Pour egg mixture into the silicone muffin molds.
3. Select Bake mode.
4. Set time to 20 minutes and temperature 400 F then press START.
5. The air fryer display will prompt you to ADD FOOD once the temperature is reached then place muffin molds in the air fryer basket.
6. Serve and enjoy.

Nutritional Value (Amount per Serving):
Calories 69; Fat 4.5 g; Carbohydrates 3.6 g; Sugar 2.6 g; Protein 4.4 g; Cholesterol 87 mg

Vanilla Raspberry Muffins

Preparation Time: 10 minutes; Cooking Time: 20 minutes; Serve: 12

Ingredients:
- 3 eggs
- 1/2 cup raspberries
- 1/2 tsp vanilla
- 1/3 cup unsweetened almond milk
- 1/3 cup coconut oil, melted
- 1 1/2 tsp baking powder
- 1/2 cup Swerve
- 2 1/2 cups almond flour

Directions:
1. In a large bowl, mix almond flour, baking powder, and sweetener.
2. Stir in the coconut oil, vanilla, eggs, and almond milk. Add raspberries and fold well.
3. Pour mixture into the silicone muffin molds.
4. Select Bake mode.
5. Set time to 20 minutes and temperature 350 F then press START.
6. The air fryer display will prompt you to ADD FOOD once the temperature is reached then place muffin molds in the air fryer basket.
7. Serve and enjoy.

Nutritional Value (Amount per Serving):
Calories 106; Fat 10.2 g; Carbohydrates 2.4 g; Sugar 0.5 g; Protein 2.7 g; Cholesterol 41 mg

Mushroom Kale Egg Cups

Preparation Time: 10 minutes; Cooking Time: 15 minutes; Serve: 8

Ingredients:
- 6 eggs
- 1 cup mushrooms, diced
- 1 cup kale, chopped
- 1 tsp olive oil
- 2 tbsp onion, minced
- 1/2 cup Swiss cheese, shredded
- Pepper
- Salt

Directions:
1. Heat oil in a pan over medium-high heat. Add mushrooms and sauté for 2-3 minutes.
2. Add onion and kale and sauté for 2 minutes. Remove pan from heat.
3. In a bowl, whisk eggs with pepper and salt. Stir in sautéed mushroom kale mixture and shredded cheese.
4. Pour egg mixture into the silicone muffin molds.
5. Select Bake mode.
6. Set time to 15 minutes and temperature 350 F then press START.

7. The air fryer display will prompt you to ADD FOOD once the temperature is reached then place muffin molds in the air fryer basket.
8. Serve and enjoy.

Nutritional Value (Amount per Serving):
Calories 85; Fat 5.8 g; Carbohydrates 2 g; Sugar 0.6 g; Protein 6.5 g; Cholesterol 129 mg

Breakfast Bake Egg

Preparation Time: 10 minutes; Cooking Time: 15 minutes; Serve: 1
Ingredients:
- 2 eggs
- 2 tbsp cheddar cheese, shredded
- 2 tbsp half and half
- 1 tbsp parmesan cheese, grated
- 1/2 tsp garlic powder
- Pepper
- Salt

Directions:
1. In a small bowl, whisk eggs and a half and half. Stir in cheddar cheese, parmesan cheese, pepper, and salt.
2. Pour egg mixture into the greased 8-ounce ramekin.
3. Select Bake mode.
4. Set time to 15 minutes and temperature 400 F then press START.
5. The air fryer display will prompt you to ADD FOOD once the temperature is reached then place the ramekin in the air fryer basket.
6. Serve and enjoy.

Nutritional Value (Amount per Serving):
Calories 245; Fat 18.1 g; Carbohydrates 3.4 g; Sugar 1.1 g; Protein 17.5 g; Cholesterol 357 mg

Sun-dried Tomatoes Kale Egg Cups

Preparation Time: 10 minutes; Cooking Time: 35 minutes; Serve: 12
Ingredients:
- 10 eggs
- 1/4 cup sun-dried tomatoes, chopped
- 1 cup unsweetened coconut milk
- 1/4 cup sausage, sliced
- 1/4 cup kale, chopped
- Pepper
- Salt

Directions:
1. In a large bowl, add all ingredients and whisk until well combined.
2. Pour egg mixture into the silicone muffin molds.
3. Select Bake mode.
4. Set time to 35 minutes and temperature 350 F then press START.
5. The air fryer display will prompt you to ADD FOOD once the temperature is reached then place muffin molds in the air fryer basket.
6. Serve and enjoy.

Nutritional Value (Amount per Serving):
Calories 114; Fat 9.6 g; Carbohydrates 1.7 g; Sugar 1.1 g; Protein 6 g; Cholesterol 140 mg

Easy Chicken Egg Cups

Preparation Time: 10 minutes; Cooking Time: 15 minutes; Serve: 12
Ingredients:
- 10 eggs
- 1 cup chicken, cooked and chopped
- 1/2 tsp garlic powder
- 1/4 tsp pepper
- 1 tsp sea salt

Directions:

1. In a large bowl, whisk eggs with pepper and salt. Add remaining ingredients and stir well.
2. Pour egg mixture into the silicone muffin molds.
3. Select Bake mode.
4. Set time to 15 minutes and temperature 400 F then press START.
5. The air fryer display will prompt you to ADD FOOD once the temperature is reached then place muffin molds in the air fryer basket.
6. Serve and enjoy.

Nutritional Value (Amount per Serving):
Calories 71; Fat 4 g; Carbohydrates 0.4 g; Sugar 0.3 g; Protein 8 g; Cholesterol 145 mg

Roasted Pepper Egg Cups

Preparation Time: 10 minutes; Cooking Time: 20 minutes; Serve: 12
Ingredients:
- 8 eggs
- 1 cup roasted red peppers, chopped
- 1/4 cup unsweetened almond milk
- 1 cup spinach, chopped
- 1/2 tsp salt

Directions:
1. In a bowl, whisk eggs with coconut milk and salt.
2. Add spinach, green onion, and red peppers to the egg mixture and stir to combine.
3. Pour egg mixture into the silicone muffin molds.
4. Select Bake mode.
5. Set time to 20 minutes and temperature 350 F then press START.
6. The air fryer display will prompt you to ADD FOOD once the temperature is reached then place muffin molds in the air fryer basket.
7. Serve and enjoy.

Nutritional Value (Amount per Serving):
Calories 47; Fat 3 g; Carbohydrates 1.3 g; Sugar 0.9 g; Protein 3.9 g; Cholesterol 109 mg

Easy Breakfast Sausage

Preparation Time: 10 minutes; Cooking Time: 15 minutes; Serve: 6
Ingredients:
- 2 lbs ground pork
- 1 tbsp dried parsley
- 1 tbsp Italian seasoning
- 2 tbsp olive oil
- 1 tsp paprika
- 1 tsp red pepper flakes
- 2 tsp salt

Directions:
1. In a large bowl, combine together ground pork, paprika, red pepper flakes, parsley, Italian seasoning, olive oil, pepper, and salt.
2. Make small patties from the meat mixture.
3. Place the cooking tray in the air fryer basket. Line air fryer basket with parchment paper.
4. Select Bake mode.
5. Set time to 15 minutes and temperature 375 F then press START.
6. The air fryer display will prompt you to ADD FOOD once the temperature is reached then place patties onto the parchment paper in the air fryer basket.
7. Serve and enjoy.

Nutritional Value (Amount per Serving):
Calories 266; Fat 10.8 g; Carbohydrates 0.7 g; Sugar 0.3 g; Protein 39.7 g; Cholesterol 112 mg

Spinach Bacon Egg Bake

Preparation Time: 10 minutes; Cooking Time: 45 minutes; Serve: 6

Ingredients:
- 10 eggs
- 3 cups baby spinach, chopped
- 1 tbsp olive oil
- 10 bacon sliced, cooked and crumbled
- 2 large tomatoes, sliced
- 1/2 tsp salt

Directions:
1. Heat oil in a pan over medium heat.
2. Add spinach and cook until spinach wilted.
3. In a mixing bowl, whisk eggs with salt. Stir in spinach.
4. Pour egg mixture into the greased 9-inch baking dish. Cover dish with foil.
5. Select Bake mode.
6. Set time to 45 minutes and temperature 350 F then press START.
7. The air fryer display will prompt you to ADD FOOD once the temperature is reached then place the baking dish in the air fryer basket.
8. Serve and enjoy.

Nutritional Value (Amount per Serving):
Calories 273; Fat 21.5 g; Carbohydrates 3.5 g; Sugar 2.2 g; Protein 18.5 g; Cholesterol 298 mg

Zucchini Breakfast Casserole

Preparation Time: 10 minutes; Cooking Time: 50 minutes; Serve: 8

Ingredients:
- 12 eggs
- 2 small zucchinis, shredded
- 1 lb ground Italian sausage
- 3 tomatoes, sliced
- 3 tbsp coconut flour
- 1/4 cup unsweetened almond milk
- 1/4 tsp pepper
- 1/2 tsp salt

Directions:
1. Cook sausage in a pan until lightly brown.
2. Transfer sausage to a large bowl. Add coconut flour, milk, eggs, zucchini, pepper, and salt and mix well.
3. Add eggs and whisk until well combined.
4. Pour egg mixture into the greased casserole dish and top with tomato slices. Cover dish with foil.
5. Select Bake mode.
6. Set time to 50 minutes and temperature 350 F then press START.
7. The air fryer display will prompt you to ADD FOOD once the temperature is reached then place a casserole dish in the air fryer basket.
8. Serve and enjoy.

Nutritional Value (Amount per Serving):
Calories 303; Fat 20.7 g; Carbohydrates 7.4 g; Sugar 3.6 g; Protein 20 g; Cholesterol 286 mg

Egg Casserole

Preparation Time: 10 minutes; Cooking Time: 30 minutes; Serve: 2

Ingredients:
- 5 eggs
- 2 tbsp heavy cream
- 3 tbsp tomato sauce
- 2 tbsp parmesan cheese, grated

Directions:
1. In a bowl, whisk eggs with cream. Stir in cheese and tomato sauce.
2. Pour egg mixture into the greased baking dish. Cover dish with foil.
3. Select Bake mode.
4. Set time to 30 minutes and temperature 350 F then press START.

5. The air fryer display will prompt you to ADD FOOD once the temperature is reached then place the baking dish in the air fryer basket.
6. Serve and enjoy.

Nutritional Value (Amount per Serving):
Calories 233; Fat 17.8 g; Carbohydrates 2.7 g; Sugar 1.9 g; Protein 16.3 g; Cholesterol 434 mg

Basil Cheese Zucchini Quiche

Preparation Time: 10 minutes; Cooking Time: 40 minutes; Serve: 6

Ingredients:
- 3 eggs
- 1 cup mozzarella, shredded
- 15 oz ricotta
- 1 onion, chopped
- 2 medium zucchinis, sliced
- 1/2 tsp dried oregano
- 1/2 tsp dried basil
- 1 tbsp olive oil
- Black pepper
- Salt

Directions:
1. Heat oil in a pan over medium heat. Add zucchini and sauté over low heat.
2. Add onion and cook for 10 minutes. Add pepper and seasoning.
3. In a bowl, whisk eggs. Stir in mozzarella, ricotta, onions, and zucchini.
4. Pour egg mixture into the greased pie dish. Cover dish with foil.
5. Select Bake mode.
6. Set time to 30 minutes and temperature 350 F then press START.
7. The air fryer display will prompt you to ADD FOOD once the temperature is reached then place the pie dish in the air fryer basket.
8. Serve and enjoy.

Nutritional Value (Amount per Serving):
Calories 181; Fat 11.1 g; Carbohydrates 8 g; Sugar 2.3 g; Protein 13.2 g; Cholesterol 106 mg

Spinach Egg Bake

Preparation Time: 10 minutes; Cooking Time: 35 minutes; Serve: 6

Ingredients:
- 8 eggs, beaten
- 1 1/2 cups mozzarella
- 1 tsp olive oil
- 5 oz fresh spinach
- 1 tsp spike seasoning
- 1/3 cup green onion, sliced
- Pepper
- Salt

Directions:
1. Heat oil in a large pan over medium heat.
2. Add spinach and cook until wilted.
3. Transfer cooked spinach into the casserole dish and spread well. Spread onion and cheese on top.
4. In a bowl, whisk together eggs, pepper, spike seasoning, and salt.
5. Pour egg mixture over spinach mixture. Cover dish with foil.
6. Select Bake mode.
7. Set time to 35 minutes and temperature 375 F then press START.
8. The air fryer display will prompt you to ADD FOOD once the temperature is reached then place a casserole dish in the air fryer basket.
9. Slice and serve.

Nutritional Value (Amount per Serving):
Calories 118; Fat 8 g; Carbohydrates 2 g; Sugar 0.7 g; Protein 10.2 g; Cholesterol 222 mg

Asparagus Quiche

Preparation Time: 10 minutes; Cooking Time: 30 minutes; Serve: 6
Ingredients:
- 4 eggs
- 4 egg whites
- 1/4 cup water
- 8 oz asparagus, cut into 1-inch pieces
- 2 tbsp feta cheese, crumbled
- 1 cup cottage cheese
- 1/2 tsp dried thyme
- 1/4 tsp pepper
- 1/4 tsp salt

Directions:
1. Add water into the large pot and bring to boil over high heat.
2. Add asparagus into the pot and cook for 2 minutes. Drain well.
3. In a large bowl, whisk egg whites, eggs, cottage cheese, thyme, water, pepper, and salt.
4. Pour egg mixture into the greased baking dish.
5. Add asparagus pieces into the egg mixture and top with feta cheese. Cover dish with foil.
6. Select Bake mode.
7. Set time to 30 minutes and temperature 375 F then press START.
8. The air fryer display will prompt you to ADD FOOD once the temperature is reached then place the baking dish in the air fryer basket.
9. Slice and serve.

Nutritional Value (Amount per Serving):
Calories 104; Fat 4.4 g; Carbohydrates 3.5 g; Sugar 1.4 g; Protein 12.6 g; Cholesterol 115 mg

Spinach Pepper Breakfast Egg Cups

Preparation Time: 10 minutes; Cooking Time: 20 minutes; Serve: 12
Ingredients:
- 9 eggs
- 1 cup bell peppers, chopped
- 1/2 cup onion, sliced
- 1 tbsp olive oil
- 8 oz ground sausage
- 1/4 cup unsweetened almond milk
- 1/2 tsp oregano
- 1 1/2 cups spinach
- Pepper
- Salt

Directions:
1. Add ground sausage in a pan and sauté over medium heat until browned.
2. Add olive oil, oregano, bell pepper, and onion and sauté until onion is translucent.
3. Add spinach and cook until spinach is wilted.
4. Remove pan from heat and set aside.
5. In a bowl, whisk eggs, milk, pepper, and salt.
6. Add sausage and vegetable mixture into the egg mixture and mix well.
7. Pour egg mixture into the silicone muffin molds.
8. Select Bake mode.
9. Set time to 20 minutes and temperature 350 F then press START.
10. The air fryer display will prompt you to ADD FOOD once the temperature is reached then place muffin molds in the air fryer basket.
11. Serve and enjoy.

Nutritional Value (Amount per Serving):
Calories 128; Fat 9.9 g; Carbohydrates 1.7 g; Sugar 0.4 g; Protein 8.1 g; Cholesterol 139 mg

Moist Pumpkin Muffins

Preparation Time: 10 minutes; Cooking Time: 15 minutes; Serve: 20
Ingredients:
- 2 scoops vanilla protein powder
- 1/2 cup almond flour

- 1/2 cup coconut oil
- 1/2 cup pumpkin puree
- 1/2 cup almond butter
- 1 tbsp cinnamon
- 1 tsp baking powder

Directions:
1. In a large bowl, mix together all dry ingredients.
2. Add wet ingredients into the dry ingredients and mix until well combined.
3. Pour batter into the silicone muffin molds.
4. Select Bake mode.
5. Set time to 15 minutes and temperature 350 F then press START.
6. The air fryer display will prompt you to ADD FOOD once the temperature is reached then place muffin molds in the air fryer basket.
7. Serve and enjoy.

Nutritional Value (Amount per Serving):
Calories 68; Fat 6.1 g; Carbohydrates 1.2 g; Sugar 0.3 g; Protein 3 g; Cholesterol 0 mg

Cheddar Cheese Ham Quiche

Preparation Time: 10 minutes; Cooking Time: 40 minutes; Serve: 6

Ingredients:
- 8 eggs
- 1 cup zucchini, shredded and squeezed
- 1 cup ham, cooked and diced
- 1/2 tsp dry mustard
- 1/2 cup heavy cream
- 1 cup cheddar cheese, shredded
- Pepper
- Salt

Directions:
1. Add ham, cheddar cheese, and zucchini in a 9-inch pie dish.
2. In a bowl, whisk together eggs, heavy cream, and seasoning.
3. Pour egg mixture over ham mixture. Cover dish with foil.
4. Select Bake mode.
5. Set time to 40 minutes and temperature 375 F then press START.
6. The air fryer display will prompt you to ADD FOOD once the temperature is reached then add food in the air fryer basket.
7. Serve and enjoy.

Nutritional Value (Amount per Serving):
Calories 235; Fat 17.8 g; Carbohydrates 2.6 g; Sugar 0.9 g; Protein 16.3 g; Cholesterol 265 mg

Healthy Zucchini Gratin

Preparation Time: 10 minutes; Cooking Time: 30 minutes; Serve: 4

Ingredients:
- 1 egg, lightly beaten
- 3 medium zucchinis, sliced
- 1/2 cup nutritional yeast
- 1 1/4 cup unsweetened almond milk
- 1 tbsp Dijon mustard
- 1 tsp sea salt

Directions:
1. Arrange zucchini slices in the oven-safe casserole dish.
2. In a saucepan, heat almond milk over low heat and stir in Dijon mustard, nutritional yeast, and sea salt. Add egg and whisk well.
3. Pour sauce over zucchini slices. Cover dish with foil.
4. Select Bake mode.
5. Set time to 30 minutes and temperature 400 F then press START.
6. The air fryer display will prompt you to ADD FOOD once the temperature is reached then place a casserole dish in the air fryer basket.
7. Serve and enjoy.

Nutritional Value (Amount per Serving):
Calories 99; Fat 3.1 g; Carbohydrates 10.8 g; Sugar 2.7 g; Protein 9.6 g; Cholesterol 41 mg

Coconut Jalapeno Muffins

Preparation Time: 10 minutes; Cooking Time: 20 minutes; Serve: 8

Ingredients:
- 5 eggs
- 3 tbsp jalapenos, sliced
- 3 tbsp erythritol
- 2/3 cup coconut flour
- 1/4 cup unsweetened coconut milk
- 1/3 cup coconut oil, melted
- 2 tsp baking powder
- 3/4 tsp sea salt

Directions:
1. In a large bowl, stir together coconut flour, baking powder, sweetener, and sea salt.
2. Stir in eggs, jalapenos, milk, and coconut oil until well combined.
3. Pour batter into the silicone muffin molds.
4. Select Bake mode.
5. Set time to 20 minutes and temperature 350 F then press START.
6. The air fryer display will prompt you to ADD FOOD once the temperature is reached then place muffin molds in the air fryer basket.
7. Serve and enjoy.

Nutritional Value (Amount per Serving):
Calories 177; Fat 15 g; Carbohydrates 6.7 g; Sugar 1.2 g; Protein 5 g; Cholesterol 102 mg

Artichoke Quiche

Preparation Time: 10 minutes; Cooking Time: 40 minutes; Serve: 4

Ingredients:
- 3 eggs
- 1 cup artichoke hearts, chopped
- 1 cup mushrooms, sliced
- 1 small onion, chopped
- 3 garlic cloves, minced
- 1/2 cup cottage cheese, fat-free
- 10 oz spinach, frozen
- 1/2 tsp olive oil
- Pepper
- Salt

Directions:
1. Heat oil in a pan over medium heat.
2. Add onion, mushrooms, garlic, and spinach and sauté for a minute.
3. In a bowl add cheese, artichoke hearts, eggs, pepper, and salt mix well.
4. Add sautéed vegetable mixture to the bowl and mix well.
5. Pour egg mixture into the greased baking dish. Cover dish with foil.
6. Select Bake mode.
7. Set time to 40 minutes and temperature 350 F then press START.
8. The air fryer display will prompt you to ADD FOOD once the temperature is reached then place the baking dish in the air fryer basket.
9. Serve and enjoy.

Nutritional Value (Amount per Serving):
Calories 123; Fat 4.8 g; Carbohydrates 10.2 g; Sugar 2 g; Protein 12 g; Cholesterol 125 mg

Breakfast Vegetable Quiche

Preparation Time: 10 minutes; Cooking Time: 40 minutes; Serve: 6

Ingredients:
- 8 egg whites
- 1 cup gruyere cheese, shredded
- 1/4 cup onion, diced
- 2 cups spinach, steamed & squeeze out excess liquid
- 4 pieces roasted red peppers, sliced

- 1/2 cup cherry tomatoes, halved
- 1 garlic cloves, minced
- 1/2 cup unsweetened coconut milk
- Pepper
- Salt

Directions:
1. Spray pan with cooking spray and heat over medium-high heat.
2. Add garlic and onion and sauté until softened.
3. In a bowl, whisk egg whites, cheese, and milk.
4. Add sautéed onion and garlic into the egg mixture and stir well.
5. Layer tomatoes, roasted peppers, and spinach in a greased baking dish.
6. Pour egg mixture over the vegetables. Cover dish with foil.
7. Select Bake mode.
8. Set time to 40 minutes and temperature 350 F then press START.
9. The air fryer display will prompt you to ADD FOOD once the temperature is reached then place the baking dish in the air fryer basket.
10. Serve and enjoy.

Nutritional Value (Amount per Serving):
Calories 153; Fat 10.8 g; Carbohydrates 3.6 g; Sugar 2 g; Protein 11.2 g; Cholesterol 20 mg

Tomato Feta Frittata

Preparation Time: 10 minutes; Cooking Time: 7 minutes; Serve: 2

Ingredients:
- 6 eggs
- 2/3 cup feta cheese, crumbled
- 1 small onion, chopped
- 1 tbsp fresh chives, chopped
- 1 tbsp olive oil
- 1 tbsp fresh basil, chopped
- 3 oz cherry tomatoes, halved
- Pepper
- Salt

Directions:
1. Heat oil in a pan over medium-high heat.
2. Add onion and sauté until lightly browned. Remove from heat.
3. In a bowl, whisk eggs, basil, chives, pepper, and salt. Stir in sauteed onion, cherry tomatoes, and crumbled cheese.
4. Pour egg mixture into the greased baking dish.
5. Select Broil mode.
6. Set time to 7 minutes and temperature 400 F then press START.
7. The air fryer display will prompt you to ADD FOOD once the temperature is reached then place the baking dish in the air fryer basket.
8. Serve and enjoy.

Nutritional Value (Amount per Serving):
Calories 403; Fat 30.9 g; Carbohydrates 8.1 g; Sugar 5.7 g; Protein 24.6 g; Cholesterol 536 mg

Chapter 4: Poultry Recipes

Healthy Chicken Tenders

Preparation Time: 10 minutes; Cooking Time: 10 minutes; Serve: 3

Ingredients:
- 1 egg
- 1 lb chicken breast, boneless & cut into strips
- 1 tsp garlic powder
- 2 tsp Italian seasoning
- 1/3 cup pecans, chopped
- 2/3 cup almond flour
- 1 tbsp water
- 1/2 tsp sea salt

Directions:
1. In a small bowl, whisk together egg and 1 tablespoon of water.
2. In a shallow bowl, mix together almond flour, pecans, Italian seasoning, garlic powder, and salt.
3. Dip each chicken strip in egg then coat with almond flour mixture.
4. Place the cooking tray in the air fryer basket.
5. Select Air Fry mode.
6. Set time to 10 minutes and temperature 350 F then press START.
7. The air fryer display will prompt you to ADD FOOD once the temperature is reached then place coated chicken strips in the air fryer basket.
8. Turn chicken strips halfway through.
9. Serve and enjoy.

Nutritional Value (Amount per Serving):
Calories 300; Fat 15.2 g; Carbohydrates 3.7 g; Sugar 1.1 g; Protein 36.3 g; Cholesterol 154 mg

Sweet & Tangy Chicken

Preparation Time: 10 minutes; Cooking Time: 15 minutes; Serve: 3

Ingredients:
- 1 lb chicken breast, boneless and cut into bite-size pieces
- 1 tbsp sesame seeds, toasted
- 2 garlic cloves, minced
- 1 tsp fresh ginger, chopped
- 1 tsp orange zest, grated
- 2 tbsp orange juice
- 1 tbsp sesame oil
- 2 tbsp vinegar
- 1/4 cup coconut amino
- 1 tsp garlic powder
- 3 1/2 tbsp arrowroot

Directions:
1. Toss chicken with 3 tablespoons of arrowroot and garlic powder.
2. Place the cooking tray in the air fryer basket.
3. Select Air Fry mode.
4. Set time to 12 minutes and temperature 370 F then press START.
5. The air fryer display will prompt you to ADD FOOD once the temperature is reached then add chicken pieces in the air fryer basket. Spray chicken pieces with cooking spray.
6. Toss chicken halfway through.
7. Meanwhile, for sauce, in a small saucepan, whisk together vinegar, garlic, ginger, orange zest, sesame oil, orange juice, and coconut aminos. Whisk in remaining arrowroot and cook over medium heat until sauce thicken. Remove from heat.
8. Once the chicken is done, toss in a mixing bowl with sauce.
9. Sprinkle with sesame seeds and serve.

Nutritional Value (Amount per Serving):
Calories 271; Fat 9.9 g; Carbohydrates 9 g; Sugar 1.2 g; Protein 33.4 g; Cholesterol 97 mg

Parmesan Chicken Breast

Preparation Time: 10 minutes; Cooking Time: 14 minutes; Serve: 4

Ingredients:
- 2 eggs, lightly beaten
- 1 lb chicken breast, skinless & boneless
- 1 cup parmesan cheese, grated
- 1/2 cup almond flour
- 1/2 tsp garlic powder
- 1 tsp Italian seasoning
- Pepper
- Salt

Directions:
1. In a shallow bowl, add eggs and whisk well.
2. In a separate shallow dish, mix together parmesan cheese, Italian seasoning, garlic powder, almond flour, pepper, and salt.
3. Dip chicken breast into the egg mixture and coat with parmesan cheese mixture.
4. Place the cooking tray in the air fryer basket.
5. Select Air Fry mode.
6. Set time to 14 minutes and temperature 360 F then press START.
7. The air fryer display will prompt you to ADD FOOD once the temperature is reached then place coated chicken breasts in the air fryer basket.
8. Serve and enjoy.

Nutritional Value (Amount per Serving):
Calories 374; Fat 19.7 g; Carbohydrates 3.4 g; Sugar 0.5 g; Protein 46.5 g; Cholesterol 197 mg

Garlic Herb Turkey Breast

Preparation Time: 10 minutes; Cooking Time: 40 minutes; Serve: 6

Ingredients:
- 3 lbs turkey breast, boneless & thawed
- 2 garlic cloves, minced
- 1 tbsp fresh parsley, chopped
- 1 tbsp fresh rosemary, chopped
- 1 tsp pepper
- 1 tsp salt

Directions:
1. In a small bowl, mix together garlic, parsley, rosemary, pepper, and salt and rub all over turkey breast.
2. Place the cooking tray in the air fryer basket.
3. Select Air Fry mode.
4. Set time to 40 minutes and temperature 350 F then press START.
5. The air fryer display will prompt you to ADD FOOD once the temperature is reached then place turkey breast in the air fryer basket.
6. Remove turkey breast from the air fryer and let it cool for 10 minutes.
7. Slice and serve.

Nutritional Value (Amount per Serving):
Calories 240; Fat 3.9 g; Carbohydrates 10.5 g; Sugar 8 g; Protein 38.9 g; Cholesterol 98 mg

Simple & Juicy Chicken Breasts

Preparation Time: 10 minutes; Cooking Time: 30 minutes; Serve: 2

Ingredients:
- 2 chicken breasts, skinless & boneless
- 1/2 tsp garlic powder
- 1 tbsp olive oil
- 1/4 tsp pepper
- 1/2 tsp salt

Directions:
1. Brush chicken breasts with oil and season with garlic powder, pepper, and salt.
2. Place the cooking tray in the air fryer basket.

3. Select Air Fry mode.
4. Set time to 30 minutes and temperature 360 F then press START.
5. The air fryer display will prompt you to ADD FOOD once the temperature is reached then place chicken breasts in the air fryer basket. Turn chicken after 20 minutes.
6. Serve and enjoy.

Nutritional Value (Amount per Serving):
Calories 329; Fat 17.4 g; Carbohydrates 0.7 g; Sugar 0.2 g; Protein 40.7 g; Cholesterol 125 mg

Cauliflower Chicken Casserole

Preparation Time: 10 minutes; Cooking Time: 30 minutes; Serve: 4
Ingredients:
- 1 lb cooked chicken, shredded
- 4 oz cream cheese, softened
- 4 cups cauliflower florets
- 1/8 tsp black pepper
- 1/4 cup Greek yogurt
- 1 cup cheddar cheese, shredded
- 1/2 cup salsa
- 1/2 tsp kosher salt

Directions:
1. Add cauliflower florets into the baking dish and microwave for 10 minutes.
2. Add cream cheese and microwave for 30 seconds more. Mix well.
3. Add chicken, yogurt, cheddar cheese, salsa, pepper, and salt and stir everything well.
4. Select Bake mode.
5. Set time to 20 minutes and temperature 375 F then press START.
6. The air fryer display will prompt you to ADD FOOD once the temperature is reached then place the baking dish in the air fryer basket.
7. Serve and enjoy.

Nutritional Value (Amount per Serving):
Calories 431; Fat 23.2 g; Carbohydrates 9.2 g; Sugar 4.3 g; Protein 46.3 g; Cholesterol 149 mg

Flavorful Greek Chicken

Preparation Time: 10 minutes; Cooking Time: 30 minutes; Serve: 4
Ingredients:
- 1 lb chicken breasts, skinless & boneless

For marinade:
- 1 tsp onion powder
- 1/4 tsp basil
- 1/4 tsp oregano
- 3 garlic cloves, minced
- 1 tbsp lemon juice
- 3 tbsp olive oil
- 1/2 tsp dill
- 1/4 tsp pepper
- 1/2 tsp salt

Directions:
1. Add all marinade ingredients into the bowl and mix well.
2. Add chicken into the marinade and coat well. Cover and place in the refrigerator overnight.
3. Arrange marinated chicken into the baking dish. Cover dish with foil.
4. Select Bake mode.
5. Set time to 30 minutes and temperature 400 F then press START.
6. The air fryer display will prompt you to ADD FOOD once the temperature is reached then place baking dish in the air fryer basket.
7. Serve and enjoy.

Nutritional Value (Amount per Serving):
Calories 313; Fat 19 g; Carbohydrates 1.5 g; Sugar 0.3 g; Protein 33.1 g; Cholesterol 101 mg

Simple Baked Chicken Breast

Preparation Time: 10 minutes; Cooking Time: 25 minutes; Serve: 6
Ingredients:
- 6 chicken breasts, skinless & boneless
- 1/4 tsp pepper
- 1/4 tsp paprika
- 1 tsp Italian seasoning
- 2 tbsp olive oil
- 1/2 tsp garlic salt

Directions:
1. Brush chicken with oil.
2. Mix together Italian seasoning, garlic salt, paprika, and pepper and rub all over the chicken.
3. Arrange chicken breasts into the baking dish. Cover dish with foil.
4. Select Bake mode.
5. Set time to 25 minutes and temperature 400 F then press START.
6. The air fryer display will prompt you to ADD FOOD once the temperature is reached then place the baking dish in the air fryer basket.
7. Serve and enjoy.

Nutritional Value (Amount per Serving):
Calories 321; Fat 15.7 g; Carbohydrates 0.4 g; Sugar 0.1 g; Protein 42.3 g; Cholesterol 130 mg

Baked Chicken Thighs

Preparation Time: 10 minutes; Cooking Time: 35 minutes; Serve: 6
Ingredients:
- 6 chicken thighs
- 2 tsp poultry seasoning
- 2 tbsp olive oil
- Pepper
- Salt

Directions:
1. Brush chicken with oil and rub with poultry seasoning, pepper, and salt.
2. Arrange chicken into the baking dish. Cover dish with foil.
3. Select Bake mode.
4. Set time to 35 minutes and temperature 400 F then press START.
5. The air fryer display will prompt you to ADD FOOD once the temperature is reached then place the baking dish in the air fryer basket.
6. Serve and enjoy.

Nutritional Value (Amount per Serving):
Calories 319; Fat 15.5 g; Carbohydrates 0.3 g; Sugar 0 g; Protein 42.3 g; Cholesterol 130 mg

Tasty Chicken Wings

Preparation Time: 10 minutes; Cooking Time: 45 minutes; Serve: 6
Ingredients:
- 3 lbs chicken wings
- 2 tbsp olive oil
- 1/2 cup dry BBQ spice rub

Directions:
1. Brush chicken wings with olive oil and place in a large bowl.
2. Add BBQ spice over chicken wings and toss well.
3. Select Bake mode.
4. Set time to 45 minutes and temperature 400 F then press START.
5. The air fryer display will prompt you to ADD FOOD once the temperature is reached then add chicken wings in the air fryer basket.
6. Serve and enjoy.

Nutritional Value (Amount per Serving):

Calories 471; Fat 21.5 g; Carbohydrates 0 g; Sugar 0 g; Protein 65.6 g; Cholesterol 202 mg

Italian Turkey Tenderloin

Preparation Time: 10 minutes; Cooking Time: 45 minutes; Serve: 4

Ingredients:
- 1 1/2 lbs turkey breast tenderloin
- 1/2 tbsp olive oil
- 1 tsp Italian seasoning
- 1/4 tsp pepper
- 1/2 tsp salt

Directions:
1. Brush turkey tenderloin with olive oil and rub with Italian seasoning, pepper, and salt.
2. Select Bake mode.
3. Set time to 45 minutes and temperature 390 F then press START.
4. The air fryer display will prompt you to ADD FOOD once the temperature is reached then place turkey tenderloin in the air fryer basket.
5. Serve and enjoy.

Nutritional Value (Amount per Serving):
Calories 200; Fat 4.3 g; Carbohydrates 0.2 g; Sugar 0.1 g; Protein 42.2 g; Cholesterol 69 mg

Pesto Parmesan Chicken

Preparation Time: 10 minutes; Cooking Time: 25 minutes; Serve: 4

Ingredients:
- 4 chicken breasts, skinless & boneless
- 1/2 cup parmesan cheese, shredded
- 1/2 cup basil pesto
- Pepper
- Salt

Directions:
1. Season chicken with pepper and salt and place into the baking dish.
2. Spread pesto on top of the chicken and sprinkle with shredded cheese.
3. Select Bake mode.
4. Set time to 25 minutes and temperature 400 F then press START.
5. The air fryer display will prompt you to ADD FOOD once the temperature is reached then place the baking dish in the air fryer basket.
6. Serve and enjoy.

Nutritional Value (Amount per Serving):
Calories 372; Fat 17.1 g; Carbohydrates 1.2 g; Sugar 0 g; Protein 51.7 g; Cholesterol 151 mg

Lemon Chicken Breasts

Preparation Time: 10 minutes; Cooking Time: 30 minutes; Serve: 4

Ingredients:
- 4 chicken breasts, skinless and boneless
- 4 tsp butter, sliced
- 1/2 tsp paprika
- 1 tsp garlic powder
- 1 tsp lemon pepper seasoning
- 4 tsp lemon juice
- Pepper
- Salt

Directions:
1. Season chicken with pepper and salt and place into the baking dish. Pour lemon juice over chicken.
2. Mix together paprika, garlic powder, and lemon pepper seasoning and sprinkle over chicken.
3. Add butter slices on top of the chicken.
4. Select Bake mode.

5. Set time to 30 minutes and temperature 350 F then press START.
6. The air fryer display will prompt you to ADD FOOD once the temperature is reached then place the baking dish in the air fryer basket.
7. Serve and enjoy.

Nutritional Value (Amount per Serving):
Calories 317; Fat 14.7 g; Carbohydrates 1.1 g; Sugar 0.3 g; Protein 42.5 g; Cholesterol 140 mg

Spicy Chicken Wings

Preparation Time: 10 minutes; Cooking Time: 20 minutes; Serve: 4

Ingredients:
- 12 chicken wings
- 1 tbsp chili powder
- 1/2 tbsp baking powder
- 1 tsp granulated garlic
- 1/2 tsp sea salt

Directions:
1. Add chicken wings into the large bowl and toss with remaining ingredients.
2. Select Air Fry mode.
3. Set time to 20 minutes and temperature 400 F then press START.
4. The air fryer display will prompt you to ADD FOOD once the temperature is reached then place chicken wings in the air fryer basket.
5. Serve and enjoy.

Nutritional Value (Amount per Serving):
Calories 760; Fat 54.3 g; Carbohydrates 2.4 g; Sugar 0.3 g; Protein 63.4 g; Cholesterol 255 mg

Meatballs

Preparation Time: 10 minutes; Cooking Time: 20 minutes; Serve: 6

Ingredients:
- 1 lb ground turkey
- 1 tbsp basil, chopped
- 1/3 cup coconut flour
- 2 cups zucchini, grated
- 1 tbsp dried onion flakes
- 2 eggs, lightly beaten
- 1 tbsp nutritional yeast
- 1 tsp dried oregano
- 1 tbsp garlic, minced
- 1 tsp cumin
- Pepper
- Salt

Directions:
1. Add all ingredients into the bowl and mix until just combined.
2. Make small balls from the meat mixture.
3. Select Bake mode.
4. Set time to 20 minutes and temperature 400 F then press START.
5. The air fryer display will prompt you to ADD FOOD once the temperature is reached then place meatballs in the air fryer basket.
6. Serve and enjoy.

Nutritional Value (Amount per Serving):
Calories 214; Fat 10.9 g; Carbohydrates 7.2 g; Sugar 1.5 g; Protein 24.9 g; Cholesterol 132 mg

Hot Chicken Wings

Preparation Time: 10 minutes; Cooking Time: 25 minutes; Serve: 4

Ingredients:
- 2 lbs chicken wings
- 1/2 tsp Worcestershire sauce
- 1/2 tsp Tabasco
- 6 tbsp butter, melted
- 12 oz hot sauce

Directions:

1. Select Air Fry mode.
2. Set time to 25 minutes and temperature 375 F then press START.
3. The air fryer display will prompt you to ADD FOOD once the temperature is reached then place chicken wings in the air fryer basket.
4. Meanwhile, in a bowl, mix together hot sauce, Worcestershire sauce, and butter. Set aside.
5. Add chicken wings into the sauce bowl and toss well.
6. Serve and enjoy.

Nutritional Value (Amount per Serving):
Calories 594; Fat 34.4 g; Carbohydrates 1.6 g; Sugar 1.2 g; Protein 66.2 g; Cholesterol 248 mg

Fajita Chicken

Preparation Time: 10 minutes; Cooking Time: 15 minutes; Serve: 4

Ingredients:
- 4 chicken breasts, make horizontal cuts on each piece
- 2 tbsp fajita seasoning
- 2 tbsp olive oil
- 1 onion, sliced
- 1 bell pepper, sliced

Directions:
1. Brush chicken with oil and season with fajita seasoning.
2. Select Bake mode.
3. Set time to 15 minutes and temperature 375 F then press START.
4. The air fryer display will prompt you to ADD FOOD once the temperature is reached then add chicken, onion, and bell pepper in the air fryer basket.
5. Serve and enjoy.

Nutritional Value (Amount per Serving):
Calories 374; Fat 17.9 g; Carbohydrates 8 g; Sugar 2.7 g; Protein 42.8 g; Cholesterol 130 mg

Meatballs

Preparation Time: 10 minutes; Cooking Time: 12 minutes; Serve: 4

Ingredients:
- 1 egg
- 1 lb ground turkey
- 1/4 cup celery, chopped
- 1/4 cup carrots, grated
- 1 garlic clove, minced
- 2 green onion, chopped
- 2 tbsp coconut flour
- Pepper
- Salt

Directions:
1. Add all ingredients into the large bowl and mix until just combined.
2. Make small balls from the meat mixture.
3. Select Air Fry mode.
4. Set time to 12 minutes and temperature 400 F then press START.
5. The air fryer display will prompt you to ADD FOOD once the temperature is reached then place meatballs in the air fryer basket.
6. Serve and enjoy.

Nutritional Value (Amount per Serving):
Calories 259; Fat 14.1 g; Carbohydrates 3.8 g; Sugar 0.9 g; Protein 33.2 g; Cholesterol 157 mg

Herb Wings

Preparation Time: 10 minutes; Cooking Time: 15 minutes; Serve: 4

Ingredients:
- 2 lbs chicken wings
- 1 tsp paprika
- 1/2 cup parmesan cheese, grated
- 1 tsp herb de Provence

- Salt

Directions:
1. In a small bowl, mix together cheese, herb de Provence, paprika, and salt.
2. Coat chicken wings with cheese mixture.
3. Select Air Fry mode.
4. Set time to 15 minutes and temperature 350 F then press START.
5. The air fryer display will prompt you to ADD FOOD once the temperature is reached then place chicken wings in the air fryer basket.
6. Serve and enjoy.

Nutritional Value (Amount per Serving):
Calories 528; Fat 23.3 g; Carbohydrates 1.4 g; Sugar 0.1 g; Protein 75.3 g; Cholesterol 223 mg

Rosemary Garlic Chicken

Preparation Time: 10 minutes; Cooking Time: 25 minutes; Serve: 4

Ingredients:
- 1 lb chicken breasts, skinless, boneless, and cubed
- 2 tbsp chives, chopped
- 1 tbsp fresh lemon juice
- 1 tsp garlic powder
- 1 tbsp rosemary, chopped
- 1 tbsp garlic, minced
- 2 tbsp olive oil
- Pepper
- Salt

Directions:
1. Add all ingredients into the bowl and toss well.
2. Select Air Fry mode.
3. Set time to 25 minutes and temperature 370 F then press START.
4. The air fryer display will prompt you to ADD FOOD once the temperature is reached then add the chicken mixture in the air fryer basket.
5. Serve and enjoy.

Nutritional Value (Amount per Serving):
Calories 285; Fat 15.6 g; Carbohydrates 1.9 g; Sugar 0.3 g; Protein 33.2 g; Cholesterol 101 mg

Easy Cajun Chicken Breasts

Preparation Time: 10 minutes; Cooking Time: 10 minutes; Serve: 2

Ingredients:
- 2 chicken breasts, skinless & boneless
- 3 tbsp Cajun spice

Directions:
1. Season chicken with Cajun spice.
2. Select Air Fry mode.
3. Set time to 10 minutes and temperature 350 F then press START.
4. The air fryer display will prompt you to ADD FOOD once the temperature is reached then place chicken in the air fryer basket.
5. Serve and enjoy.

Nutritional Value (Amount per Serving):
Calories 277; Fat 10.8 g; Carbohydrates 0 g; Sugar 0 g; Protein 42.4 g; Cholesterol 130 mg

Veggie Turkey Breast

Preparation Time: 10 minutes; Cooking Time: 45 minutes; Serve: 4

Ingredients:
- 1 lb turkey breast, cut into 1-inch cubes
- 1 cup mushrooms, cleaned
- 1/2 lb Brussels sprouts, cut in half
- 1 tsp garlic powder
- 2 tbsp olive oil

- Pepper
- Salt

Directions:
1. In a small bowl, mix oil, garlic powder, pepper, and salt.
2. In a baking dish, mix together turkey, mushrooms, and Brussels sprouts. Pour oil mixture on top.
3. Cover dish with foil.
4. Select Bake mode.
5. Set time to 45 minutes and temperature 350 F then press START.
6. The air fryer display will prompt you to ADD FOOD once the temperature is reached then place the baking dish in the air fryer basket.
7. Serve and enjoy.

Nutritional Value (Amount per Serving):
Calories 209; Fat 9.1 g; Carbohydrates 11 g; Sugar 5.7 g; Protein 22 g; Cholesterol 49 mg

Flavorful Asian Chicken Thighs

Preparation Time: 10 minutes; Cooking Time: 20 minutes; Serve: 4

Ingredients:
- 1 lb chicken thighs
- 1 tsp garlic, minced
- 1/2 cup water
- 1 tsp ginger, minced
- 1 tbsp sriracha sauce
- 2 tbsp lime juice
- 2 tbsp sweet chili sauce
- 1 tbsp soy sauce
- 1/4 cup creamy peanut butter
- 1/2 tsp salt

Directions:
1. In a large bowl, whisk together peanut butter, sriracha sauce, ginger, water, soy sauce, sweet chili sauce, lime juice, garlic, and salt.
2. Add chicken into the bowl and coat well.
3. Cover and place in the refrigerator overnight.
4. Select Air Fry mode.
5. Set time to 20 minutes and temperature 350 F then press START.
6. The air fryer display will prompt you to ADD FOOD once the temperature is reached then place the marinated chicken in the air fryer basket.
7. Serve and enjoy.

Nutritional Value (Amount per Serving):
Calories 335; Fat 16.6 g; Carbohydrates 8.9 g; Sugar 5 g; Protein 37.3 g; Cholesterol 101 mg

Mustard Chicken Drumsticks

Preparation Time: 10 minutes; Cooking Time: 12 minutes; Serve: 2

Ingredients:
- 2 chicken drumsticks
- 1/2 tsp ginger garlic paste
- 1/2 tsp mustard
- 1/2 tbsp olive oil
- Pepper
- Salt

Directions:
1. Add chicken wings into the bowl. Add remaining ingredients and toss well.
2. Select Air Fry mode.
3. Set time to 12 minutes and temperature 350 F then press START.
4. The air fryer display will prompt you to ADD FOOD once the temperature is reached then place chicken in the air fryer basket. Turn chicken halfway through.
5. Serve and enjoy.

Nutritional Value (Amount per Serving):
Calories 118; Fat 6.6 g; Carbohydrates 1.1 g; Sugar 0.1 g; Protein 13.1 g; Cholesterol 40 mg

Meatballs

Preparation Time: 10 minutes; Cooking Time: 10 minutes; Serve: 4
Ingredients:
- 1 egg
- 1 lb ground chicken
- 1/2 cup parmesan cheese, shredded
- 1/2 tsp onion powder
- 1/2 cup almond flour
- Pepper
- Salt

Directions:
1. Add all ingredients into the large bowl and mix until well combined.
2. Make small balls from the meat mixture.
3. Select Air Fry mode.
4. Set time to 10 minutes and temperature 370 F then press START.
5. The air fryer display will prompt you to ADD FOOD once the temperature is reached then place meatballs in the air fryer basket. Turn meatballs halfway through.
6. Serve and enjoy.

Nutritional Value (Amount per Serving):
Calories 346; Fat 17.5 g; Carbohydrates 2.1 g; Sugar 0.3 g; Protein 44.4 g; Cholesterol 163 mg

Burger Patties

Preparation Time: 10 minutes; Cooking Time: 22 minutes; Serve: 4
Ingredients:
- 1 lb ground turkey
- 4 oz feta cheese, crumbled
- 1 1/4 cup spinach, chopped
- 1 tsp Italian seasoning
- 1 tbsp olive oil
- 1 tbsp garlic paste
- Pepper
- Salt

Directions:
1. Add all ingredients into the mixing bowl and mix until well combined.
2. Make 4 equal shapes of patties from the mixture.
3. Select Air Fry mode.
4. Set time to 22 minutes and temperature 390 F then press START.
5. The air fryer display will prompt you to ADD FOOD once the temperature is reached then place chicken patties in the air fryer basket. Turn patties halfway through.
6. Serve and enjoy.

Nutritional Value (Amount per Serving):
Calories 268; Fat 17.9 g; Carbohydrates 1.9 g; Sugar 1.1 g; Protein 28.4 g; Cholesterol 113 mg

Chicken Burgers

Preparation Time: 10 minutes; Cooking Time: 18 minutes; Serve: 4
Ingredients:
- 1 lb ground chicken
- 3 oz almond flour
- 1 tbsp oregano
- 2 oz mozzarella cheese, shredded
- Pepper
- Salt

Directions:
1. Add all ingredients into the mixing bowl and mix until well combined.
2. Make 4 equal shapes of patties from meat mixture.
3. Select Air Fry mode.
4. Set time to 18 minutes and temperature 360 F then press START.
5. The air fryer display will prompt you to ADD FOOD once the temperature is reached then place chicken patties in the air fryer basket.
6. Serve and enjoy.

Nutritional Value (Amount per Serving):
Calories 379; Fat 21.5 g; Carbohydrates 5.8 g; Sugar 0.8 g; Protein 41.4 g; Cholesterol 108 mg

Italian Chicken

Preparation Time: 10 minutes; Cooking Time: 25 minutes; Serve: 4

Ingredients:
- 4 chicken breasts, skinless & boneless
- 1 tbsp olive oil

For rub:
- 1 tsp oregano
- 1 tsp thyme
- 1 tsp parsley
- 1 tsp onion powder
- 1 tsp basil
- Pepper
- Salt

Directions:
1. Brush chicken breast with oil.
2. In a small bowl, mix together all rub ingredients and rub all over chicken breasts.
3. Select Air Fry mode.
4. Set time to 25 minutes and temperature 390 F then press START.
5. The air fryer display will prompt you to ADD FOOD once the temperature is reached then place chicken in the air fryer basket. Turn chicken halfway through.
6. Serve and enjoy.

Nutritional Value (Amount per Serving):
Calories 312; Fat 14.4 g; Carbohydrates 0.9 g; Sugar 0.2 g; Protein 42.4 g; Cholesterol 130 mg

Tasty Chicken Tenders

Preparation Time: 10 minutes; Cooking Time: 16 minutes; Serve: 4

Ingredients:
- 1 lb chicken tenders

For rub:
- 1/2 tbsp dried thyme
- 1 tbsp garlic powder
- 1 tbsp paprika
- 1/2 tbsp onion powder
- 1/2 tsp cayenne pepper
- Pepper
- Salt

Directions:
1. In a bowl, add all rub ingredients and mix well.
2. Add chicken tenders into the bowl and coat with rub.
3. Select Air Fry mode.
4. Set time to 16 minutes and temperature 370 F then press START.
5. The air fryer display will prompt you to ADD FOOD once the temperature is reached then place chicken tenders in the air fryer basket.
6. Turn chicken tenders halfway through.
7. Serve and enjoy.

Nutritional Value (Amount per Serving):
Calories 232; Fat 8.7 g; Carbohydrates 3.6 g; Sugar 1 g; Protein 33.6 g; Cholesterol 101 mg

Air Fry Chicken Drumsticks

Preparation Time: 10 minutes; Cooking Time: 25 minutes; Serve: 5

Ingredients:
- 5 chicken drumsticks
- 1/4 tsp paprika
- 1/2 tsp garlic powder
- 2 tbsp olive oil
- 1/2 cup BBQ sauce, sugar-free
- 1/4 tsp onion powder

- Pepper
- Salt

Directions:
1. In a bowl, add chicken drumsticks, onion powder, garlic powder, olive oil, paprika, pepper, and salt and toss well.
2. Select Air Fry mode.
3. Set time to 15 minutes and temperature 390 F then press START.
4. The air fryer display will prompt you to ADD FOOD once the temperature is reached then place chicken drumsticks in the air fryer basket.
5. Turn chicken drumsticks and air fry for 5 minutes more. Brush chicken drumsticks with BBQ sauce air fry for 5 minutes more.
6. Serve and enjoy.

Nutritional Value (Amount per Serving):
Calories 165; Fat 8.3 g; Carbohydrates 9.4 g; Sugar 6.6 g; Protein 12.7 g; Cholesterol 40 mg

Jerk Chicken

Preparation Time: 10 minutes; Cooking Time: 20 minutes; Serve: 2

Ingredients:
- 1 lb chicken wings
- 1 tbsp jerk seasoning
- 1 tsp olive oil
- Pepper
- Salt

Directions:
1. In a mixing bowl, add chicken wings. Add remaining ingredients on top of chicken wings and toss to coat.
2. Select Air Fry mode.
3. Set time to 20 minutes and temperature 380 F then press START.
4. The air fryer display will prompt you to ADD FOOD once the temperature is reached then place chicken wings in the air fryer basket.
5. Serve and enjoy.

Nutritional Value (Amount per Serving):
Calories 451; Fat 19.1 g; Carbohydrates 4.5 g; Sugar 4 g; Protein 65.6 g; Cholesterol 202 mg

Garlic Ranch Chicken Wings

Preparation Time: 10 minutes; Cooking Time: 25 minutes; Serve: 2

Ingredients:
- 1 lb chicken wings
- 1 1/2 tbsp ranch seasoning
- 3 garlic cloves, minced
- 2 tbsp butter, melted

Directions:
1. In a bowl, mix together butter, garlic, and ranch seasoning. Add chicken wings and toss to coat.
2. Cover bowl and place in the refrigerator overnight.
3. Select Air Fry mode.
4. Set time to 25 minutes and temperature 360 F then press START.
5. The air fryer display will prompt you to ADD FOOD once the temperature is reached then add chicken wings in the air fryer basket.
6. Serve and enjoy.

Nutritional Value (Amount per Serving):
Calories 562; Fat 28.4 g; Carbohydrates 1.5 g; Sugar 0.1 g; Protein 66 g; Cholesterol 232 mg

Chicken Fritters

Preparation Time: 10 minutes; Cooking Time: 25 minutes; Serve: 4

Ingredients:
- 1 lb ground chicken
- 1 1/2 cups mozzarella cheese, shredded
- 1/2 cup onion, chopped
- 2 cups broccoli, chopped
- 3/4 cup almond flour
- 2 garlic cloves, minced
- 1 egg, lightly beaten
- Pepper
- Salt

Directions:
1. Add all ingredients into the mixing bowl and mix until well combined.
2. Make small patties from the meat mixture.
3. Select Bake mode.
4. Set time to 25 minutes and temperature 380 F then press START.
5. The air fryer display will prompt you to ADD FOOD once the temperature is reached then place chicken patties in the air fryer basket. Turn patties halfway through.
6. Serve and enjoy.

Nutritional Value (Amount per Serving):
Calories 285; Fat 14.2 g; Carbohydrates 6.5 g; Sugar 1.7 g; Protein 39.9 g; Cholesterol 147 mg

Tandoori Chicken

Preparation Time: 10 minutes; Cooking Time: 15 minutes; Serve: 4

Ingredients:
- 4 chicken drumsticks

For marinade:
- 1/2 tsp garam masala
- 1/2 tsp ground turmeric
- 1 tsp chili powder
- 1 tbsp ginger garlic paste
- 1 tbsp fresh lime juice
- 1 tsp ground cumin
- 1/4 cup yogurt
- 1 tsp salt

Directions:
1. In a bowl, mix together all marinade ingredients until well combined.
2. Add chicken in marinade and mix until well coated.
3. Cover and place in the refrigerator overnight.
4. Select Air Fry mode.
5. Set time to 10 minutes and temperature 360 F then press START.
6. The air fryer display will prompt you to ADD FOOD once the temperature is reached then place chicken in the air fryer basket. Turn chicken halfway through and cook for 5 minutes more.
7. Serve and enjoy.

Nutritional Value (Amount per Serving):
Calories 100; Fat 3.3 g; Carbohydrates 2.6 g; Sugar 1.2 g; Protein 14 g; Cholesterol 41 mg

Chicken Nuggets

Preparation Time: 10 minutes; Cooking Time: 25 minutes; Serve: 4

Ingredients:
- 1 1/2 lbs chicken breast, boneless & cut into chunks
- 1/2 tsp garlic powder
- 1/4 cup parmesan cheese, shredded
- 1/4 cup mayonnaise
- 1/4 tsp salt

Directions:
1. In a bowl, mix together mayonnaise, cheese, garlic powder, and salt.
2. Add chicken and mix until well coated.
3. Select Air Fry mode.
4. Set time to 25 minutes and temperature 400 F then press START.

5. The air fryer display will prompt you to ADD FOOD once the temperature is reached then add chicken in the air fryer basket.
6. Serve and enjoy.

Nutritional Value (Amount per Serving):
Calories 299; Fat 12.3 g; Carbohydrates 4.3 g; Sugar 1 g; Protein 40.9 g; Cholesterol 123 mg

Ranch Chicken Wings

Preparation Time: 10 minutes; Cooking Time: 20 minutes; Serve: 2
Ingredients:
- 1 lb chicken wings
- 2 tbsp butter, melted
- 1 1/2 tbsp ranch seasoning

Directions:
1. In a bowl, mix together butter, and ranch seasoning.
2. Add chicken wings and toss well.
3. Cover and place in the refrigerator for 1 hour.
4. Select Air Fry mode.
5. Set time to 20 minutes and temperature 360 F then press START.
6. The air fryer display will prompt you to ADD FOOD once the temperature is reached then place chicken wings in the air fryer basket.
7. Serve and enjoy.

Nutritional Value (Amount per Serving):
Calories 555; Fat 28.3 g; Carbohydrates 0 g; Sugar 0 g; Protein 65.7 g; Cholesterol 232 mg

Garlic Butter Wings

Preparation Time: 10 minutes; Cooking Time: 25 minutes; Serve: 3
Ingredients:
- 1 lb chicken wings
- 1/2 tsp Italian seasoning
- 1 tsp garlic powder
- 1/4 tsp pepper
- 1/2 tsp salt

For sauce:
- 1 tbsp butter, melted
- 1/8 tsp garlic powder

Directions:
1. In a bowl, toss chicken wings with Italian seasoning, garlic powder, pepper, and salt.
2. Select Air Fry mode.
3. Set time to 25 minutes and temperature 390 F then press START.
4. The air fryer display will prompt you to ADD FOOD once the temperature is reached then add chicken wings in the air fryer basket.
5. In a large bowl, mix together melted butter and garlic powder. Add chicken wings and toss until well coated.
6. Serve and enjoy.

Nutritional Value (Amount per Serving):
Calories 328; Fat 15.3 g; Carbohydrates 1 g; Sugar 0.3 g; Protein 44 g; Cholesterol 145 mg

Chicken Vegetable Burger Patties

Preparation Time: 10 minutes; Cooking Time: 25 minutes; Serve: 4
Ingredients:
- 1 lb ground chicken
- 3/4 cup almond flour
- 1 egg, lightly beaten
- 1 cup Monterey jack cheese, grated
- 1 cup carrot, grated
- 1 cup cauliflower, grated
- 1/8 tsp red pepper flakes
- 2 garlic cloves, minced

- 1/2 cup onion, minced
- Pepper
- Salt

Directions:
1. Add all ingredients into the mixing bowl and mix until well combined.
2. Make small patties from the mixture.
3. Select Bake mode.
4. Set time to 25 minutes and temperature 400 F then press START.
5. The air fryer display will prompt you to ADD FOOD once the temperature is reached then place chicken patties in the air fryer basket.
6. Serve and enjoy.

Nutritional Value (Amount per Serving):
Calories 392; Fat 20.7 g; Carbohydrates 7.3 g; Sugar 3 g; Protein 43.2 g; Cholesterol 167 mg

Meatballs

Preparation Time: 10 minutes; Cooking Time: 18 minutes; Serve: 6
Ingredients:
- 1 lb ground turkey
- 1/3 cup almond flour
- 2 cups zucchini, grated
- 1 tsp dried oregano
- 1 tbsp garlic, minced
- 1 tsp cumin
- 1 tbsp dried onion flakes
- 2 eggs, lightly beaten
- 1 tbsp basil, chopped
- Pepper
- Salt

Directions:
1. Add all ingredients into the mixing bowl and mix until well combined.
2. Make small balls from the meat mixture.
3. Select Bake mode.
4. Set time to 18 minutes and temperature 400 F then press START.
5. The air fryer display will prompt you to ADD FOOD once the temperature is reached then place meatballs in the air fryer basket.
6. Serve and enjoy.

Nutritional Value (Amount per Serving):
Calories 191; Fat 10.7 g; Carbohydrates 3.2 g; Sugar 1.2 g; Protein 23.6 g; Cholesterol 132 mg

Jalapeno Meatballs

Preparation Time: 10 minutes; Cooking Time: 25 minutes; Serve: 4
Ingredients:
- 1 lb ground chicken
- 1/2 cup cilantro, chopped
- 1 jalapeno pepper, minced
- 1 habanero pepper, minced
- 1 poblano chili pepper, minced
- Salt

Directions:
1. Add all ingredients into the large bowl and mix until well combined.
2. Make small balls from the meat mixture.
3. Select Air Fry mode.
4. Set time to 25 minutes and temperature 400 F then press START.
5. The air fryer display will prompt you to ADD FOOD once the temperature is reached then place meatballs in the air fryer basket.
6. Serve and enjoy.

Nutritional Value (Amount per Serving):
Calories 226; Fat 8.5 g; Carbohydrates 2.3 g; Sugar 1.3 g; Protein 33.3 g; Cholesterol 101 mg

Chicken Skewers

Preparation Time: 10 minutes; Cooking Time: 20 minutes; Serve: 4
Ingredients:
- 1 1/2 lbs chicken breast, cut into 1-inch cubes

For marinade:
- 2 tbsp dried oregano
- 1/4 cup fresh mint leaves
- 5 garlic cloves
- 1/2 cup lemon juice
- 1/4 tsp cayenne
- 1 tbsp red wine vinegar
- 1/2 cup low-fat yogurt
- 2 tbsp fresh rosemary, chopped
- 1 cup olive oil
- Pepper
- Salt

Directions:
1. Add all marinade ingredients into the blender and blend until smooth.
2. Pour marinade in a large bowl.
3. Add chicken to the bowl and coat well, cover and place in the refrigerator for 1 hour.
4. Remove marinated chicken from the refrigerator and slide onto the skewers.
5. Select Bake mode.
6. Set time to 20 minutes and temperature 400 F then press START.
7. The air fryer display will prompt you to ADD FOOD once the temperature is reached then place chicken skewers in the air fryer basket.
8. Serve and enjoy.

Nutritional Value (Amount per Serving):
Calories 677; Fat 55.8 g; Carbohydrates 7.1 g; Sugar 3 g; Protein 38.8 g; Cholesterol 111 mg

Meatballs

Preparation Time: 10 minutes; Cooking Time: 18 minutes; Serve: 6
Ingredients:
- 1 1/2 cups zucchini, grated
- 1/4 cup almond flour
- 1 egg, lightly beaten
- 1 lb ground chicken
- 1 1/2 tsp Italian seasoning
- 2 tbsp chives, chopped
- 1/2 tsp salt

Directions:
1. Add all ingredients into the mixing bowl and mix until well combined.
2. Make small balls from the meat mixture.
3. Select Bake mode.
4. Set time to 18 minutes and temperature 350 F then press START.
5. The air fryer display will prompt you to ADD FOOD once the temperature is reached then place meatballs in the air fryer basket.
6. Serve and enjoy.

Nutritional Value (Amount per Serving):
Calories 169; Fat 7.3 g; Carbohydrates 1.4 g; Sugar 0.7 g; Protein 23.4 g; Cholesterol 95 mg

Tasty Chicken Tenders

Preparation Time: 10 minutes; Cooking Time: 20 minutes; Serve: 4
Ingredients:
- 1 lbs chicken tenders
- 2 tbsp fresh tarragon, chopped
- 1/2 oz fresh lemon juice
- 1/2 tsp pepper
- 1/2 cup whole grain mustard
- 1/2 tsp paprika
- 1 garlic clove, minced
- 1/4 tsp kosher salt

Directions:

1. Add all ingredients except chicken to the large bowl and mix well.
2. Add chicken to the bowl and stir until well coated.
3. Place chicken on a baking dish and cover dish with foil.
4. Select Bake mode.
5. Set time to 20 minutes and temperature 400 F then press START.
6. The air fryer display will prompt you to ADD FOOD once the temperature is reached then place the baking dish in the air fryer basket.
7. Serve and enjoy.

Nutritional Value (Amount per Serving):
Calories 242; Fat 9.5 g; Carbohydrates 3.1 g; Sugar 0.1 g; Protein 33.2 g; Cholesterol 101 mg

Baked Feta Dill Chicken

Preparation Time: 10 minutes; Cooking Time: 35 minutes; Serve: 4

Ingredients:
- 2 lbs chicken tenders
- 2 tbsp olive oil
- 3 dill sprigs
- 1 large zucchini
- 1 cup grape tomatoes

For topping:
- 1 tbsp fresh lemon juice
- 1 tbsp fresh dill, chopped
- 2 tbsp feta cheese, crumbled
- 1 tbsp olive oil

Directions:
1. Drizzle the olive oil on a baking dish then place chicken, zucchini, dill, and tomatoes in the dish. Season with salt.
2. Select Bake mode.
3. Set time to 30 minutes and temperature 400 F then press START.
4. The air fryer display will prompt you to ADD FOOD once the temperature is reached then place the baking dish in the air fryer basket.
5. Meanwhile, in a small bowl, stir together all topping ingredients.
6. Sprinkle topping mixture on top of the chicken and Serve.

Nutritional Value (Amount per Serving):
Calories 559; Fat 28.6 g; Carbohydrates 5.6 g; Sugar 2.9 g; Protein 68 g; Cholesterol 206 mg

Thyme Sage Turkey Breast

Preparation Time: 10 minutes; Cooking Time: 60 minutes; Serve: 8

Ingredients:
- 2 lbs turkey breast
- 1/4 tsp pepper
- 1 tbsp butter
- 1/2 tsp sage leaves, chopped
- 1/2 tsp thyme leaves, chopped
- 1 tsp salt

Directions:
1. Rub butter all over the turkey breast and season with pepper, sage, thyme, and salt.
2. Select Bake mode.
3. Set time to 60 minutes and temperature 325 F then press START.
4. The air fryer display will prompt you to ADD FOOD once the temperature is reached then place turkey breast in the air fryer basket. Turn turkey breast halfway through.
5. Serve and enjoy.

Nutritional Value (Amount per Serving):
Calories 131; Fat 3.3 g; Carbohydrates 4.9 g; Sugar 4 g; Protein 19.4 g; Cholesterol 53 mg

Meatballs

Preparation Time: 10 minutes; Cooking Time: 12 minutes; Serve: 4

Ingredients:
- 1 egg
- 2 tbsp coconut flour
- 1 lb ground turkey
- 1 garlic clove, minced
- 2 green onion, chopped
- 1/4 cup celery, chopped
- 1/4 cup carrots, grated
- Pepper
- Salt

Directions:
1. Add all ingredients into the large bowl and mix until well combined.
2. Make small balls from the meat mixture.
3. Select Air Fry mode.
4. Set time to 12 minutes and temperature 400 F then press START.
5. The air fryer display will prompt you to ADD FOOD once the temperature is reached then place meatballs in the air fryer basket.
6. Serve and enjoy.

Nutritional Value (Amount per Serving):
Calories 259; Fat 14.1 g; Carbohydrates 3.8 g; Sugar 0.9 g; Protein 33.2 g; Cholesterol 157 mg

Pecan Mustard Chicken Tenders

Preparation Time: 10 minutes; Cooking Time: 12 minutes; Serve: 4

Ingredients:
- 1 lb chicken tenders
- 1 egg, lightly beaten
- 1/2 tsp paprika
- 1 cup pecans, crushed
- 1/4 cup ground mustard
- 1 tsp pepper
- 1 tsp salt

Directions:
1. Add chicken into the large bowl.
2. Season with paprika, pepper, and salt. Add mustard mix well.
3. In another bowl, add egg and whisk well.
4. In a shallow dish, add crushed pecans.
5. Dip chicken into the egg then coats with crushed pecans.
6. Select Air Fry mode.
7. Set time to 12 minutes and temperature 350 F then press START.
8. The air fryer display will prompt you to ADD FOOD once the temperature is reached then place coated chicken tenders in the air fryer basket.
9. Serve and enjoy.

Nutritional Value (Amount per Serving):
Calories 454; Fat 30.3 g; Carbohydrates 7.6 g; Sugar 1.7 g; Protein 39.4 g; Cholesterol 142 mg

Flavorful Spiced Chicken

Preparation Time: 10 minutes; Cooking Time: 10 minutes; Serve: 8

Ingredients:
- 3 lbs chicken thigh, skinless and boneless
- 1/2 tsp ground ginger
- 1 tbsp cayenne
- 1 tbsp cinnamon
- 1 tbsp coriander powder
- 3 tbsp coconut oil, melted
- 1/2 tsp ground nutmeg
- Pepper
- Salt

Directions:
1. In a small bowl, mix together all spices. Brush chicken with oil and rub with spice mixture. Season with salt.
2. Select Air Fry mode.

3. Set time to 10 minutes and temperature 390 F then press START.
4. The air fryer display will prompt you to ADD FOOD once the temperature is reached then place chicken in the air fryer basket.
5. Serve and enjoy.

Nutritional Value (Amount per Serving):
Calories 373; Fat 17.9 g; Carbohydrates 1.2 g; Sugar 0.1 g; Protein 49.3 g; Cholesterol 151 mg

Easy Lemon Chicken

Preparation Time: 10 minutes; Cooking Time: 20 minutes; Serve: 4
Ingredients:
- 4 chicken breasts, skinless and boneless
- 1 preserved lemon
- 1 tbsp olive oil

Directions:
1. Add all ingredients into the bowl and mix well. Set aside for 10 minutes.
2. Select Air Fry mode.
3. Set time to 20 minutes and temperature 400 F then press START.
4. The air fryer display will prompt you to ADD FOOD once the temperature is reached then place chicken in the air fryer basket.
5. Serve and enjoy.

Nutritional Value (Amount per Serving):
Calories 312; Fat 14.4 g; Carbohydrates 1.4 g; Sugar 0.4 g; Protein 42.4 g; Cholesterol 130 mg

Persian Kabab

Preparation Time: 10 minutes; Cooking Time: 6 minutes; Serve: 3
Ingredients:
- 1 lb ground chicken
- 1/4 cup almond flour
- 2 green onion, chopped
- 1 egg, lightly beaten
- 1/3 cup fresh parsley, chopped
- 2 garlic cloves
- 4 oz onion, chopped
- 1/4 tsp turmeric powder
- 1/2 tsp black pepper
- 1 tbsp fresh lemon juice

Directions:
1. Add all ingredients into the food processor and process until well combined.
2. Transfer chicken mixture to the bowl and place it in the refrigerator for 30 minutes.
3. Divide mixture into the six equal portions and roll around the soaked wooden skewers.
4. Select Air Fry mode.
5. Set time to 6 minutes and temperature 400 F then press START.
6. The air fryer display will prompt you to ADD FOOD once the temperature is reached then place chicken skewers in the air fryer basket.
7. Serve and enjoy.

Nutritional Value (Amount per Serving):
Calories 348; Fat 14 g; Carbohydrates 6.4 g; Sugar 2.2 g; Protein 47.1 g; Cholesterol 189 mg

Whole Chicken

Preparation Time: 10 minutes; Cooking Time: 35 minutes; Serve: 4
Ingredients:
- 4 lbs whole chicken, cut into pieces
- 2 tsp ground sumac
- 4 garlic cloves, minced
- 2 tbsp olive oil
- 1 tsp lemon zest
- 2 tsp kosher salt

Directions:

1. Rub chicken with oil, sumac, lemon zest, and salt. Marinate in the refrigerator for 3 hours.
2. Select Air Fry mode.
3. Set time to 35 minutes and temperature 350 F then press START.
4. The air fryer display will prompt you to ADD FOOD once the temperature is reached then place the marinated chicken in the air fryer basket.
5. Serve and enjoy.

Nutritional Value (Amount per Serving):
Calories 227; Fat 16.2 g; Carbohydrates 1.1 g; Sugar 0.1 g; Protein 20 g; Cholesterol 98 mg

Asian Chicken Wings

Preparation Time: 10 minutes; Cooking Time: 30 minutes; Serve: 2
Ingredients:
- 4 chicken wings
- 1 tbsp soy sauce
- 1 tbsp Chinese spice
- 1 tsp mixed spice
- Pepper
- Salt

Directions:
1. Add chicken wings into the bowl.
2. Add remaining ingredients and toss well.
3. Select Air Fry mode.
4. Set time to 30 minutes and temperature 350 F then press START.
5. The air fryer display will prompt you to ADD FOOD once the temperature is reached then place chicken wings in the air fryer basket. Turn chicken wings halfway through.
6. Serve and enjoy.

Nutritional Value (Amount per Serving):
Calories 387; Fat 15 g; Carbohydrates 0.8 g; Sugar 0.2 g; Protein 58.4 g; Cholesterol 177 mg

Cheese Fajita Chicken

Preparation Time: 10 minutes; Cooking Time: 15 minutes; Serve: 4
Ingredients:
- 4 chicken breasts, make horizontal cuts on each piece
- 1 bell pepper, sliced
- 2 tbsp fajita seasoning
- 2 tbsp olive oil
- 1/2 cup cheddar cheese, shredded
- 1 onion, sliced

Directions:
1. Rub oil and seasoning all over the chicken breast.
2. Add chicken, bell pepper, and onion into the baking dish.
3. Select Air Fry mode.
4. Set time to 10 minutes and temperature 380 F then press START.
5. The air fryer display will prompt you to ADD FOOD once the temperature is reached then place the baking dish in the air fryer basket.
6. Sprinkle cheese on top of the chicken and cook for 5 minutes more.
7. Serve and enjoy.

Nutritional Value (Amount per Serving):
Calories 431; Fat 22.6 g; Carbohydrates 8.2 g; Sugar 2.7 g; Protein 46.4 g; Cholesterol 145 mg

Spicy Chicken Wings

Preparation Time: 10 minutes; Cooking Time: 25 minutes; Serve: 4
Ingredients:
- 2 lbs chicken wings
- 6 tbsp butter, melted

- 12 oz hot sauce
- 1 tsp chili powder

Directions:
1. Select Air Fry mode.
2. Set time to 25 minutes and temperature 380 F then press START.
3. The air fryer display will prompt you to ADD FOOD once the temperature is reached then place chicken wings in the air fryer basket.
4. Meanwhile, in a bowl, mix together hot sauce, butter, and chili powder.
5. Add cooked chicken wings into the sauce bowl and toss well.
6. Serve and enjoy.

Nutritional Value (Amount per Serving):
Calories 595; Fat 34.5 g; Carbohydrates 1.9 g; Sugar 1.1 g; Protein 66.3 g; Cholesterol 248 mg

Cheesy Chicken Casserole

Preparation Time: 10 minutes; Cooking Time: 40 minutes; Serve: 8

Ingredients:
- 2 lbs cooked chicken, shredded
- 6 oz cream cheese, softened
- 4 oz butter, melted
- 6 oz ham, cut into small pieces
- 5 oz Swiss cheese
- 1 oz fresh lemon juice
- 1 tbsp Dijon mustard
- 1/2 tsp salt

Directions:
1. Arrange chicken in the bottom of the baking dish then layer ham pieces on top.
2. Add butter, lemon juice, mustard, cream cheese, and salt into the blender and blend until a thick sauce.
3. Spread sauce over top of chicken and ham mixture in the baking dish.
4. Arrange cheese slices on top of sauce.
5. Select Bake mode.
6. Set time to 40 minutes and temperature 350 F then press START.
7. The air fryer display will prompt you to ADD FOOD once the temperature is reached then place the baking dish in the air fryer basket.
8. Serve and enjoy.

Nutritional Value (Amount per Serving):
Calories 451; Fat 29.2 g; Carbohydrates 2.5 g; Sugar 0.4 g; Protein 43 g; Cholesterol 170 mg

Chicken Sun-dried Tomatoes & Mushrooms

Preparation Time: 10 minutes; Cooking Time: 30 minutes; Serve: 4

Ingredients:
- 2 lbs chicken breasts, halved
- 8 oz mushrooms, sliced
- 1/2 cup mayonnaise
- 1/3 cup sun-dried tomatoes
- 1 tsp salt

Directions:
1. Place chicken breasts into the baking dish and top with sun-dried tomatoes, mushrooms, mayonnaise, and salt. Mix well.
2. Select Bake mode.
3. Set time to 30 minutes and temperature 400 F then press START.
4. The air fryer display will prompt you to ADD FOOD once the temperature is reached then place the baking dish in the air fryer basket.
5. Serve and enjoy.

Nutritional Value (Amount per Serving):
Calories 560; Fat 26.8 g; Carbohydrates 9.5 g; Sugar 3.2 g; Protein 67.8 g; Cholesterol 209 mg

Meatloaf

Preparation Time: 10 minutes; Cooking Time: 40 minutes; Serve: 8

Ingredients:
- 2 eggs
- 1/2 cup parmesan cheese, grated
- 1/2 cup marinara sauce, without sugar
- 1 cup cottage cheese
- 1 lb mozzarella cheese, cut into cubes
- 2 lbs ground turkey
- 2 tsp Italian seasoning
- 1/4 cup basil pesto
- 1 tsp salt

Directions:
1. Add all ingredients into the large bowl and mix until well combined.
2. Transfer bowl mixture into the loaf pan.
3. Select Bake mode.
4. Set time to 40 minutes and temperature 400 F then press START.
5. The air fryer display will prompt you to ADD FOOD once the temperature is reached then place the coated loaf pan in the air fryer basket.
6. Serve and enjoy.

Nutritional Value (Amount per Serving):
Calories 337; Fat 18.6 g; Carbohydrates 4.1 g; Sugar 1.7 g; Protein 42.3 g; Cholesterol 172 mg

BBQ Meatloaf

Preparation Time: 10 minutes; Cooking Time: 35 minutes; Serve: 8

Ingredients:
- 1 egg
- 1 tsp chili powder
- 1 tsp garlic powder
- 1 tsp garlic, minced
- 1 tbsp onion, minced
- 2 lbs ground turkey
- 2 oz BBQ sauce, sugar-free
- 1 tsp ground mustard
- 1 cup cheddar cheese, shredded
- 1 tsp salt

Directions:
1. In a large bowl, combine together all ingredients then transfer to the greased casserole dish.
2. Select Bake mode.
3. Set time to 35 minutes and temperature 400 F then press START.
4. The air fryer display will prompt you to ADD FOOD once the temperature is reached then place a casserole dish in the air fryer basket.
5. Serve and enjoy.

Nutritional Value (Amount per Serving):
Calories 302; Fat 17.9 g; Carbohydrates 3.6 g; Sugar 2.2 g; Protein 35.5 g; Cholesterol 151 mg

Chicken Pepper Zucchini Casserole

Preparation Time: 10 minutes; Cooking Time: 40 minutes; Serve: 8

Ingredients:
- 2 1/2 lbs chicken breasts, boneless and cubed
- 12 oz roasted red peppers, drained and chopped
- 10 garlic cloves
- 2/3 cup mayonnaise
- 5 zucchini, cut into cubes
- 1 tsp xanthan gum
- 1 tbsp tomato paste
- 5 oz coconut cream
- 1 tsp salt

Directions:
1. Add zucchini and chicken to a casserole dish.
2. Select Bake mode.

3. Set time to 25 minutes and temperature 400 F then press START.
4. The air fryer display will prompt you to ADD FOOD once the temperature is reached then place a casserole dish in the air fryer basket.
5. Stir well and cook for 10 minutes more.
6. Meanwhile, in a bowl, stir together the remaining ingredients.
7. Pour bowl mixture over chicken mixture and broil for 5 minutes.
8. Serve and enjoy.

Nutritional Value (Amount per Serving):
Calories 483; Fat 29.7 g; Carbohydrates 9.8 g; Sugar 4.9 g; Protein 43.7 g; Cholesterol 137 mg

Delicious Chicken Fajita Casserole

Preparation Time: 10 minutes; Cooking Time: 15 minutes; Serve: 4

Ingredients:
- 1 lb cooked chicken, shredded
- 1 bell pepper, sliced
- 1/3 cup mayonnaise
- 7 oz cream cheese
- 7 oz cheese, shredded
- 2 tbsp tex-mix seasoning
- 1 onion, sliced
- Pepper
- Salt

Directions:
1. Mix all ingredients except 2 oz shredded cheese in a greased baking dish.
2. Spread remaining cheese on top.
3. Select Bake mode.
4. Set time to 15 minutes and temperature 400 F then press START.
5. The air fryer display will prompt you to ADD FOOD once the temperature is reached then place the baking dish in the air fryer basket.
6. Serve and enjoy.

Nutritional Value (Amount per Serving):
Calories 478; Fat 39.8 g; Carbohydrates 7.3 g; Sugar 4.8 g; Protein 38.8 g; Cholesterol 149 mg

Chapter 5: Meat Recipes

Pecan Dijon Pork Chops

Preparation Time: 10 minutes; Cooking Time: 12 minutes; Serve: 6
Ingredients:
- 1 egg
- 6 pork chops, boneless
- 2 garlic cloves, minced
- 1 tbsp water
- 1 tsp Dijon mustard
- 1 tsp garlic powder
- 1 tsp onion powder
- 2 tsp Italian seasoning
- 1/3 cup arrowroot
- 1 cup pecans, finely chopped
- 1/4 tsp salt

Directions:
1. In a shallow bowl, whisk the egg with garlic, water, and Dijon mustard.
2. In a separate shallow bowl, mix together arrowroot, pecans, Italian seasoning, onion powder, garlic powder, and salt.
3. Dip pork chop in the egg mixture and coat with arrowroot mixture.
4. Place the cooking tray in the air fryer basket.
5. Select Air Fry mode.
6. Set time to 12 minutes and temperature 400 F then press START.
7. The air fryer display will prompt you to ADD FOOD once the temperature is reached then place coated pork chops in the air fryer basket.
8. Turn pork chops halfway through.
9. Serve and enjoy.

Nutritional Value (Amount per Serving):
Calories 410; Fat 34.1 g; Carbohydrates 4.8 g; Sugar 1.1 g; Protein 21.4 g; Cholesterol 97 mg

Simple & Juicy Steak

Preparation Time: 10 minutes; Cooking Time: 13 minutes; Serve: 2
Ingredients:
- 12 oz ribeye steak
- 1 tsp steak seasoning
- 1 tbsp olive oil
- Pepper
- Salt

Directions:
1. Coat steak with oil and season with steak seasoning, pepper, and salt.
2. Place the cooking tray in the air fryer basket.
3. Select Air Fry mode.
4. Set time to 13 minutes and temperature 400 F then press START.
5. The air fryer display will prompt you to ADD FOOD once the temperature is reached then place steak in the air fryer basket.
6. Serve and enjoy.

Nutritional Value (Amount per Serving):
Calories 241; Fat 11.6 g; Carbohydrates 0 g; Sugar 0 g; Protein 39.1 g; Cholesterol 90 mg

Marinated Ribeye Steaks

Preparation Time: 10 minutes; Cooking Time: 12 minutes; Serve: 4
Ingredients:
- 2 large ribeye steaks, 1 1/2-inch thick
- 1 1/2 tbsp Montreal steak seasoning
- 1/2 cup low-sodium soy sauce
- 1/4 cup olive oil

Directions:
1. Add soy sauce, oil, and Montreal steak seasoning in a large zip-lock bag.

2. Add steaks in a zip-lock bag. Seal bag shakes well and places in the refrigerator for 2 hours.
3. Place the cooking tray in the air fryer basket.
4. Select Air Fry mode.
5. Set time to 12 minutes and temperature 400 F then press START.
6. The air fryer display will prompt you to ADD FOOD once the temperature is reached then remove steaks from marinade and place in the air fryer basket.
7. Turn steaks halfway through.
8. Serve and enjoy.

Nutritional Value (Amount per Serving):
Calories 186; Fat 14.1 g; Carbohydrates 2 g; Sugar 2 g; Protein 15 g; Cholesterol 30 mg

Pork Chop Fries

Preparation Time: 10 minutes; Cooking Time: 15 minutes; Serve: 4
Ingredients:
- 1 lb pork chops, cut into fries
- 1/2 cup parmesan cheese, grated
- 3.5 oz pork rinds, crushed
- 1/2 cup ranch dressing
- Pepper
- Salt

Directions:
1. In a shallow dish, mix together crushed pork rinds, parmesan cheese, pepper, and salt.
2. Add pork chop pieces and ranch dressing into the zip-lock bag, seal bag, and shake well.
3. Remove pork chop pieces from zip-lock bag and coat with crushed pork rind mixture.
4. Place the cooking tray in the air fryer basket. Line air fryer basket with parchment paper.
5. Select Bake mode.
6. Set time to 15 minutes and temperature 400 F then press START.
7. The air fryer display will prompt you to ADD FOOD once the temperature is reached then place breaded pork chop fries in the air fryer basket.
8. Serve and enjoy.

Nutritional Value (Amount per Serving):
Calories 608; Fat 43.4 g; Carbohydrates 2.7 g; Sugar 0.8 g; Protein 51.2 g; Cholesterol 154 mg

Pork Kebabs

Preparation Time: 10 minutes; Cooking Time: 15 minutes; Serve: 6
Ingredients:
- 2 lbs country-style pork ribs, cut into cubes
- 1/4 cup soy sauce
- 1/2 cup olive oil
- 1 tbsp Italian seasoning

Directions:
1. Add soy sauce, oil, Italian seasoning, and pork cubes into the zip-lock bag, seal bag and place in the refrigerator for 4 hours.
2. Remove pork cubes from marinade and place the cubes on wooden skewers.
3. Place the cooking tray in the air fryer basket. Line air fryer basket with parchment paper.
4. Select Bake mode.
5. Set time to 15 minutes and temperature 380 F then press START.
6. The air fryer display will prompt you to ADD FOOD once the temperature is reached then place pork skewers in the air fryer basket.
7. Serve and enjoy.

Nutritional Value (Amount per Serving):
Calories 438; Fat 34.9 g; Carbohydrates 1.1 g; Sugar 0.4 g; Protein 30.1 g; Cholesterol 115 mg

Meatballs

Preparation Time: 10 minutes; Cooking Time: 10 minutes; Serve: 4
Ingredients:
- 2 eggs
- 1 tsp sesame oil
- 1 tsp ginger, minced
- 1 tsp garlic, minced
- 1/2 cup almond flour
- 2 lbs ground pork
- 1/3 tsp red chili pepper flakes
- 1 tbsp scallions, diced
- 1 tsp soy sauce
- Pepper
- Salt

Directions:
1. Add all ingredients into the large bowl and mix until well combined.
2. Male small balls from meat mixture.
3. Select Air Fry mode.
4. Set time to 10 minutes and temperature 400 F then press START.
5. The air fryer display will prompt you to ADD FOOD once the temperature is reached then place meatballs in the air fryer basket.
6. Serve and enjoy.

Nutritional Value (Amount per Serving):
Calories 390; Fat 13.1 g; Carbohydrates 1.7 g; Sugar 0.4 g; Protein 63.1 g; Cholesterol 247 mg

Feta Cheese Meatballs

Preparation Time: 10 minutes; Cooking Time: 12 minutes; Serve: 8
Ingredients:
- 2 lbs ground pork
- 2 eggs, lightly beaten
- 1/4 cup fresh parsley, chopped
- 1 tbsp garlic, minced
- 1 onion, chopped
- 1 tbsp Worcestershire sauce
- 1/2 cup feta cheese, crumbled
- 1/2 cup almond flour
- Pepper
- Salt

Directions:
1. Add all ingredients into the mixing bowl and mix until well combined.
2. Make small balls from the meat mixture.
3. Select Air Fry mode.
4. Set time to 12 minutes and temperature 400 F then press START.
5. The air fryer display will prompt you to ADD FOOD once the temperature is reached then place meatballs in the air fryer basket.
6. Serve and enjoy.

Nutritional Value (Amount per Serving):
Calories 222; Fat 8 g; Carbohydrates 3 g; Sugar 1.5 g; Protein 33.1 g; Cholesterol 132 mg

Asian Meatballs

Preparation Time: 10 minutes; Cooking Time: 15 minutes; Serve: 4
Ingredients:
- 1 lb ground pork
- 1/2 lime juice
- 2 tsp curry paste
- 1 tbsp Worcestershire sauce
- 1 tbsp soy sauce
- 1 tsp garlic puree
- 1 tsp coriander
- 1 tsp Chinese spice
- 1 onion, chopped
- Pepper
- Salt

Directions:

1. Add ground meat and remaining ingredients into the large bowl and mix until well combined.
2. Make small meatballs from meat mixture.
3. Select Air Fry mode.
4. Set time to 15 minutes and temperature 350 F then press START.
5. The air fryer display will prompt you to ADD FOOD once the temperature is reached then place meatballs in the air fryer basket.
6. Serve and enjoy.

Nutritional Value (Amount per Serving):
Calories 201; Fat 5.8 g; Carbohydrates 4.9 g; Sugar 2.1 g; Protein 30.5 g; Cholesterol 83 mg

Spicy Pork Patties

Preparation Time: 10 minutes; Cooking Time: 10 minutes; Serve: 2
Ingredients:
- 1/2 lb ground pork
- 1 tbsp Cajun seasoning
- 1 egg, lightly beaten
- 1/2 cup almond flour
- Pepper
- Salt

Directions:
1. Add all ingredients into the large bowl and mix until well combined.
2. Make two equal shapes of patties from the meat mixture.
3. Select Air Fry mode.
4. Set time to 10 minutes and temperature 360 F then press START.
5. The air fryer display will prompt you to ADD FOOD once the temperature is reached then place patties in the air fryer basket.
6. Serve and enjoy.

Nutritional Value (Amount per Serving):
Calories 234; Fat 9.7 g; Carbohydrates 1.7 g; Sugar 0.4 g; Protein 34 g; Cholesterol 165 mg

Herb Pork Chops

Preparation Time: 10 minutes; Cooking Time: 15 minutes; Serve: 4
Ingredients:
- 4 pork chops
- 2 tsp oregano
- 2 tsp thyme
- 2 tsp sage
- 1 tsp garlic powder
- 1 tsp paprika
- 1 tsp rosemary
- Pepper
- Salt

Directions:
1. Spray pork chops with cooking spray.
2. Mix together garlic powder, paprika, rosemary, oregano, thyme, sage, pepper, and salt and rub over pork chops.
3. Select Air Fry mode.
4. Set time to 15 minutes and temperature 360 F then press START.
5. The air fryer display will prompt you to ADD FOOD once the temperature is reached then place pork chops in the air fryer basket. Turn pork chops halfway through.
6. Serve and enjoy.

Nutritional Value (Amount per Serving):
Calories 266; Fat 20.2 g; Carbohydrates 2 g; Sugar 0.3 g; Protein 18.4 g; Cholesterol 69 mg

Spicy Parmesan Pork Chops

Preparation Time: 10 minutes; Cooking Time: 9 minutes; Serve: 2

Ingredients:
- 2 pork chops, boneless
- 1 tsp paprika
- 3 tbsp parmesan cheese, grated
- 1/3 cup almond flour
- 1 tsp Cajun seasoning
- 1 tsp dried mixed herbs

Directions:
1. In a shallow bowl, mix together parmesan cheese, almond flour, paprika, mixed herbs, and Cajun seasoning.
2. Spray pork chops with cooking spray and coat with parmesan cheese.
3. Select Air Fry mode.
4. Set time to 9 minutes and temperature 350 F then press START.
5. The air fryer display will prompt you to ADD FOOD once the temperature is reached then place breaded pork chops in the air fryer basket. Turn pork chops halfway through.
6. Serve and enjoy.

Nutritional Value (Amount per Serving):
Calories 359; Fat 27.2 g; Carbohydrates 2.6 g; Sugar 0.3 g; Protein 26.4 g; Cholesterol 85 mg

Moist Pork Chops

Preparation Time: 10 minutes; Cooking Time: 14 minutes; Serve: 2

Ingredients:
- 2 pork chops
- 1 tsp paprika
- 1 tsp garlic powder
- 1 tsp olive oil
- Pepper
- Salt

Directions:
1. Brush pork chops with olive oil and season with garlic powder, paprika, pepper, and salt.
2. Select Air Fry mode.
3. Set time to 14 minutes and temperature 360 F then press START.
4. The air fryer display will prompt you to ADD FOOD once the temperature is reached then place pork chops in the air fryer basket. Turn pork chops halfway through.
5. Serve and enjoy.

Nutritional Value (Amount per Serving):
Calories 284; Fat 22.4 g; Carbohydrates 1.6 g; Sugar 0.5 g; Protein 18.4 g; Cholesterol 69 mg

Air Fried Pork Bites

Preparation Time: 10 minutes; Cooking Time: 15 minutes; Serve: 4

Ingredients:
- 1 lb pork belly, cut into 1-inch cubes
- 1 tsp soy sauce
- Pepper
- Salt

Directions:
1. In a bowl, toss pork cubes with soy sauce, pepper, and salt.
2. Select Air Fry mode.
3. Set time to 15 minutes and temperature 400 F then press START.
4. The air fryer display will prompt you to ADD FOOD once the temperature is reached then place pork cubes in the air fryer basket.
5. Serve and enjoy.

Nutritional Value (Amount per Serving):
Calories 524; Fat 30.5 g; Carbohydrates 0.1 g; Sugar 0 g; Protein 52.4 g; Cholesterol 131 mg

Meatballs

Preparation Time: 10 minutes; Cooking Time: 10 minutes; Serve: 4

Ingredients:

- 1 lb ground beef
- 1/2 cup cheddar cheese, shredded
- 1 egg, lightly beaten
- 1/4 cup cilantro, chopped
- 1/4 cup onion, chopped
- 2 tbsp taco seasoning
- 1 tbsp garlic, minced
- Pepper
- Salt

Directions:
1. Add ground beef and remaining ingredients into the large bowl and mix until well combined.
2. Make small meatballs from meat mixture.
3. Select Air Fry mode.
4. Set time to 10 minutes and temperature 400 F then press START.
5. The air fryer display will prompt you to ADD FOOD once the temperature is reached then place meatballs in the air fryer basket.
6. Serve and enjoy.

Nutritional Value (Amount per Serving):
Calories 301; Fat 13.5 g; Carbohydrates 2.5 g; Sugar 0.5 g; Protein 40.1 g; Cholesterol 159 mg

Beef Kebabs

Preparation Time: 10 minutes; Cooking Time: 15 minutes; Serve: 4
Ingredients:
- 1 lb ground beef
- 1/2 cup onion, minced
- 1/4 tsp ground cinnamon
- 1/4 tsp ground cardamom
- 1/2 tsp cayenne
- 1/2 tsp turmeric
- 1/2 tbsp ginger paste
- 1/2 tbsp garlic paste
- 1/4 cup cilantro, chopped
- 1 tsp salt

Directions:
1. Add meat and remaining ingredients into the large bowl and mix until well combined.
2. Make sausage shape kebabs.
3. Select Bake mode.
4. Set time to 15 minutes and temperature 350 F then press START.
5. The air fryer display will prompt you to ADD FOOD once the temperature is reached then place kebabs in the air fryer basket.
6. Serve and enjoy.

Nutritional Value (Amount per Serving):
Calories 223; Fat 7.2 g; Carbohydrates 2.7 g; Sugar 0.7 g; Protein 34.8 g; Cholesterol 101 mg

Steak Tips

Preparation Time: 10 minutes; Cooking Time: 5 minutes; Serve: 3
Ingredients:
- 1 lb steak, cut into cubes
- 1 tsp olive oil
- 1 tsp Montreal steak seasoning
- Pepper
- Salt

Directions:
1. In a bowl, add steak cubes and remaining ingredients and toss well.
2. Select Air Fry mode.
3. Set time to 5 minutes and temperature 400 F then press START.
4. The air fryer display will prompt you to ADD FOOD once the temperature is reached then place steak cubes in the air fryer basket.
5. Serve and enjoy.

Nutritional Value (Amount per Serving):

Calories 317; Fat 9.1 g; Carbohydrates 0 g; Sugar 0 g; Protein 54.6 g; Cholesterol 136 mg

Rosemary Beef Tips

Preparation Time: 10 minutes; Cooking Time: 12 minutes; Serve: 4
Ingredients:
- 1 lb steak, cut into 1-inch cubes
- 1 tsp paprika
- 2 tsp onion powder
- 1 tsp garlic powder
- 2 tbsp coconut aminos
- 2 tsp rosemary, crushed
- Pepper
- Salt

Directions:
1. Add meat and remaining ingredients into the mixing bowl and mix well and let it sit for 5 minutes.
2. Select Air Fry mode.
3. Set time to 12 minutes and temperature 380 F then press START.
4. The air fryer display will prompt you to ADD FOOD once the temperature is reached then place steak cubes in the air fryer basket. Stir halfway through.
5. Serve and enjoy.

Nutritional Value (Amount per Serving):
Calories 243; Fat 5.9 g; Carbohydrates 3.7 g; Sugar 0.7 g; Protein 41.3 g; Cholesterol 102 mg

Ranch Patties

Preparation Time: 10 minutes; Cooking Time: 12 minutes; Serve: 4
Ingredients:
- 1 lb ground beef
- 1/2 tsp dried dill
- 1/2 tsp onion powder
- 1/2 tsp garlic powder
- 2 tsp dried parsley
- 1/8 tsp dried dill
- 1/2 tsp paprika
- Pepper
- Salt

Directions:
1. Add all ingredients into the large bowl and mix until well combined.
2. Make 4 even shape patties from meat mixture.
3. Select Air Fry mode.
4. Set time to 12 minutes and temperature 350 F then press START.
5. The air fryer display will prompt you to ADD FOOD once the temperature is reached then place patties in the air fryer basket.
6. Serve and enjoy.

Nutritional Value (Amount per Serving):
Calories 214; Fat 7.1 g; Carbohydrates 0.8 g; Sugar 0.2 g; Protein 34.6 g; Cholesterol 101 mg

Sirloin Steak

Preparation Time: 10 minutes; Cooking Time: 14 minutes; Serve: 2
Ingredients:
- 1 lb sirloin steaks
- 1/2 tsp garlic powder
- 1/4 tsp onion powder
- 1 tsp olive oil
- Pepper
- Salt

Directions:
1. Brush steak with olive oil and rub with garlic powder, onion powder, pepper, and salt.
2. Select Air Fry mode.
3. Set time to 14 minutes and temperature 400 F then press START.

4. The air fryer display will prompt you to ADD FOOD once the temperature is reached then place steaks in the air fryer basket. Turn steak halfway through.
5. Serve and enjoy.

Nutritional Value (Amount per Serving):
Calories 445; Fat 16.5 g; Carbohydrates 0.8 g; Sugar 0.3 g; Protein 69 g; Cholesterol 203 mg

Easy Beef Kebabs

Preparation Time: 10 minutes; Cooking Time: 10 minutes; Serve: 4

Ingredients:
- 1 lb beef chuck ribs, cut into 1-inch pieces
- 1/2 onion, cut into 1-inch pieces
- 2 tbsp soy sauce
- 1/3 cup sour cream
- 1 bell pepper, cut into 1-inch pieces

Directions:
1. Add meat pieces, soy sauce, and sour cream into the mixing bowl and mix well.
2. Cover bowl and place in the refrigerator overnight.
3. Thread marinated meat, onion, and bell peppers pieces onto the soaked wooden skewers.
4. Select Air Fry mode.
5. Set time to 10 minutes and temperature 400 F then press START.
6. The air fryer display will prompt you to ADD FOOD once the temperature is reached then place skewers in the air fryer basket. Turn halfway through.
7. Serve and enjoy.

Nutritional Value (Amount per Serving):
Calories 271; Fat 11.2 g; Carbohydrates 5 g; Sugar 2.3 g; Protein 36 g; Cholesterol 110 mg

Steak & Mushrooms

Preparation Time: 10 minutes; Cooking Time: 18 minutes; Serve: 4

Ingredients:
- 1 lb steaks, cut into 1-inch cubes
- 2 tbsp olive oil
- 8 oz mushrooms, halved
- 1/2 tsp garlic powder
- 1 tsp Worcestershire sauce
- Pepper
- Salt

Directions:
1. Add steak cubes and remaining ingredients into the mixing bowl and toss until well coated.
2. Select Air Fry mode.
3. Set time to 18 minutes and temperature 400 F then press START.
4. The air fryer display will prompt you to ADD FOOD once the temperature is reached then place steak and mushrooms in the air fryer basket. Stir halfway through.
5. Serve and enjoy.

Nutritional Value (Amount per Serving):
Calories 300; Fat 12.8 g; Carbohydrates 2.4 g; Sugar 1.3 g; Protein 42.8 g; Cholesterol 102 mg

Meatballs

Preparation Time: 10 minutes; Cooking Time: 12 minutes; Serve: 6

Ingredients:
- 2 lbs ground beef
- 2 oz pork rind, crushed
- 2 eggs, lightly beaten
- 3 oz parmesan cheese, shredded
- Pepper
- Salt

Directions:
1. Add all ingredients into the mixing bowl and mix until well combined.

2. Make small balls from the meat mixture.
3. Select Air Fry mode.
4. Set time to 12 minutes and temperature 350 F then press START.
5. The air fryer display will prompt you to ADD FOOD once the temperature is reached then place meatballs in the air fryer basket.
6. Serve and enjoy.

Nutritional Value (Amount per Serving):
Calories 401; Fat 17.3 g; Carbohydrates 17.3 g; Sugar 0.1 g; Protein 58.4 g; Cholesterol 213 mg

Air Fryer Beef Fajitas

Preparation Time: 10 minutes; Cooking Time: 8 minutes; Serve: 4
Ingredients:
- 1 lb steak, sliced
- 1/2 tbsp chili powder
- 3 tbsp olive oil
- 2 bell peppers, sliced
- 1 tsp garlic powder
- 1 tsp paprika
- 1 tsp cumin
- Pepper
- Salt

Directions:
1. In a mixing bowl, toss sliced steak with remaining ingredients.
2. Select Air Fry mode.
3. Set time to 8 minutes and temperature 390 F then press START.
4. The air fryer display will prompt you to ADD FOOD once the temperature is reached then place fajitas in the air fryer basket.
5. Serve and enjoy.

Nutritional Value (Amount per Serving):
Calories 344; Fat 16.7 g; Carbohydrates 6.1 g; Sugar 3.3 g; Protein 42 g; Cholesterol 102 mg

Flavorful Burger Patties

Preparation Time: 10 minutes; Cooking Time: 15 minutes; Serve: 4
Ingredients:
- 1 lb ground lamb
- 1/4 tsp cayenne pepper
- 1/4 cup fresh parsley, chopped
- 1/4 cup onion, minced
- 1 tbsp garlic, minced
- 1/2 tsp ground allspice
- 1 tsp ground cinnamon
- 1 tsp ground coriander
- 1 tsp ground cumin
- 1/4 tsp pepper
- 1 tsp kosher salt

Directions:
1. Add all ingredients into the large bowl and mix until well combined.
2. Make 4 patties from the meat mixture.
3. Select Bake mode.
4. Set time to 14 minutes and temperature 375 F then press START.
5. The air fryer display will prompt you to ADD FOOD once the temperature is reached then place patties in the air fryer basket. Turn patties halfway through.
6. Serve and enjoy.

Nutritional Value (Amount per Serving):
Calories 223; Fat 8.5 g; Carbohydrates 2.6 g; Sugar 0.4 g; Protein 32.3 g; Cholesterol 102 mg

Meatballs

Preparation Time: 10 minutes; Cooking Time: 20 minutes; Serve: 4
Ingredients:

- 1 lb ground lamb
- 2 tbsp fresh parsley, chopped
- 1 tbsp garlic, minced
- 1 egg, lightly beaten
- 1/4 tsp red pepper flakes
- 1 tsp ground cumin
- 2 tsp fresh oregano, chopped
- 1/4 tsp pepper
- 1 tsp kosher salt

Directions:
1. Add all ingredients into the mixing bowl and mix until well combined.
2. Make small meatballs from meat mixture.
3. Select Bake mode.
4. Set time to 20 minutes and temperature 400 F then press START.
5. The air fryer display will prompt you to ADD FOOD once the temperature is reached then place meatballs in the air fryer basket.
6. Serve and enjoy.

Nutritional Value (Amount per Serving):
Calories 235; Fat 9.7 g; Carbohydrates 1.7 g; Sugar 0.2 g; Protein 33.6 g; Cholesterol 143 mg

Juicy Pork Tenderloin

Preparation Time: 10 minutes; Cooking Time: 20 minutes; Serve: 4
Ingredients:
- 1 1/2 lbs pork tenderloin
- 2 tbsp olive oil
- 1 tsp garlic powder
- 1 tsp Italian seasoning
- 1/4 tsp pepper
- 1 tsp sea salt

Directions:
1. Rub pork tenderloin with 1 tablespoon of olive oil.
2. Mix together garlic powder, Italian seasoning, pepper, and salt and rub over pork tenderloin.
3. Heat remaining oil in a pan over medium-high heat.
4. Add pork tenderloin in hot oil and cook until brown
5. Select Bake mode.
6. Set time to 15 minutes and temperature 400 F then press START.
7. The air fryer display will prompt you to ADD FOOD once the temperature is reached then place pork tenderloin in the air fryer basket.
8. Serve and enjoy.

Nutritional Value (Amount per Serving):
Calories 309; Fat 13.3 g; Carbohydrates 0.7 g; Sugar 0.3 g; Protein 44.7 g; Cholesterol 125 mg

Meatloaf

Preparation Time: 10 minutes; Cooking Time: 20 minutes; Serve: 4
Ingredients:
- 1 egg, lightly beaten
- 3 tbsp almond flour
- 1 onion, chopped
- 1 lb ground pork
- 1 tbsp thyme, chopped
- 1/4 tsp garlic powder
- Pepper
- Salt

Directions:
1. Add all ingredients into the mixing bowl and mix until well combined.
2. Pour meat mixture into the greased loaf pan.
3. Select Bake mode.
4. Set time to 20 minutes and temperature 390 F then press START.
5. The air fryer display will prompt you to ADD FOOD once the temperature is reached then place the loaf pan in the air fryer basket.

6. Serve and enjoy.

Nutritional Value (Amount per Serving):
Calories 311; Fat 15.7 g; Carbohydrates 7.7 g; Sugar 2.1 g; Protein 36 g; Cholesterol 124 mg

Baked Beef & Broccoli

Preparation Time: 10 minutes; Cooking Time: 25 minutes; Serve: 2

Ingredients:
- 1/2 cup broccoli florets
- 1/2 lb beef stew meat, cut into pieces
- 1 onion, sliced
- 1 tbsp vinegar
- 1 tbsp olive oil
- Pepper
- Salt

Directions:
1. Add meat and remaining ingredients into the large bowl and toss well.
2. Select Bake mode.
3. Set time to 25 minutes and temperature 390 F then press START.
4. The air fryer display will prompt you to ADD FOOD once the temperature is reached then place beef and broccoli in the air fryer basket.
5. Serve and enjoy.

Nutritional Value (Amount per Serving):
Calories 302; Fat 14.2 g; Carbohydrates 6.8 g; Sugar 2.8 g; Protein 35.7 g; Cholesterol 101 mg

Lemon Pepper Pork

Preparation Time: 10 minutes; Cooking Time: 15 minutes; Serve: 4

Ingredients:
- 4 pork chops, boneless
- 1 tsp lemon pepper seasoning
- Salt

Directions:
1. Season pork chops with lemon pepper seasoning, and salt.
2. Select Air Fry mode.
3. Set time to 15 minutes and temperature 400 F then press START.
4. The air fryer display will prompt you to ADD FOOD once the temperature is reached then place pork chops in the air fryer basket.
5. Serve and enjoy.

Nutritional Value (Amount per Serving):
Calories 257; Fat 19.9 g; Carbohydrates 0.3 g; Sugar 0 g; Protein 18 g; Cholesterol 69 mg

Meatballs

Preparation Time: 10 minutes; Cooking Time: 20 minutes; Serve: 6

Ingredients:
- 1 lb ground pork
- 1 lb ground beef
- 1 tsp oregano
- 1 tsp cinnamon
- 2 tsp cumin
- 2 tsp coriander
- 1 tsp garlic, minced
- 1 small onion, grated
- 1 egg, lightly beaten
- 1 tbsp fresh mint, chopped
- 1/4 cup fresh parsley, minced
- 1/2 tsp allspice
- 1 tsp paprika
- 1/4 tsp pepper
- 1/2 tsp salt

Directions:
1. Add all ingredients into the large mixing bowl and mix until well combined.
2. Make small balls from the meat mixture.

3. Select Bake mode.
4. Set time to 20 minutes and temperature 400 F then press START.
5. The air fryer display will prompt you to ADD FOOD once the temperature is reached then place meatballs in the air fryer basket.
6. Serve and enjoy.

Nutritional Value (Amount per Serving):
Calories 272; Fat 8.4 g; Carbohydrates 2.7 g; Sugar 0.7 g; Protein 44.1 g; Cholesterol 150 mg

Meatloaf

Preparation Time: 10 minutes; Cooking Time: 55 minutes; Serve: 6
Ingredients:
- 1 lb ground beef
- 1 lb ground pork
- 1 tsp oregano
- 1 tsp paprika
- 1 tsp cumin
- 1/4 cup fresh cilantro, chopped
- 1/2 cup sunflower seed flour
- 1/2 cup salsa, low-fodmap
- 2 eggs, lightly beaten
- 2 tbsp olive oil
- 1 red bell pepper, diced
- 1/2 tsp salt

Directions:
1. Add meat in a bowl. Cook bell pepper in olive oil over medium heat, about 5 minutes.
2. Transfer bell pepper in meat bowl. Add remaining ingredients to the meat mixture and mix until well combined.
3. Transfer meat mixture into the loaf pan.
4. Select Bake mode.
5. Set time to 55 minutes and temperature 375 F then press START.
6. The air fryer display will prompt you to ADD FOOD once the temperature is reached then place the loaf pan in the air fryer basket.
7. Serve and enjoy.

Nutritional Value (Amount per Serving):
Calories 342; Fat 13.8 g; Carbohydrates 5.4 g; Sugar 1.8 g; Protein 47.8 g; Cholesterol 177 mg

Spiced Pork Tenderloin

Preparation Time: 10 minutes; Cooking Time: 35 minutes; Serve: 6
Ingredients:
- 2 lbs pork tenderloin
- For the spice mix:
- 1/2 tsp allspice
- 1 tsp cinnamon
- 1 tsp cumin
- 1 tsp coriander
- 1/4 tsp cayenne
- 1 tsp oregano
- 1/4 tsp cloves

Directions:
1. In a small bowl, mix together all spice ingredients and set aside.
2. Using a sharp knife make slits on pork tenderloin and insert chopped garlic into each slit.
3. Rub spice mixture over pork tenderloin. Sprinkle with pepper and salt.
4. Select Bake mode.
5. Set time to 35 minutes and temperature 375 F then press START.
6. The air fryer display will prompt you to ADD FOOD once the temperature is reached then place pork tenderloin in the air fryer basket.
7. Serve and enjoy.

Nutritional Value (Amount per Serving):
Calories 220; Fat 5.5 g; Carbohydrates 0.9 g; Sugar 0 g; Protein 39.7 g; Cholesterol 110 mg

Stuffed Pork Chops

Preparation Time: 10 minutes; Cooking Time: 35 minutes; Serve: 4

Ingredients:
- 4 pork chops, boneless and thick-cut
- 2 tbsp olives, chopped
- 2 tbsp sun-dried tomatoes, chopped
- 1/2 cup feta cheese, crumbled
- 2 garlic cloves, minced
- 2 tbsp fresh parsley, chopped

Directions:
1. In a bowl, combine together feta cheese, garlic, parsley, olives, and sun-dried tomatoes.
2. Stuff cheese mixture all the pork chops. Season pork chops with pepper and salt.
3. Select Bake mode.
4. Set time to 35 minutes and temperature 375 F then press START.
5. The air fryer display will prompt you to ADD FOOD once the temperature is reached then place stuffed pork chops in the air fryer basket.
6. Serve and enjoy.

Nutritional Value (Amount per Serving):
Calories 314; Fat 24.4 g; Carbohydrates 1.9 g; Sugar 1 g; Protein 20.9 g; Cholesterol 85 mg

Spicy Pork Chops

Preparation Time: 10 minutes; Cooking Time: 10 minutes; Serve: 4

Ingredients:
- 4 pork chops
- 1/2 tsp black pepper
- 1/2 tsp ground cumin
- 1 1/2 tsp olive oil
- 1/2 tsp dried sage
- 1 tsp cayenne pepper
- 1 tsp paprika
- 1/2 tsp garlic salt

Directions:
1. In a small bowl, mix together paprika, garlic salt, sage, pepper, cayenne pepper, and cumin.
2. Rub pork chops with spice mixture.
3. Spray pork chops with cooking spray.
4. Select Bake mode.
5. Set time to 10 minutes and temperature 400 F then press START.
6. The air fryer display will prompt you to ADD FOOD once the temperature is reached then place pork chops in the air fryer basket. Turn pork chops halfway through.
7. Serve and enjoy.

Nutritional Value (Amount per Serving):
Calories 277; Fat 21.9 g; Carbohydrates 1.1 g; Sugar 0.2 g; Protein 18.3 g; Cholesterol 69 mg

Meatballs

Preparation Time: 10 minutes; Cooking Time: 15 minutes; Serve: 4

Ingredients:
- 4 oz sausage meat
- 3 tbsp almond flour
- 1 tsp sage
- 1 tsp Italian seasoning
- 1/2 tsp garlic paste
- 1/2 onion, diced
- Pepper
- Salt

Directions:
1. Add all ingredients into the mixing bowl and mix until well combined.
2. Make small balls from bowl mixture.
3. Select Air Fry mode.
4. Set time to 15 minutes and temperature 360 F then press START.

5. The air fryer display will prompt you to ADD FOOD once the temperature is reached then place meatballs in the air fryer basket.
6. Serve and enjoy.

Nutritional Value (Amount per Serving):
Calories 226; Fat 18.9 g; Carbohydrates 6.2 g; Sugar 1.4 g; Protein 10.2 g; Cholesterol 25 mg

Air Fryer Lamb Chops

Preparation Time: 10 minutes; Cooking Time: 12 minutes; Serve: 4
Ingredients:
- 4 lamb chops
- 2 garlic clove, minced
- 3 tbsp olive oil
- Pepper
- Salt

Directions:
1. In a small bowl, mix together thyme and oil.
2. Season lamb chops with pepper and salt and rubs with thyme mixture.
3. Select Air Fry mode.
4. Set time to 12 minutes and temperature 400 F then press START.
5. The air fryer display will prompt you to ADD FOOD once the temperature is reached then place lamb chops in the air fryer basket. Turn halfway through.
6. Serve and enjoy.

Nutritional Value (Amount per Serving):
Calories 701; Fat 34.5 g; Carbohydrates 0.5 g; Sugar 0 g; Protein 91.9 g; Cholesterol 294 mg

Lemon Herb Lamb Chops

Preparation Time: 10 minutes; Cooking Time: 16 minutes; Serve: 4
Ingredients:
- 1 lb lamb chops
- 1 tsp coriander
- 1 tsp oregano
- 1 tsp thyme
- 1 tsp rosemary
- 2 tbsp fresh lemon juice
- 2 tbsp olive oil
- 1 tsp salt

Directions:
1. Add all ingredients except lamb chops into the zip-lock bag.
2. Add lamb chops to the bag. Seal bag and place in the refrigerator overnight.
3. Select Air Fry mode.
4. Set time to 16 minutes and temperature 390 F then press START.
5. The air fryer display will prompt you to ADD FOOD once the temperature is reached then place lamb chops in the air fryer basket. Turn lamb chops halfway through.
6. Serve and enjoy.

Nutritional Value (Amount per Serving):
Calories 276; Fat 15.5 g; Carbohydrates 0.8 g; Sugar 0.2 g; Protein 32 g; Cholesterol 102 mg

Breaded Pork Chops

Preparation Time: 10 minutes; Cooking Time: 20 minutes; Serve: 4
Ingredients:
- 4 pork chops, boneless
- 1/4 cup parmesan cheese, grated
- 1 cup almond meal
- 1/2 tbsp black pepper
- 1 tbsp onion powder
- 1 tbsp garlic powder
- 2 eggs, lightly beaten
- 1/2 tsp sea salt

Directions:

1. In a bowl, mix together almond meal, parmesan cheese, onion powder, garlic powder, pepper, and salt.
2. Whisk eggs in a shallow dish.
3. Dip pork chops into the egg then coat with almond meal mixture.
4. Select Air Fry mode.
5. Set time to 20 minutes and temperature 350 F then press START.
6. The air fryer display will prompt you to ADD FOOD once the temperature is reached then place breaded pork chops in the air fryer basket. Turn pork chops halfway through.
7. Serve and enjoy.

Nutritional Value (Amount per Serving):
Calories 486; Fat 37.1 g; Carbohydrates 9.2 g; Sugar 2.3 g; Protein 31.1 g; Cholesterol 161 mg

Cajun Herb Pork Chops

Preparation Time: 10 minutes; Cooking Time: 9 minutes; Serve: 2
Ingredients:
- 2 pork chops, boneless
- 1 tsp herb de Provence
- 1 tsp paprika
- 1/2 tsp Cajun seasoning
- 3 tbsp parmesan cheese, grated
- 1/3 cup almond flour

Directions:
1. Mix together almond flour, Cajun seasoning, herb de Provence, paprika, and parmesan cheese.
2. Spray both the pork chops with cooking spray.
3. Coat both the pork chops with almond flour mixture.
4. Select Bake mode.
5. Set time to 8 minutes and temperature 350 F then press START.
6. The air fryer display will prompt you to ADD FOOD once the temperature is reached then place pork chops in the air fryer basket. Turn pork chops halfway through.
7. Serve and enjoy.

Nutritional Value (Amount per Serving):
Calories 332; Fat 25.3 g; Carbohydrates 2 g; Sugar 0.3 g; Protein 24 g; Cholesterol 77 mg

Creole Seasoned Pork Chops

Preparation Time: 10 minutes; Cooking Time: 12 minutes; Serve: 6
Ingredients:
- 1 1/2 lbs pork chops, boneless
- 1/4 cup parmesan cheese, grated
- 1/3 cup almond flour
- 1 tsp paprika
- 1 tsp Creole seasoning
- 1 tsp garlic powder

Directions:
1. Add all ingredients except pork chops into the zip-lock bag.
2. Add pork chops into the bag. Seal bag and shake well.
3. Remove pork chops from the zip-lock bag.
4. Select Air Fry mode.
5. Set time to 12 minutes and temperature 360 F then press START.
6. The air fryer display will prompt you to ADD FOOD once the temperature is reached then place pork chops in the air fryer basket.
7. Serve and enjoy.

Nutritional Value (Amount per Serving):
Calories 405; Fat 31.1 g; Carbohydrates 1.2 g; Sugar 0.2 g; Protein 29.1 g; Cholesterol 104 mg

Thai Pork Chops

Preparation Time: 10 minutes; Cooking Time: 12 minutes; Serve: 2

Ingredients:
- 2 pork chops
- 1 tsp black pepper
- 3 tbsp lemongrass, chopped
- 1 tbsp shallot, chopped
- 1 tbsp garlic, chopped
- 1 tsp liquid stevia
- 1 tbsp sesame oil
- 1 tbsp fish sauce
- 1 tsp soy sauce

Directions:
1. Add pork chops in a mixing bowl.
2. Pour remaining ingredients over the pork chops and mix well.
3. Place in refrigerator for 2 hours.
4. Select Air Fry mode.
5. Set time to 12 minutes and temperature 400 F then press START.
6. The air fryer display will prompt you to ADD FOOD once the temperature is reached then place marinated pork chops in the air fryer basket.
7. Serve and enjoy.

Nutritional Value (Amount per Serving):
Calories 340; Fat 26.8 g; Carbohydrates 5.3 g; Sugar 0.4 g; Protein 19.3 g; Cholesterol 69 mg

Coconut Pork Chops

Preparation Time: 10 minutes; Cooking Time: 14 minutes; Serve: 4

Ingredients:
- 4 pork chops
- 1 tbsp coconut oil
- 1 tbsp coconut butter
- 2 tsp parsley
- 2 tsp garlic, grated
- Pepper
- Salt

Directions:
1. In a large bowl, mix together with seasonings, garlic, butter, and coconut oil.
2. Add pork chops to the bowl and mix well. Place in refrigerator overnight.
3. Select Air Fry mode.
4. Set time to 14 minutes and temperature 350 F then press START.
5. The air fryer display will prompt you to ADD FOOD once the temperature is reached then place marinated pork chops in the air fryer basket. Turn pork chops halfway through.
6. Serve and enjoy.

Nutritional Value (Amount per Serving):
Calories 299; Fat 23.8 g; Carbohydrates 2.3 g; Sugar 1.3 g; Protein 18.3 g; Cholesterol 69 mg

Savory Dash Seasoned Pork Chops

Preparation Time: 10 minutes; Cooking Time: 20 minutes; Serve: 4

Ingredients:
- 4 pork chops, boneless
- 2 tbsp dash seasoning

Directions:
1. Coat pork chops with seasoning.
2. Select Air Fry mode.
3. Set time to 20 minutes and temperature 360 F then press START.
4. The air fryer display will prompt you to ADD FOOD once the temperature is reached then place pork chops in the air fryer basket. Turn pork chops halfway through.
5. Serve and enjoy.

Nutritional Value (Amount per Serving):
Calories 256; Fat 19.9 g; Carbohydrates 0 g; Sugar 0 g; Protein 18 g; Cholesterol 69 mg

Jerk Pork Cubes

Preparation Time: 10 minutes; Cooking Time: 20 minutes; Serve: 4

Ingredients:
- 1 1/2 lbs pork butt, cut into pieces
- 1/4 cup jerk paste
- Pepper
- Salt

Directions:
1. Add meat and jerk paste into the bowl and mix well and place in refrigerator overnight.
2. Select Air Fry mode.
3. Set time to 20 minutes and temperature 390 F then press START.
4. The air fryer display will prompt you to ADD FOOD once the temperature is reached then place marinated pork pieces in the air fryer basket. Stir halfway through.
5. Serve and enjoy.

Nutritional Value (Amount per Serving):
Calories 339; Fat 12.1 g; Carbohydrates 0.8 g; Sugar 0.6 g; Protein 53 g; Cholesterol 156 mg

Spicy Asian Lamb

Preparation Time: 10 minutes; Cooking Time: 10 minutes; Serve: 4

Ingredients:
- 1 lb lamb, cut into 2-inch pieces
- 1 tbsp soy sauce
- 2 tbsp vegetable oil
- 1/2 tsp cayenne
- 1 1/2 tbsp ground cumin
- 1/4 tsp liquid stevia
- 2 red chili peppers, chopped
- 1 tbsp garlic, minced
- 1 tsp salt

Directions:
1. Mix together cumin and cayenne in a small bowl.
2. Rub meat with cumin mixture and place in a large bowl.
3. Add oil, soy sauce, garlic, chili peppers, stevia, and salt over the meat. Mix well and place in the refrigerator overnight.
4. Select Air Fry mode.
5. Set time to 10 minutes and temperature 360 F then press START.
6. The air fryer display will prompt you to ADD FOOD once the temperature is reached then place marinated meat in the air fryer basket.
7. Serve and enjoy.

Nutritional Value (Amount per Serving):
Calories 229; Fat 12.5 g; Carbohydrates 1.8 g; Sugar 0.2 g; Protein 26.1 g; Cholesterol 82 mg

Meatballs

Preparation Time: 10 minutes; Cooking Time: 11 minutes; Serve: 4

Ingredients:
- 1 egg
- 1 lb ground beef
- 1 tsp Italian seasoning
- 1 tbsp onion, minced
- 1/4 cup marinara sauce, sugar-free
- 1/3 cup parmesan cheese, shredded
- 1 tsp garlic, minced
- Pepper
- Salt

Directions:
1. Add all ingredients into the mixing bowl and mix until well combined.
2. Make small balls from the meat mixture.

3. Select Air Fry mode.
   4. Set time to 11 minutes and temperature 350 F then press START.
   5. The air fryer display will prompt you to ADD FOOD once the temperature is reached then place meatballs in the air fryer basket.
   6. Serve and enjoy.

Nutritional Value (Amount per Serving):
Calories 270; Fat 10.5 g; Carbohydrates 3.1 g; Sugar 1.7 g; Protein 38.5 g; Cholesterol 149 mg

Smokey Steaks

Preparation Time: 10 minutes; Cooking Time: 7 minutes; Serve: 2

Ingredients:
- 12 oz steaks
- 1 tbsp Montreal steak seasoning
- 1 tsp liquid smoke
- 1 tbsp soy sauce
- 1/2 tbsp cocoa powder
- Pepper
- Salt

Directions:
1. Add steak, liquid smoke, soy sauce, and steak seasonings into the large zip-lock bag. Shake well and place it in the refrigerator overnight.
2. Select Air Fry mode.
3. Set time to 7 minutes and temperature 375 F then press START.
4. The air fryer display will prompt you to ADD FOOD once the temperature is reached then place steaks in the air fryer basket. Turn steaks after 5 minutes.
5. Serve and enjoy.

Nutritional Value (Amount per Serving):
Calories 356; Fat 8.7 g; Carbohydrates 1.4 g; Sugar 0.2 g; Protein 62.2 g; Cholesterol 153 mg

Meatloaf

Preparation Time: 10 minutes; Cooking Time: 25 minutes; Serve: 4

Ingredients:
- 1 lb ground beef
- 2 oz chorizo sausage, chopped
- 3 tbsp almond flour
- 1 egg, lightly beaten
- 2 mushrooms, sliced
- 1 tbsp thyme, chopped
- 1 onion, chopped
- Pepper
- Salt

Directions:
1. Add all ingredients into the large bowl and mix until well combined.
2. Transfer meat mixture into the baking dish. Cover dish with foil.
3. Select Bake mode.
4. Set time to 25 minutes and temperature 390 F then press START.
5. The air fryer display will prompt you to ADD FOOD once the temperature is reached then place the baking dish in the air fryer basket.
6. Serve and enjoy.

Nutritional Value (Amount per Serving):
Calories 409; Fat 22.8 g; Carbohydrates 7.9 g; Sugar 2.2 g; Protein 43.7 g; Cholesterol 154 mg

Chipotle Steak

Preparation Time: 10 minutes; Cooking Time: 10 minutes; Serve: 3

Ingredients:
- 1 lb ribeye steak
- 1/4 tsp onion powder
- 1/4 tsp garlic powder
- 1/4 tsp chili powder

- 1/2 tsp black pepper
- 1/2 tsp coffee powder
- 1/8 tsp cocoa powder
- 1/8 tsp coriander powder
- 1/4 tsp chipotle powder
- 1/4 tsp paprika
- 1 1/2 tsp sea salt

Directions:
1. In a small bowl, mix together all ingredients except steak.
2. Rub spice mixture all over the steak and let sit the steak for 30 minutes.
3. Select Air Fry mode.
4. Set time to 10 minutes and temperature 390 F then press START.
5. The air fryer display will prompt you to ADD FOOD once the temperature is reached then place steak in the air fryer basket. Turn steak halfway through.
6. Serve and enjoy.

Nutritional Value (Amount per Serving):
Calories 967; Fat 66.7 g; Carbohydrates 7 g; Sugar 0.2 g; Protein 83.6 g; Cholesterol 1 mg

Simple Beef Kabab

Preparation Time: 10 minutes; Cooking Time: 10 minutes; Serve: 4
Ingredients:
- 1 lb ground beef
- 2 tbsp kabab spice mix
- 1 tbsp garlic, minced
- 1 tbsp olive oil
- 1 tsp salt

Directions:
1. Add all ingredients into the mixing bowl and mix until well combined. Place in refrigerator for 30 minutes.
2. Divide mixture into the 4 equal portions and make sausage shape kabab.
3. Select Air Fry mode.
4. Set time to 10 minutes and temperature 370 F then press START.
5. The air fryer display will prompt you to ADD FOOD once the temperature is reached then place kabab in the air fryer basket.
6. Serve and enjoy.

Nutritional Value (Amount per Serving):
Calories 254; Fat 10.4 g; Carbohydrates 1.8 g; Sugar 0.1 g; Protein 35 g; Cholesterol 101 mg

Meatballs

Preparation Time: 10 minutes; Cooking Time: 15 minutes; Serve: 2
Ingredients:
- 5 oz pork minced
- 1/2 tbsp cheddar cheese, grated
- 1 tbsp fresh basil, chopped
- 1/2 onion, diced
- 1/2 tsp mustard
- 1/2 tsp garlic paste
- Pepper
- Salt

Directions:
1. Add all ingredients into the large bowl and mix well to combine.
2. Make small balls from the meat mixture.
3. Select Air Fry mode.
4. Set time to 15 minutes and temperature 400 F then press START.
5. The air fryer display will prompt you to ADD FOOD once the temperature is reached then place meatballs in the air fryer basket.
6. Serve and enjoy.

Nutritional Value (Amount per Serving):
Calories 243; Fat 20.2 g; Carbohydrates 5.3 g; Sugar 1.3 g; Protein 10.4 g; Cholesterol 51 mg

Baked Lamb Chops

Preparation Time: 10 minutes; Cooking Time: 20 minutes; Serve: 5
Ingredients:
- 5 lamb rib chops
- 1 garlic clove, grated
- 2 tbsp olive oil
- 1 tsp paprika
- 1/2 tsp smoked paprika
- 1 tsp cumin
- 1/2 tbsp oregano

Directions:
1. In a small bowl, mix together paprika, smoked paprika, cumin, oregano, garlic, and 1 tbsp olive oil.
2. Coat lamb chops with spice mixture and place in the refrigerator for 3 hours.
3. Heat remaining 1 tbsp olive oil in a pan over medium-high heat.
4. Once the oil is hot then place lamb chops and cook for 3 minutes or until browned.
5. Select Bake mode.
6. Set time to 16 minutes and temperature 375 F then press START.
7. The air fryer display will prompt you to ADD FOOD once the temperature is reached then place lamb chops in the air fryer basket. Turn lamb chops halfway through.
8. Serve and enjoy.

Nutritional Value (Amount per Serving):
Calories 262; Fat 13.4 g; Carbohydrates 0.9 g; Sugar 0.1 g; Protein 33 g; Cholesterol 105 mg

Spicy Pork Tenderloin

Preparation Time: 10 minutes; Cooking Time: 35 minutes; Serve: 6
Ingredients:
- 2 pork tenderloin
- For rub:
- 1 tbsp smoked paprika
- 1 tbsp garlic powder
- 1 tbsp onion powder
- 1/2 tbsp salt

Directions:
1. In a small bowl, combine together all rub ingredients.
2. Coat pork tenderloin with the rub.
3. Heat ovenproof pan over medium-high heat. Spray pan with cooking spray.
4. Sear pork on all sides until lightly golden brown.
5. Select Bake mode.
6. Set time to 30 minutes and temperature 400 F then press START.
7. The air fryer display will prompt you to ADD FOOD once the temperature is reached then place pork tenderloin in the air fryer basket.
8. Serve and enjoy.

Nutritional Value (Amount per Serving):
Calories 83; Fat 1.9 g; Carbohydrates 2.6 g; Sugar 0.9 g; Protein 13.6 g; Cholesterol 37 mg

Lemon Garlic Sirloin Steak

Preparation Time: 10 minutes; Cooking Time: 30 minutes; Serve: 6
Ingredients:
- 2 lbs sirloin steak, cut into 1-inch pieces
- 2 garlic cloves, minced
- 1 1/2 cups fresh parsley, chopped
- 1/2 tsp black pepper
- 3 tbsp fresh lemon juice
- 1 tsp dried oregano
- 1/4 cup water
- 1/4 cup olive oil
- 1 tsp salt

Directions:
1. Add all ingredients except beef into the large bowl and mix well together.

2. Pour bowl mixture into the large zip-lock bag.
   3. Add beef into the bag and shake well and refrigerate for 1 hour.
   4. Select Bake mode.
   5. Set time to 30 minutes and temperature 400 F then press START.
   6. The air fryer display will prompt you to ADD FOOD once the temperature is reached then place marinated beef in the air fryer basket.
   7. Serve and enjoy.

Nutritional Value (Amount per Serving):
   Calories 363; Fat 18.1 g; Carbohydrates 1.7 g; Sugar 0.3 g; Protein 46.5 g; Cholesterol 135 mg

Meatloaf

Preparation Time: 10 minutes; Cooking Time: 45 minutes; Serve: 6
Ingredients:
- 2 large eggs
- 1 tbsp fresh rosemary
- 1/2 cup sun-dried tomatoes, chopped
- 1 1/2 lbs ground lamb
- 3 garlic cloves, minced
- 2 tbsp balsamic vinegar
- 2 onion, chopped
- Pepper
- Salt

Directions:
   1. In a bowl, whisk together eggs, salt, pepper, and vinegar.
   2. Add rosemary, sun-dried tomatoes, onion, and garlic and mix well.
   3. Add lamb and mix just until combined.
   4. Pour meatloaf mixture into the greased loaf pan.
   5. Select Bake mode.
   6. Set time to 45 minutes and temperature 390 F then press START.
   7. The air fryer display will prompt you to ADD FOOD once the temperature is reached then place the loaf pan in the air fryer basket.
   8. Serve and enjoy.

Nutritional Value (Amount per Serving):
   Calories 257; Fat 10.1 g; Carbohydrates 5 g; Sugar 2.1 g; Protein 34.6 g; Cholesterol 164 mg

Meatloaf

Preparation Time: 10 minutes; Cooking Time: 60 minutes; Serve: 8
Ingredients:
- 2 lbs ground beef
- 1 tsp garlic powder
- 2 large eggs
- 1 small onion, chopped
- 1/2 cup parmesan cheese, grated
- 1/4 tsp pepper
- 2 tsp salt

Directions:
   1. In mixing bowl, add all ingredients and mix well until combined.
   2. Add beef mixture into the loaf pan.
   3. Select Bake mode.
   4. Set time to 60 minutes and temperature 350 F then press START.
   5. The air fryer display will prompt you to ADD FOOD once the temperature is reached then place the loaf pan in the air fryer basket.
   6. Serve and enjoy.

Nutritional Value (Amount per Serving):
   Calories 280; Fat 11.5 g; Carbohydrates 1.7 g; Sugar 0.6 g; Protein 40.8 g; Cholesterol 158 mg

Garlic Thyme Lamb Chops

Preparation Time: 5 minutes; Cooking Time: 12 minutes; Serve: 4
Ingredients:
- 4 lamb chops
- 4 garlic clove, minced
- 3 tbsp olive oil
- Pepper
- Salt

Directions:
1. In a small bowl, mix together oil and garlic.
2. Season lamb chops with pepper and salt and rubs with oil and garlic mixture.
3. Select Bake mode.
4. Set time to 12 minutes and temperature 400 F then press START.
5. The air fryer display will prompt you to ADD FOOD once the temperature is reached then place lamb chops in the air fryer basket. Turn lamb chops halfway through.
6. Serve and enjoy.

Nutritional Value (Amount per Serving):
Calories 416; Fat 36.6 g; Carbohydrates 1 g; Sugar 0 g; Protein 19.3 g; Cholesterol 80 mg

Flavorful Air Fryer Kabab

Preparation Time: 10 minutes; Cooking Time: 10 minutes; Serve: 4
Ingredients:
- 1/2 lb ground beef
- 1/2 lb ground pork
- 4 garlic cloves, minced
- 1/2 tsp onion powder
- 1 tsp chili powder
- 1/4 tsp paprika
- 1/4 cup fresh parsley, chopped
- 1 tbsp olive oil
- 1 tsp salt

Directions:
1. Add all ingredients into the mixing bowl and mix until well combined. Place in refrigerator for 30 minutes.
2. Divide mixture into the 4 portions and make sausage shape kabab.
3. Select Air Fry mode.
4. Set time to 10 minutes and temperature 375 F then press START.
5. The air fryer display will prompt you to ADD FOOD once the temperature is reached then place kabab in the air fryer basket. Turn kabab halfway through.
6. Serve and enjoy.

Nutritional Value (Amount per Serving):
Calories 226; Fat 9.2 g; Carbohydrates 1.9 g; Sugar 0.2 g; Protein 32.5 g; Cholesterol 92 mg

Meatballs

Preparation Time: 10 minutes; Cooking Time: 15 minutes; Serve: 4
Ingredients:
- 4 oz sausage meat
- 1/2 tsp garlic paste
- 1/2 tsp ginger paste
- 1/2 small onion, diced
- 3 tbsp almond flour
- 1/4 tsp oregano
- 1/2 tsp sage
- Pepper
- Salt

Directions:
1. Add all ingredients into the mixing bowl and mix until well combined.
2. Make balls from the meat mixture.
3. Select Air Fryer mode.
4. Set time to 15 minutes and temperature 350 F then press START.

5. The air fryer display will prompt you to ADD FOOD once the temperature is reached then place meatballs in the air fryer basket.
6. Serve and enjoy.

Nutritional Value (Amount per Serving):
Calories 133; Fat 10.6 g; Carbohydrates 2.4 g; Sugar 0.4 g; Protein 6.8 g; Cholesterol 24 mg

Delicious Herb Beef Patties

Preparation Time: 10 minutes; Cooking Time: 45 minutes; Serve: 4
Ingredients:
- 10 oz beef minced
- 1/4 tsp ginger paste
- 1 1/2 tsp mixed herbs
- 1 tsp basil
- 1 tsp tomato puree
- 1 tsp garlic puree
- 1/2 tsp mustard
- Pepper
- Salt

Directions:
1. Add all ingredients into the large bowl and mix until well combined.
2. Make patties from meat mixture.
3. Select Air Fry mode.
4. Set time to 45 minutes and temperature 375 F then press START.
5. The air fryer display will prompt you to ADD FOOD once the temperature is reached then place patties in the air fryer basket.
6. Serve and enjoy.

Nutritional Value (Amount per Serving):
Calories 122; Fat 7.7 g; Carbohydrates 3.5 g; Sugar 0.1 g; Protein 9.4 g; Cholesterol 0 mg

Baked Lamb Patties

Preparation Time: 10 minutes; Cooking Time: 15 minutes; Serve: 4
Ingredients:
- 1 lb ground lamb
- 1 tsp chili pepper
- ½ tsp ground allspice
- 1 tsp ground cumin
- 1/4 cup fresh parsley, chopped
- 1/4 cup onion, minced
- 1 tbsp ginger garlic paste
- 1/4 tsp pepper
- 1 tsp kosher salt

Directions:
1. Add all ingredients into the large bowl and mix until well combined.
2. Make four equal shapes of patties from meat mixture.
3. Select Bake mode.
4. Set time to 15 minutes and temperature 400 F then press START.
5. The air fryer display will prompt you to ADD FOOD once the temperature is reached then place patties in the air fryer basket. Turn patties after 8 minutes.
6. Serve and enjoy.

Nutritional Value (Amount per Serving):
Calories 225; Fat 8.8 g; Carbohydrates 2.3 g; Sugar 0.4 g; Protein 32.4 g; Cholesterol 102 mg

Roasted Sirloin Steak

Preparation Time: 10 minutes; Cooking Time: 30 minutes; Serve: 6
Ingredients:
- 2 lbs sirloin steak, cut into 1-inch cubes
- 2 garlic cloves, minced
- 3 tbsp fresh lemon juice
- 1 tsp dried oregano
- 1/4 tsp thyme

- 1/4 cup water
- 1/4 cup olive oil
- 2 cups fresh parsley, chopped
- 1/2 tsp pepper
- 1 tsp salt

Directions:
1. Add all ingredients except beef into the large bowl and mix well.
2. Pour bowl mixture into the large zip-lock bag.
3. Add steak cubes into the bag and seal bag and place in refrigerator for 1 hour.
4. Place marinated beef on a baking dish and cover dish with foil.
5. Select Bake mode.
6. Set time to 30 minutes and temperature 400 F then press START.
7. The air fryer display will prompt you to ADD FOOD once the temperature is reached then place the baking dish in the air fryer basket.
8. Serve and enjoy.

Nutritional Value (Amount per Serving):
Calories 365; Fat 18.1 g; Carbohydrates 2.1 g; Sugar 0.4 g; Protein 46.6 g; Cholesterol 135 mg

Greek Beef Casserole

Preparation Time: 10 minutes; Cooking Time: 1 hour 30 minutes; Serve: 6

Ingredients:
- 1 lb lean stew beef, cut into chunks
- 4 oz black olives, sliced
- 7 oz can tomatoes, chopped
- 1 tbsp tomato puree
- 2 cups beef stock
- 2 tbsp olive oil
- 1/4 tsp garlic powder
- 2 tsp herb de Provence
- 3 tsp paprika

Directions:
1. Heat oil in a pan over medium heat.
2. Add meat to the pan and cook until browned.
3. Add stock, olives, tomatoes, tomato puree, garlic powder, herb de Provence, and paprika. Stir well and bring to boil.
4. Transfer meat mixture into the baking dish. Cover dish with foil.
5. Select Bake mode.
6. Set time to 60 minutes and temperature 350 F then press START.
7. The air fryer display will prompt you to ADD FOOD once the temperature is reached then place the baking dish in the air fryer basket.
8. Stir well and cook for 30 minutes more.
9. Serve and enjoy.

Nutritional Value (Amount per Serving):
Calories 223; Fat 11.8 g; Carbohydrates 3.8 g; Sugar 1.4 g; Protein 26.3 g; Cholesterol 0 mg

Basil Cheese Lamb Patties

Preparation Time: 10 minutes; Cooking Time: 8 minutes; Serve: 4

Ingredients:
- 1 lb ground lamb
- 1 cup goat cheese, crumbled
- 1 tbsp garlic, minced
- 6 basil leaves, minced
- 1 tsp chili powder
- 1/4 cup mint leaves, minced
- 1/4 cup fresh parsley, chopped
- 1 tsp dried oregano
- 1/4 tsp pepper
- 1/2 tsp kosher salt

Directions:
1. Add all ingredients into the mixing bowl and mix until well combined.
2. Make four equal shape patties from the meat mixture.

3. Select Bake mode.
4. Set time to 8 minutes and temperature 400 F then press START.
5. The air fryer display will prompt you to ADD FOOD once the temperature is reached then place patties in the air fryer basket. Turn patties halfway through.
6. Serve and enjoy.

Nutritional Value (Amount per Serving):
Calories 335; Fat 17.4 g; Carbohydrates 2.7 g; Sugar 0.7 g; Protein 40.1 g; Cholesterol 128 mg

Mini Meatloaf

Preparation Time: 10 minutes; Cooking Time: 25 minutes; Serve: 2
Ingredients:
- 1/2 lb ground beef
- 1 1/2 tbsp almond flour
- 1 egg, lightly beaten
- 2 olives, chopped
- 1 tbsp green onion, chopped
- 1/2 small onion, chopped
- 1 tbsp chorizo, chopped
- Pepper
- Salt

Directions:
1. In a large bowl, mix together all ingredients until well combined.
2. Transfer meat mixture into the small baking dish. Cover dish with foil.
3. Select Bake mode.
4. Set time to 25 minutes and temperature 400 F then press START.
5. The air fryer display will prompt you to ADD FOOD once the temperature is reached then place the baking dish in the air fryer basket.
6. Serve and enjoy.

Nutritional Value (Amount per Serving):
Calories 398; Fat 22.2 g; Carbohydrates 6.9 g; Sugar 1.7 g; Protein 43.2 g; Cholesterol 188 mg

Air Fryer Stew Meat

Preparation Time: 10 minutes; Cooking Time: 25 minutes; Serve: 4
Ingredients:
- 1 lb beef stew meat, cut into strips
- 1/2 lime juice
- 1 tbsp olive oil
- 1/2 tbsp ground cumin
- 1 tbsp garlic powder
- 1/2 tsp onion powder
- Pepper
- Salt

Directions:
1. Add meat and remaining ingredients into the mixing bowl and mix well.
2. Select Air Fry mode.
3. Set time to 25 minutes and temperature 380 F then press START.
4. The air fryer display will prompt you to ADD FOOD once the temperature is reached then place stew meat in the air fryer basket. Stir halfway through
5. Serve and enjoy.

Nutritional Value (Amount per Serving):
Calories 253; Fat 10.8 g; Carbohydrates 2.6 g; Sugar 0.7 g; Protein 34.9 g; Cholesterol 101 mg

Flavorful Beef Satay

Preparation Time: 10 minutes; Cooking Time: 8 minutes; Serve: 2
Ingredients:
- 1 lb beef flank steak, sliced into long strips
- 1 tbsp fish sauce
- 2 tbsp olive oil
- 1 tsp hot sauce
- 1 tbsp Swerve

- 1 tbsp ginger garlic paste
- 1 tbsp soy sauce
- 1/2 cup parsley, chopped
- 1 tsp ground coriander

Directions:
1. Add all ingredients into the zip-lock bag and shake well. Place into the refrigerator for 1 hour.
2. Select Air Fry mode.
3. Set time to 8 minutes and temperature 400 F then press START.
4. The air fryer display will prompt you to ADD FOOD once the temperature is reached then place marinated meat in the air fryer basket. Stir halfway through.
5. Serve and enjoy.

Nutritional Value (Amount per Serving):
Calories 569; Fat 28.8 g; Carbohydrates 4.4 g; Sugar 0.6 g; Protein 70.7 g; Cholesterol 203 mg

Stuffed Bell Peppers

Preparation Time: 10 minutes; Cooking Time: 20 minutes; Serve: 2

Ingredients:
- 8 oz ground pork
- 2 bell peppers, remove stems and seeds
- 1/2 cup tomato sauce
- 4 oz mozzarella cheese, shredded
- 1 tsp olive oil
- 1 garlic clove, minced
- 1/2 onion, chopped
- 1/2 tsp pepper
- 1/2 tsp salt

Directions:
1. Sauté garlic and onion in the olive oil in a small pan until softened.
2. Add meat, 1/4 cup tomato sauce, half cheese, pepper, and salt and stir to combine.
3. Stuff meat mixture into each pepper and top with remaining cheese and tomato sauce.
4. Select Air Fry mode.
5. Set time to 20 minutes and temperature 390 F then press START.
6. The air fryer display will prompt you to ADD FOOD once the temperature is reached then place stuffed pepper in the air fryer basket.
7. Serve and enjoy.

Nutritional Value (Amount per Serving):
Calories 148; Fat 6.3 g; Carbohydrates 16.2 g; Sugar 9.8 g; Protein 9 g; Cholesterol 15 mg

Steak Fajitas

Preparation Time: 10 minutes; Cooking Time: 15 minutes; Serve: 6

Ingredients:
- 1 lb steak, sliced
- 1/2 cup onion, sliced
- 1 red bell peppers, sliced
- 1 yellow bell peppers, sliced
- 1 green bell peppers, sliced
- 1 tbsp olive oil
- 1/4 tsp chili powder
- 1 tbsp fajita seasoning

Directions:
1. Add all ingredients large bowl and toss until well coated.
2. Select Air Fry mode.
3. Set time to 15 minutes and temperature 390 F then press START.
4. The air fryer display will prompt you to ADD FOOD once the temperature is reached then place fajita mixture in the air fryer basket. Stir after 10 minutes.
5. Serve and enjoy.

Nutritional Value (Amount per Serving):
Calories 199; Fat 6.3 g; Carbohydrates 6.5 g; Sugar 3.4 g; Protein 28 g; Cholesterol 68 mg

Ranch Pork Chops

Preparation Time: 10 minutes; Cooking Time: 35 minutes; Serve: 4
Ingredients:
- 4 pork chops, boneless
- 1 oz ranch seasoning
- 1 1/2 tbsp olive oil

Directions:
1. Brush pork chops with oil and rub with ranch seasoning.
2. Select Air Fry mode.
3. Set time to 35 minutes and temperature 400 F then press START.
4. The air fryer display will prompt you to ADD FOOD once the temperature is reached then place pork chops in the air fryer basket.
5. Serve and enjoy.

Nutritional Value (Amount per Serving):
Calories 323; Fat 25.1 g; Carbohydrates 0 g; Sugar 0 g; Protein 18 g; Cholesterol 69 mg

Buttery Steak Bites

Preparation Time: 10 minutes; Cooking Time: 7 minutes; Serve: 4
Ingredients:
- 1 lb steak, cut into 1-inch cubes
- 2 tbsp steak seasoning
- 4 tbsp butter, melted
- Pepper
- Salt

Directions:
1. Add steak, butter, seasoning, pepper, and salt into the bowl and mix well.
2. Select Air Fry mode.
3. Set time to 7 minutes and temperature 350 F then press START.
4. The air fryer display will prompt you to ADD FOOD once the temperature is reached then add steak bites in the air fryer basket. Stir after 5 minutes.
5. Serve and enjoy.

Nutritional Value (Amount per Serving):
Calories 328; Fat 17.2 g; Carbohydrates 0 g; Sugar 0 g; Protein 41.1 g; Cholesterol 133 mg

Taco Stuffed Peppers

Preparation Time: 10 minutes; Cooking Time: 8 minutes; Serve: 12
Ingredients:
- 6 jalapeno peppers, cut in half & remove seeds
- 1 1/2 tbsp taco seasoning
- 1/2 lb ground beef
- 1/4 cup goat cheese, crumbled

Directions:
1. Browned the meat in a large pan.
2. Remove pan from heat. Add taco seasoning to the ground meat and mix well.
3. Stuff meat into each jalapeno half.
4. Select Air Fry mode.
5. Set time to 6 minutes and temperature 320 F then press START.
6. The air fryer display will prompt you to ADD FOOD once the temperature is reached then place jalapeno halves in the air fryer basket.
7. Sprinkle cheese on top of peppers and cook for 2 minutes more.
8. Serve and enjoy.

Nutritional Value (Amount per Serving):
Calories 51; Fat 2.2 g; Carbohydrates 0.8 g; Sugar 0.3 g; Protein 6.6 g; Cholesterol 20 mg

Meatballs

Preparation Time: 10 minutes; Cooking Time: 15 minutes; Serve: 2
Ingredients:
- 5 oz pork minced
- 1/2 tsp ginger garlic paste
- 1 tbsp feta cheese, crumbled
- 1 tbsp fresh basil
- 1/2 onion, diced
- Pepper
- Salt

Directions:
1. Add all ingredients into the large bowl and mix until well combined.
2. Make small meatballs from mixture.
3. Select Air Fry mode.
4. Set time to 15 minutes and temperature 390 F then press START.
5. The air fryer display will prompt you to ADD FOOD once the temperature is reached then place meatballs in the air fryer basket.
6. Serve and enjoy.

Nutritional Value (Amount per Serving):
Calories 250; Fat 20.6 g; Carbohydrates 5.7 g; Sugar 1.4 g; Protein 10.7 g; Cholesterol 54 mg

Greek Meatballs

Preparation Time: 10 minutes; Cooking Time: 20 minutes; Serve: 6
Ingredients:
- 2 lbs ground pork
- 1 egg, lightly beaten
- 1 tbsp lemon zest
- 1/4 cup shallot, diced
- 1 tsp garlic powder
- 1 tsp dried oregano
- 1 tsp dried thyme
- 1/4 cup bell pepper, diced
- 1/4 cup yogurt
- 1 cup feta cheese, crumbled
- 1 cup spinach, cooked, squeezed & chopped
- Pepper
- Salt

Directions:
1. Add all ingredients into the mixing bowl and mix until well combined.
2. Make small balls from the meat mixture.
3. Select Bake mode.
4. Set time to 30 minutes and temperature 375 F then press START.
5. The air fryer display will prompt you to ADD FOOD once the temperature is reached then place meatballs in the air fryer basket. Stir halfway through.
6. Serve and enjoy.

Nutritional Value (Amount per Serving):
Calories 311; Fat 11.6 g; Carbohydrates 4.3 g; Sugar 2.3 g; Protein 45.1 g; Cholesterol 161 mg

Breaded Pork Chops

Preparation Time: 10 minutes; Cooking Time: 15 minutes; Serve: 2
Ingredients:
- 2 pork chops, bone-in
- 1 tbsp olive oil
- 1 cup pork rinds, crushed
- 1/2 tsp paprika
- 1/2 tsp dried parsley
- 1/2 tsp garlic powder
- 1/2 tsp onion powder
- 1/4 tsp chili powder

Directions:
1. In a large bowl, mix together pork rinds, garlic powder, onion powder, parsley, chili powder, and paprika.
2. Brush pork chops with oil and coat with pork rind mixture.

3. Select Air Fry mode.
4. Set time to 15 minutes and temperature 400 F then press START.
5. The air fryer display will prompt you to ADD FOOD once the temperature is reached then place pork chops in the air fryer basket. Turn pork chops after 10 minutes.
6. Serve and enjoy.

Nutritional Value (Amount per Serving):
Calories 415; Fat 32.7 g; Carbohydrates 1.5 g; Sugar 0.5 g; Protein 28.6 g; Cholesterol 92 mg

Pecan Crusted Pork Chops

Preparation Time: 10 minutes; Cooking Time: 20 minutes; Serve: 6

Ingredients:
- 1 1/2 lbs pork chops, boneless
- 2 eggs, lightly beaten
- 2 cups pecans, crushed
- 1/4 cup Dijon mustard

Directions:
1. Rub pork chops with mustard and set aside for 5 minutes.
2. In a shallow bowl, whisk eggs.
3. In a separate shallow dish, add finely crushed pecans.
4. Dip pork chops in egg and coat with crushed pecans.
5. Select Bake mode.
6. Set time to 20 minutes and temperature 350 F then press START.
7. The air fryer display will prompt you to ADD FOOD once the temperature is reached then place pork chops in the air fryer basket.
8. Serve and enjoy.

Nutritional Value (Amount per Serving):
Calories 623; Fat 53.9 g; Carbohydrates 5.4 g; Sugar 1.4 g; Protein 31.4 g; Cholesterol 152 mg

Garlicky Pork Chops

Preparation Time: 10 minutes; Cooking Time: 20 minutes; Serve: 8

Ingredients:
- 8 pork chops, boneless
- 6 garlic cloves, minced
- 1/4 tsp pepper
- 3/4 cup parmesan cheese
- 2 tbsp butter, melted
- 2 tbsp coconut oil
- 1 tsp thyme
- 1 tbsp parsley
- 1/2 tsp sea salt

Directions:
1. In a small bowl, mix together butter, garlic, pepper, thyme, parsley, parmesan cheese, coconut oil, and salt.
2. Brush butter mixture on top of pork chops.
3. Select Air Fry mode.
4. Set time to 20 minutes and temperature 400 F then press START.
5. The air fryer display will prompt you to ADD FOOD once the temperature is reached then place pork chops in the air fryer basket. Turn pork chops halfway through.
6. Serve and enjoy.

Nutritional Value (Amount per Serving):
Calories 467; Fat 40.4 g; Carbohydrates 4.1 g; Sugar 1 g; Protein 23.5 g; Cholesterol 114 mg

Meatballs

Preparation Time: 10 minutes; Cooking Time: 15 minutes; Serve: 6

Ingredients:
- 1 1/2 lbs ground beef
- 1/4 tsp red pepper, crushed

- 2 tbsp parsley, chopped
- 1 garlic clove, minced
- 2 tbsp onion, grated
- 1/4 cup unsweetened almond milk
- 1 egg, lightly beaten
- 1/4 cup parmesan cheese, grated
- 1/4 cup almond flour
- 1 tsp Italian seasoning

Directions:
1. Add all ingredients into the mixing bowl and mix until well combined.
2. Select Bake mode.
3. Set time to 15 minutes and temperature 400 F then press START.
4. The air fryer display will prompt you to ADD FOOD once the temperature is reached then place meatballs in the air fryer basket.
5. Serve and enjoy.

Nutritional Value (Amount per Serving):
Calories 249; Fat 9.7 g; Carbohydrates 1.6 g; Sugar 0.6 g; Protein 37.1 g; Cholesterol 132 mg

Asian Pork Steak

Preparation Time: 10 minutes; Cooking Time: 15 minutes; Serve: 4
Ingredients:
- 1 lb pork steaks, boneless
- 1 tsp garam masala
- 1 tbsp ginger garlic paste
- 1/2 tsp cayenne
- 1/2 tsp ground cardamom
- 1 tsp cinnamon
- 1/2 onion, diced
- 1 tsp salt

Directions:
1. Add all ingredients except meat into the mixing bowl and mix well.
2. Add the meat into the bowl and coat well.
3. Place meat into the refrigerator overnight.
4. Select Air Fry mode.
5. Set time to 15 minutes and temperature 330 F then press START.
6. The air fryer display will prompt you to ADD FOOD once the temperature is reached then place steaks in the air fryer basket. Turn halfway through.
7. Serve and enjoy.

Nutritional Value (Amount per Serving):
Calories 272; Fat 14.6 g; Carbohydrates 2.8 g; Sugar 0.6 g; Protein 30.8 g; Cholesterol 107 mg

Dijon Pork Chops

Preparation Time: 10 minutes; Cooking Time: 12 minutes; Serve: 4
Ingredients:
- 4 pork chops
- 1 tbsp garlic, minced
- 4 tbsp Dijon mustard
- Pepper
- Salt

Directions:
1. In a small bowl, mix together mustard, garlic, pepper, and salt
2. Brush pork chops with mustard mixture.
3. Select Air Fry mode.
4. Set time to 12 minutes and temperature 350 F then press START.
5. The air fryer display will prompt you to ADD FOOD once the temperature is reached then place pork chops in the air fryer basket. Turn pork chops halfway through.
6. Serve and enjoy.

Nutritional Value (Amount per Serving):
Calories 270; Fat 20.5 g; Carbohydrates 1.5 g; Sugar 0.2 g; Protein 18.8 g; Cholesterol 69 mg

Chapter 6: Vegetable Recipes

Crisp & Crunchy Asparagus

Preparation Time: 10 minutes; Cooking Time: 10 minutes; Serve: 4

Ingredients:
- 1 lb asparagus, trim ends & cut in half
- 1 tbsp vinegar
- 2 tbsp coconut aminos
- 1 tbsp butter, melted
- 1 tbsp olive oil
- 1/2 tsp sea salt

Directions:
1. In a bowl, toss asparagus with olive oil and salt.
2. Place the cooking tray in the air fryer basket.
3. Select Air Fry mode.
4. Set time to 10 minutes and temperature 400 F then press START.
5. The air fryer display will prompt you to ADD FOOD once the temperature is reached then add asparagus in the air fryer basket.
6. Meanwhile, for the sauce in a bowl, mix together coconut aminos, melted butter, and vinegar.
7. Pour sauce over hot asparagus and serve.

Nutritional Value (Amount per Serving):
Calories 86; Fat 6.5 g; Carbohydrates 5.9 g; Sugar 2.2 g; Protein 2.5 g; Cholesterol 8 mg

Balsamic Brussels Sprouts

Preparation Time: 10 minutes; Cooking Time: 20 minutes; Serve: 4

Ingredients:
- 1 lb brussels sprouts, cut in half
- 1 small onion, sliced
- 3 bacon slices, cut into pieces
- 1 tsp garlic powder
- 2 tbsp fresh lemon juice
- 2 tbsp balsamic vinegar
- 3 tbsp olive oil
- 1/2 tsp sea salt

Directions:
1. In a small bowl, whisk together balsamic vinegar, olive oil, lemon juice, garlic powder, and salt.
2. Toss brussels sprouts with 3 tablespoons of the balsamic vinegar mixture.
3. Place the cooking tray in the air fryer basket.
4. Select Air Fry mode.
5. Set time to 20 minutes and temperature 370 F then press START.
6. The air fryer display will prompt you to ADD FOOD once the temperature is reached then add brussels sprouts in the air fryer basket.
7. After 10 minutes toss Brussels sprouts and top with bacon and onion and air fry for 10 minutes more.
8. Drizzle remaining balsamic vinegar mixture over brussels sprouts and serve.

Nutritional Value (Amount per Serving):
Calories 229; Fat 16.9 g; Carbohydrates 12.9 g; Sugar 3.6 g; Protein 9.5 g; Cholesterol 16 mg

Healthy Roasted Vegetables

Preparation Time: 10 minutes; Cooking Time: 14 minutes; Serve: 4

Ingredients:
- 8 oz asparagus, cut the ends
- 8 oz mushrooms, halved
- 1 zucchini, sliced
- 6 oz grape tomatoes
- 1/2 tsp pepper
- 1 tbsp Dijon mustard
- 1 tbsp soy sauce
- 1/4 cup balsamic vinegar

- 4 tbsp olive oil

Directions:
1. In a large bowl, mix together olive oil, vinegar, soy sauce, Dijon mustard, and pepper.
2. Add asparagus, tomatoes, zucchini, and mushrooms into the bowl and toss until well coated.
3. Place vegetables in the refrigerator for 30 minutes.
4. Place the cooking tray in the air fryer basket.
5. Select Air Fry mode.
6. Set time to 14 minutes and temperature 400 F then press START.
7. The air fryer display will prompt you to ADD FOOD once the temperature is reached then add marinated vegetables in the air fryer basket. Stir vegetables halfway through.
8. Serve and enjoy.

Nutritional Value (Amount per Serving):
Calories 168; Fat 14.6 g; Carbohydrates 8.2 g; Sugar 4.2 g; Protein 4.4 g; Cholesterol 0 mg

Parmesan Zucchini Noodles

Preparation Time: 10 minutes; Cooking Time: 10 minutes; Serve: 2

Ingredients:
- 4 cups zucchini noodles
- 1/2 cup parmesan cheese, grated
- 2 tbsp mayonnaise

Directions:
1. Add zucchini noodles into the microwave-safe bowl and microwave for 3 minutes. Pat dry zucchini noodles with a paper towel.
2. In a mixing bowl, toss zucchini noodles with parmesan cheese and mayonnaise.
3. Place the cooking tray in the air fryer basket. Line air fryer basket with parchment paper.
4. Select Air Fry mode.
5. Set time to 10 minutes and temperature 400 F then press START.
6. The air fryer display will prompt you to ADD FOOD once the temperature is reached then add zucchini noodles onto the parchment paper in the air fryer basket. Stir zucchini noodles halfway through.
7. Serve and enjoy.

Nutritional Value (Amount per Serving):
Calories 261; Fat 17.6 g; Carbohydrates 8.9 g; Sugar 2.6 g; Protein 20.1 g; Cholesterol 46 mg

Rosemary Basil Mushrooms

Preparation Time: 10 minutes; Cooking Time: 14 minutes; Serve: 4

Ingredients:
- 1 lb mushrooms
- 1/2 tbsp vinegar
- 1/2 tsp ground coriander
- 1 tsp rosemary, chopped
- 1 tbsp basil, minced
- 1 garlic clove, minced
- Pepper
- Salt

Directions:
1. Add all ingredients into the large bowl and toss well.
2. Select Air Fry mode.
3. Set time to 14 minutes and temperature 350 F then press START.
4. The air fryer display will prompt you to ADD FOOD once the temperature is reached then add mushrooms in the air fryer basket.
5. Serve and enjoy.

Nutritional Value (Amount per Serving):
Calories 27; Fat 0.4 g; Carbohydrates 4.2 g; Sugar 2 g; Protein 3.6 g; Cholesterol 0 mg

Baked Brussels Sprouts

Preparation Time: 10 minutes; Cooking Time: 35 minutes; Serve: 6
Ingredients:
- 2 cups Brussels sprouts, halved
- 1/4 tsp garlic powder
- 1/4 cup olive oil
- 1/2 tsp cayenne pepper
- 1/4 tsp salt

Directions:
1. Add all ingredients into the large bowl and toss well.
2. Select Bake mode.
3. Set time to 35 minutes and temperature 400 F then press START.
4. The air fryer display will prompt you to ADD FOOD once the temperature is reached then add brussels sprouts in the air fryer basket.
5. Serve and enjoy.

Nutritional Value (Amount per Serving):
Calories 86; Fat 8.5 g; Carbohydrates 2.8 g; Sugar 0.7 g; Protein 1 g; Cholesterol 0 mg

Old Bay Cauliflower Florets

Preparation Time: 10 minutes; Cooking Time: 15 minutes; Serve: 4
Ingredients:
- 1 medium cauliflower head, cut into florets
- 1/2 tsp old bay seasoning
- 1/4 tsp paprika
- 1 tbsp garlic, minced
- 3 tbsp olive oil
- Pepper
- Salt

Directions:
1. In a large bowl, toss cauliflower with remaining ingredients.
2. Select Air Fry mode.
3. Set time to 15 minutes and temperature 400 F then press START.
4. The air fryer display will prompt you to ADD FOOD once the temperature is reached then add cauliflower florets in the air fryer basket.
5. Serve and enjoy.

Nutritional Value (Amount per Serving):
Calories 130; Fat 10.7 g; Carbohydrates 8.4 g; Sugar 3.5 g; Protein 3 g; Cholesterol 0 mg

Rosemary Mushrooms

Preparation Time: 10 minutes; Cooking Time: 14 minutes; Serve: 4
Ingredients:
- 1 lb mushroom caps
- 1/2 tsp ground coriander
- 1 tsp rosemary, chopped
- 1/2 tsp garlic powder
- Pepper
- Salt

Directions:
1. Add all ingredients into the mixing bowl and toss well.
2. Select Air Fry mode.
3. Set time to 14 minutes and temperature 350 F then press START.
4. The air fryer display will prompt you to ADD FOOD once the temperature is reached then add mushrooms in the air fryer basket.
5. Serve and enjoy.

Nutritional Value (Amount per Serving):
Calories 27; Fat 0.4 g; Carbohydrates 4.2 g; Sugar 2 g; Protein 3.6 g; Cholesterol 0 mg

Air Fry Bell Peppers

Preparation Time: 10 minutes; Cooking Time: 8 minutes; Serve: 3
Ingredients:
- 1 cup red bell peppers, cut into chunks
- 1 cup green bell peppers, cut into chunks
- 1 cup yellow bell peppers, cut into chunks
- 1 tsp olive oil
- 1/4 tsp garlic powder
- Pepper
- Salt

Directions:
1. Add all ingredients into the large bowl and toss well.
2. Select Air Fry mode.
3. Set time to 8 minutes and temperature 360 F then press START.
4. The air fryer display will prompt you to ADD FOOD once the temperature is reached then add bell peppers in the air fryer basket. Stir halfway through.
5. Serve and enjoy.

Nutritional Value (Amount per Serving):
Calories 52; Fat 1.9 g; Carbohydrates 9.2 g; Sugar 6.1 g; Protein 1.2 g; Cholesterol 0 mg

Asian Green Beans

Preparation Time: 10 minutes; Cooking Time: 10 minutes; Serve: 2
Ingredients:
- 8 oz green beans, trimmed and cut in half
- 1 tbsp tamari
- 1 tsp sesame oil

Directions:
1. Add all ingredients into the large bowl and toss well.
2. Select Air Fry mode.
3. Set time to 10 minutes and temperature 350 F then press START.
4. The air fryer display will prompt you to ADD FOOD once the temperature is reached then add green beans in the air fryer basket. Stir halfway through.
5. Serve and enjoy.

Nutritional Value (Amount per Serving):
Calories 61; Fat 2.4 g; Carbohydrates 8.6 g; Sugar 1.7 g; Protein 3 g; Cholesterol 0 mg

Mushrooms Cauliflower Roast

Preparation Time: 10 minutes; Cooking Time: 25 minutes; Serve: 6
Ingredients:
- 1 lb mushrooms, cleaned
- 10 garlic cloves, peeled
- 2 cups cherry tomatoes
- 2 cups cauliflower florets
- 1 tbsp fresh parsley, chopped
- 1 tbsp Italian seasoning
- 2 tbsp olive oil
- Pepper
- Salt

Directions:
1. Add cauliflower, mushrooms, Italian seasoning, olive oil, garlic, cherry tomatoes, pepper, and salt into the mixing bowl and toss well.
2. Transfer cauliflower and mushroom mixture in baking dish.
3. Select Bake mode.
4. Set time to 25 minutes and temperature 400 F then press START.
5. The air fryer display will prompt you to ADD FOOD once the temperature is reached then place the baking dish in the air fryer basket.

6. Serve and enjoy.

Nutritional Value (Amount per Serving):
Calories 90; Fat 5.8 g; Carbohydrates 8.5 g; Sugar 3.9 g; Protein 3.9 g; Cholesterol 0 mg

Roasted Cauliflower Cherry Tomatoes

Preparation Time: 10 minutes; Cooking Time: 20 minutes; Serve: 4

Ingredients:
- 4 cups cauliflower florets
- 3 tbsp olive oil
- 1/2 cup cherry tomatoes, halved
- 2 tbsp fresh parsley, chopped
- 2 garlic cloves, sliced
- 1 tbsp capers, drained
- Pepper
- Salt

Directions:
1. In a bowl, toss together cherry tomatoes, cauliflower, oil, garlic, capers, pepper, and salt and spread in baking dish.
2. Select Bake mode.
3. Set time to 20 minutes and temperature 400 F then press START.
4. The air fryer display will prompt you to ADD FOOD once the temperature is reached then place the baking dish in the air fryer basket.
5. Serve and enjoy.

Nutritional Value (Amount per Serving):
Calories 123; Fat 10.7 g; Carbohydrates 6.9 g; Sugar 3 g; Protein 2.4 g; Cholesterol 0 mg

Healthy Roasted Broccoli

Preparation Time: 10 minutes; Cooking Time: 20 minutes; Serve: 6

Ingredients:
- 4 cups broccoli florets
- 3 tbsp olive oil
- 1/2 tsp pepper
- 1/2 tsp garlic powder
- 1 tsp Italian seasoning
- 1 tsp salt

Directions:
1. Add broccoli in a baking dish and drizzle with oil and season with garlic powder, Italian seasoning, pepper, and salt.
2. Select Bake mode.
3. Set time to 20 minutes and temperature 400 F then press START.
4. The air fryer display will prompt you to ADD FOOD once the temperature is reached then place the baking dish in the air fryer basket.
5. Serve and enjoy.

Nutritional Value (Amount per Serving):
Calories 84; Fat 7.4 g; Carbohydrates 4.4 g; Sugar 1.2 g; Protein 1.8 g; Cholesterol 1 mg

Air Fry Baby Carrots

Preparation Time: 10 minutes; Cooking Time: 12 minutes; Serve: 4

Ingredients:
- 3 cups baby carrots
- 1 tbsp olive oil
- Pepper
- Salt

Directions:
1. Add carrots, oil, pepper, and salt into the mixing bowl and toss well.
2. Select Bake mode.
3. Set time to 12 minutes and temperature 390 F then press START.
4. The air fryer display will prompt you to ADD FOOD once the temperature is reached then add baby carrots in the air fryer basket. Stir halfway through.

5. Serve and enjoy.

Nutritional Value (Amount per Serving):
Calories 52; Fat 3.6 g; Carbohydrates 5.3 g; Sugar 3 g; Protein 0.4 g; Cholesterol 0 mg

Crispy Brussels Sprouts

Preparation Time: 10 minutes; Cooking Time: 14 minutes; Serve: 2

Ingredients:
- 1/2 lb Brussels sprouts, trimmed and halved
- 1/2 tsp chili powder
- 1/2 tbsp olive oil
- Pepper
- Salt

Directions:
1. Add all ingredients into the large bowl and toss well.
2. Select Air Fry mode.
3. Set time to 14 minutes and temperature 350 F then press START.
4. The air fryer display will prompt you to ADD FOOD once the temperature is reached then add brussels sprouts in the air fryer basket.
5. Serve and enjoy.

Nutritional Value (Amount per Serving):
Calories 81; Fat 4 g; Carbohydrates 10.7 g; Sugar 2.5 g; Protein 4 g; Cholesterol 0 mg

Broccoli Fritters

Preparation Time: 10 minutes; Cooking Time: 30 minutes; Serve: 4

Ingredients:
- 2 eggs, lightly beaten
- 2 garlic cloves, minced
- 3 cups broccoli florets, steam & chopped
- 1 cup cheddar cheese, shredded
- 1 cup mozzarella cheese, shredded
- 1/4 cup almond flour
- Pepper
- Salt

Directions:
1. Add all ingredients into the large bowl and mix until well combined.
2. Make patties from the broccoli mixture.
3. Select Bake mode.
4. Set time to 30 minutes and temperature 375 F then press START.
5. The air fryer display will prompt you to ADD FOOD once the temperature is reached then place broccoli patties in the air fryer basket.
6. Serve and enjoy.

Nutritional Value (Amount per Serving):
Calories 201; Fat 13.9 g; Carbohydrates 6.2 g; Sugar 1.6 g; Protein 14.2 g; Cholesterol 115 mg

Baked Artichoke Hearts

Preparation Time: 10 minutes; Cooking Time: 25 minutes; Serve: 6

Ingredients:
- 18 oz frozen artichoke hearts, defrosted
- 1 tbsp olive oil
- Pepper
- Salt

Directions:
1. Brush artichoke hearts with oil and season with pepper and salt.
2. Select Bake mode.
3. Set time to 25 minutes and temperature 400 F then press START.

4. The air fryer display will prompt you to ADD FOOD once the temperature is reached then place artichoke hearts in the air fryer basket.
5. Serve and enjoy.

Nutritional Value (Amount per Serving):
Calories 60; Fat 2.5 g; Carbohydrates 9 g; Sugar 0.8 g; Protein 2.8 g; Cholesterol 0 mg

Roasted Veggies

Preparation Time: 10 minutes; Cooking Time: 30 minutes; Serve: 6
Ingredients:
- 1 bell pepper, cut into strips
- 2 zucchini, sliced
- 2 tomatoes, quartered
- 1 eggplant, sliced
- 1 onion, sliced
- 5 fresh basil leaves, sliced
- 2 tsp Italian seasoning
- 2 tbsp olive oil
- Pepper
- Salt

Directions:
1. Add all ingredients except basil leaves into the mixing bowl and toss well.
2. Select Roast mode.
3. Set time to 30 minutes and temperature 400 F then press START.
4. The air fryer display will prompt you to ADD FOOD once the temperature is reached then place vegetable mixture in the air fryer basket. Stir halfway through.
5. Garnish with basil and serve.

Nutritional Value (Amount per Serving):
Calories 95; Fat 5.5 g; Carbohydrates 11.7 g; Sugar 6.4 g; Protein 2.3 g; Cholesterol 1 mg

Lemon Garlic Cauliflower

Preparation Time: 10 minutes; Cooking Time: 35 minutes; Serve: 4
Ingredients:
- 6 cups cauliflower florets
- 5 garlic cloves, chopped
- 1/4 fresh lemon juice
- 2 tbsp olive oil
- 1/2 tsp onion powder
- 1/4 tsp cayenne
- Pepper
- Salt

Directions:
1. Add all ingredients into the large bowl and toss well.
2. Select Roast mode.
3. Set time to 35 minutes and temperature 400 F then press START.
4. The air fryer display will prompt you to ADD FOOD once the temperature is reached then add cauliflower florets in the air fryer basket. Stir halfway through.
5. Serve and enjoy.

Nutritional Value (Amount per Serving):
Calories 105; Fat 7.2 g; Carbohydrates 9.6 g; Sugar 3.8 g; Protein 3.3 g; Cholesterol 0 mg

Delicious Ratatouille

Preparation Time: 10 minutes; Cooking Time: 15 minutes; Serve: 6
Ingredients:
- 1 eggplant, diced
- 1 tbsp vinegar
- 1 onion, diced
- 3 tomatoes, diced
- 2 bell peppers, diced
- 1 1/2 tbsp olive oil
- 2 tbsp herb de Provence
- 3 garlic cloves, chopped
- Pepper
- Salt

Directions:

1. Add all ingredients into the bowl and toss well and transfer into the baking dish.
2. Select Air Fry mode.
3. Set time to 15 minutes and temperature 400 F then press START.
4. The air fryer display will prompt you to ADD FOOD once the temperature is reached then place the baking dish in the air fryer basket. Stir halfway through.
5. Serve and enjoy.

Nutritional Value (Amount per Serving):
Calories 72; Fat 4 g; Carbohydrates 8.5 g; Sugar 4.9 g; Protein 2 g; Cholesterol 0 mg

Air Fry Parmesan Tomatoes

Preparation Time: 10 minutes; Cooking Time: 25 minutes; Serve: 4
Ingredients:
- 4 large tomatoes, halved
- 2 tbsp parmesan cheese, grated
- 1 tbsp vinegar
- 1 tbsp olive oil
- 1/2 tsp fresh parsley, chopped
- 1 tsp fresh basil, minced
- 1 garlic clove, minced
- Pepper
- Salt

Directions:
1. In a bowl, mix together oil, basil, garlic, vinegar, pepper, and salt.
2. Add tomatoes and stir well to coat.
3. Select Air Fry mode.
4. Set time to 25 minutes and temperature 320 F then press START.
5. The air fryer display will prompt you to ADD FOOD once the temperature is reached then place tomato halves in the air fryer basket.
6. Sprinkle tomatoes with parmesan cheese and cook for 5 minutes more.
7. Serve and enjoy.

Nutritional Value (Amount per Serving):
Calories 79; Fat 4.8 g; Carbohydrates 7.6 g; Sugar 4.8 g; Protein 3 g; Cholesterol 3 mg

Spiced Green Beans

Preparation Time: 10 minutes; Cooking Time: 10 minutes; Serve: 2
Ingredients:
- 2 cups green beans
- 1/8 tsp cayenne pepper
- 1/8 tsp ground allspice
- 1/4 tsp ground cinnamon
- 1/2 tsp dried oregano
- 2 tbsp olive oil
- 1/4 tsp ground coriander
- 1/4 tsp ground cumin
- 1/2 tsp salt

Directions:
1. Add all ingredients into the mixing bowl and toss well.
2. Select Air Fry mode.
3. Set time to 10 minutes and temperature 370 F then press START.
4. The air fryer display will prompt you to ADD FOOD once the temperature is reached then add green beans in the air fryer basket. Stir Halfway through.
5. Serve and enjoy.

Nutritional Value (Amount per Serving):
Calories 158; Fat 14.3 g; Carbohydrates 8.6 g; Sugar 1.6 g; Protein 2.1 g; Cholesterol 0 mg

Roasted Squash

Preparation Time: 10 minutes; Cooking Time: 60 minutes; Serve: 4
Ingredients:

- 2 lbs summer squash, cut into 1-inch pieces
- 1/8 tsp garlic powder
- 3 tbsp olive oil
- 1 large lemon
- 1/8 tsp paprika
- 1/8 tsp pepper
- Pepper
- Salt

Directions:
1. Place squash pieces into the baking dish and drizzle with olive oil.
2. Season with paprika, pepper, and garlic powder.
3. Squeeze lemon juice over the squash.
4. Select Bake mode.
5. Set time to 60 minutes and temperature 400 F then press START.
6. The air fryer display will prompt you to ADD FOOD once the temperature is reached then place the baking dish in the air fryer basket.
7. Serve and enjoy.

Nutritional Value (Amount per Serving):
Calories 138; Fat 11.2 g; Carbohydrates 10.3 g; Sugar 8.4 g; Protein 2.5 g; Cholesterol 0 mg

Parmesan Baked Zucchini

Preparation Time: 10 minutes; Cooking Time: 35 minutes; Serve: 6
Ingredients:
- 2 1/2 lbs zucchini, cut into quarters
- 1/2 cup parmesan cheese, shredded
- 6 garlic cloves, crushed
- 10 oz cherry tomatoes cut in half
- 1/2 tsp black pepper
- 1/3 cup parsley, chopped
- 1 tsp dried basil
- 3/4 tsp salt

Directions:
1. Add all ingredients except parsley into the large mixing bowl and stir well to combine.
2. Pour egg mixture into the greased baking dish.
3. Select Bake mode.
4. Set time to 35 minutes and temperature 350 F then press START.
5. The air fryer display will prompt you to ADD FOOD once the temperature is reached then place the baking dish in the air fryer basket.
6. Serve and enjoy.

Nutritional Value (Amount per Serving):
Calories 108; Fat 4.7 g; Carbohydrates 10.2 g; Sugar 4.6 g; Protein 9.3 g; Cholesterol 14 mg

Parmesan Eggplant Zucchini

Preparation Time: 10 minutes; Cooking Time: 35 minutes; Serve: 6
Ingredients:
- 1 medium eggplant, sliced
- 3 medium zucchini, sliced
- 3 oz Parmesan cheese, grated
- 1 tbsp olive oil
- 1 cup cherry tomatoes, halved
- 4 garlic cloves, minced
- 4 tbsp parsley, chopped
- 4 tbsp basil, chopped
- 1/4 tsp pepper
- 1/4 tsp salt

Directions:
1. In a mixing bowl, add chopped cherry tomatoes, eggplant, zucchini, olive oil, garlic, cheese, basil, pepper, and salt toss well until combined.
2. Transfer the eggplant mixture into the baking dish.
3. Select Bake mode.
4. Set time to 35 minutes and temperature 350 F then press START.

5. The air fryer display will prompt you to ADD FOOD once the temperature is reached then place the baking dish in the air fryer basket.
6. Serve and enjoy.

Nutritional Value (Amount per Serving):
Calories 110; Fat 5.8 g; Carbohydrates 10.4 g; Sugar 4.8 g; Protein 7 g; Cholesterol 10 mg

Cheese Broccoli Stuffed Pepper

Preparation Time: 10 minutes; Cooking Time: 25 minutes; Serve: 4

Ingredients:
- 4 eggs
- 2.5 oz cheddar cheese, grated
- 2 medium bell peppers, cut in half and deseeded
- 2 tbsp olive oil
- 1/4 cup baby broccoli florets
- 1/4 cup cherry tomatoes
- 1 tsp dried sage
- 7 oz unsweetened almond milk
- Pepper
- Salt

Directions:
1. In a bowl, whisk together eggs, milk, broccoli, cherry tomatoes, sage, pepper, and salt.
2. Add olive oil to the baking dish.
3. Place bell pepper halves in the baking dish.
4. Pour egg mixture into the bell pepper halves.
5. Sprinkle cheese on top of bell pepper.
6. Select Bake mode.
7. Set time to 25 minutes and temperature 390 F then press START.
8. The air fryer display will prompt you to ADD FOOD once the temperature is reached then place the baking dish in the air fryer basket.
9. Serve and enjoy.

Nutritional Value (Amount per Serving):
Calories 226; Fat 18.1 g; Carbohydrates 6.3 g; Sugar 3.9 g; Protein 10.9 g; Cholesterol 182 mg

Creamy Spinach

Preparation Time: 10 minutes; Cooking Time: 20 minutes; Serve: 6

Ingredients:
- 1 lb fresh spinach
- 1 tbsp onion, minced
- 8 oz cream cheese
- 6 oz gouda cheese, shredded
- 1 tsp garlic powder
- Pepper
- Salt

Directions:
1. Spray a large pan with cooking spray and heat over medium heat.
2. Add spinach to the pan and cook until wilted.
3. Add cream cheese, garlic powder, and onion and stir until cheese is melted.
4. Remove pan from heat and add Gouda cheese and season with pepper and salt.
5. Transfer spinach mixture into the greased baking dish.
6. Select Bake mode.
7. Set time to 20 minutes and temperature 400 F then press START.
8. The air fryer display will prompt you to ADD FOOD once the temperature is reached then place the baking dish in the air fryer basket.
9. Serve and enjoy.

Nutritional Value (Amount per Serving):
Calories 253; Fat 21.3 g; Carbohydrates 4.9 g; Sugar 1.2 g; Protein 12.2 g; Cholesterol 74 mg

Beans with Mushrooms

Preparation Time: 10 minutes; Cooking Time: 25 minutes; Serve: 4
Ingredients:
- 2 cups mushrooms, sliced
- 2 tsp garlic, minced
- 2 cups green beans, clean and cut into pieces
- 1/4 cup olive oil
- 1 tsp black pepper
- 1 tsp sea salt

Directions:
1. In a bowl, mix together olive oil, pepper, garlic, and salt.
2. Pour olive oil mixture over green beans and mushrooms and stir to coat.
3. Spread green beans and mushroom mixture into the baking dish.
4. Select Bake mode.
5. Set time to 25 minutes and temperature 400 F then press START.
6. The air fryer display will prompt you to ADD FOOD once the temperature is reached then place the baking dish in the air fryer basket.
7. Serve and enjoy.

Nutritional Value (Amount per Serving):
Calories 136; Fat 12.8 g; Carbohydrates 5.9 g; Sugar 1.4 g; Protein 2.3 g; Cholesterol 0 mg

Broccoli Nuggets

Preparation Time: 10 minutes; Cooking Time: 20 minutes; Serve: 4
Ingredients:
- 2 cups broccoli florets, cooked until soften
- 1/4 cup almond flour
- 2 egg whites
- 1 cup cheddar cheese, shredded
- 1/8 tsp salt

Directions:
1. Add cooked broccoli florets into the large bowl and using potato masher mash into small pieces.
2. Add remaining ingredients into the bowl and mix until well combined.
3. Make small nuggets from the broccoli mixture.
4. Select Bake mode.
5. Set time to 20 minutes and temperature 350 F then press START.
6. The air fryer display will prompt you to ADD FOOD once the temperature is reached then place broccoli nuggets in the air fryer basket.
7. Serve and enjoy.

Nutritional Value (Amount per Serving):
Calories 148; Fat 10.4 g; Carbohydrates 3.9 g; Sugar 1.1 g; Protein 10.5 g; Cholesterol 30 mg

Tasty Baked Cauliflower

Preparation Time: 10 minutes; Cooking Time: 45 minutes; Serve: 2
Ingredients:
- 1/2 cauliflower head, cut into florets
- 2 tbsp olive oil

For seasoning:
- 1/2 tsp garlic powder
- 1 tsp onion powder
- 1 tbsp ground cayenne pepper
- 2 tbsp ground paprika
- 1/2 tsp ground cumin
- 1/2 tsp black pepper
- 1/2 tsp white pepper
- 2 tsp salt

Directions:
1. In a large bowl, mix together all seasoning ingredients.
2. Add oil and stir well. Add cauliflower to the bowl seasoning mixture and stir well to coat.

3. Transfer the cauliflower florets into the baking dish.
4. Select Bake mode.
5. Set time to 45 minutes and temperature 400 F then press START.
6. The air fryer display will prompt you to ADD FOOD once the temperature is reached then place the baking dish in the air fryer basket.
7. Serve and enjoy.

Nutritional Value (Amount per Serving):
Calories 176; Fat 15.6 g; Carbohydrates 11.3 g; Sugar 3.2 g; Protein 3.1 g; Cholesterol 0 mg

Cauliflower Tomato Rice

Preparation Time: 10 minutes; Cooking Time: 15 minutes; Serve: 3
Ingredients:
- 1 cauliflower head, cut into florets
- 1 tomato, chopped
- 1 onion, chopped
- 2 tbsp tomato paste
- 2 tbsp olive oil
- 1 tsp white pepper
- 1 tsp black pepper
- 1 tbsp dried thyme
- 2 chilies, chopped
- 2 garlic cloves, chopped
- 1/2 tsp salt

Directions:
1. Add cauliflower florets into the food processor and process until it looks like rice.
2. Stir in tomato paste, tomatoes, and spices and mix well.
3. Spread cauliflower mixture into the baking dish and drizzle with olive oil.
4. Select Bake mode.
5. Set time to 15 minutes and temperature 400 F then press START.
6. The air fryer display will prompt you to ADD FOOD once the temperature is reached then place the baking dish in the air fryer basket.
7. Serve and enjoy.

Nutritional Value (Amount per Serving):
Calories 149; Fat 9.9 g; Carbohydrates 15.4 g; Sugar 6.9 g; Protein 3.5 g; Cholesterol 0 mg

Squash Noodles

Preparation Time: 10 minutes; Cooking Time: 25 minutes; Serve: 2
Ingredients:
- 1 medium butternut squash, peel and spiralized
- 3 tbsp cream
- 1/4 cup parmesan cheese
- 1 tsp thyme, chopped
- 1 tbsp sage, chopped
- 1 tsp garlic powder
- 2 tbsp cream cheese

Directions:
1. In a bowl, mix together cream cheese, parmesan, thyme, sage, cream, and garlic powder.
2. Add noodles to a baking dish.
3. Select Bake mode.
4. Set time to 20 minutes and temperature 400 F then press START.
5. The air fryer display will prompt you to ADD FOOD once the temperature is reached then place the baking dish in the air fryer basket.
6. Spread the cream cheese mixture over noodles and bake for 5 minutes more.
7. Serve and enjoy.

Nutritional Value (Amount per Serving):
Calories 180; Fat 11 g; Carbohydrates 12 g; Sugar 2.3 g; Protein 11.3 g; Cholesterol 35 mg

Cheesy Zucchini Noodles

Preparation Time: 10 minutes; Cooking Time: 45 minutes; Serve: 3
Ingredients:
- 1 egg
- 2 medium zucchini, trimmed and spiralized
- 1/2 cup parmesan cheese, grated
- 1/2 cup feta cheese, crumbled
- 2 tbsp olive oil
- 1 cup mozzarella cheese, grated
- 1 tbsp thyme
- 1 garlic clove, chopped
- 1 onion, chopped
- 1/2 tsp pepper
- 1/2 tsp salt

Directions:
1. Add spiralized zucchini and salt in a colander and set aside for 10 minutes.
2. Gently wash zucchini noodles and pat dry with a paper towel.
3. Heat oil in a pan over medium heat. Add garlic and onion and sauté for 3-4 minutes.
4. Add zucchini noodles and cook for 4 minutes or until softened.
5. Add zucchini mixture into a baking dish add the eggs, thyme, cheeses. Mix well and season with pepper and salt.
6. Select Bake mode.
7. Set time to 45 minutes and temperature 375 F then press START.
8. The air fryer display will prompt you to ADD FOOD once the temperature is reached then place the baking dish in the air fryer basket.
9. Serve and enjoy.

Nutritional Value (Amount per Serving):
Calories 359; Fat 26.5 g; Carbohydrates 11.8 g; Sugar 5 g; Protein 22.8 g; Cholesterol 110 mg

Roasted Carrots

Preparation Time: 10 minutes; Cooking Time: 35 minutes; Serve: 6
Ingredients:
- 16 small carrots
- 1 tbsp fresh parsley, chopped
- 1 tbsp dried basil
- 6 garlic cloves, minced
- 4 tbsp olive oil
- 1 1/2 tsp salt

Directions:
1. In a bowl, combine together oil, carrots, basil, garlic, and salt.
2. Spread the carrots into a baking dish.
3. Select Bake mode.
4. Set time to 35 minutes and temperature 375 F then press START.
5. The air fryer display will prompt you to ADD FOOD once the temperature is reached then place the baking dish in the air fryer basket.
6. Garnish with parsley and serve.

Nutritional Value (Amount per Serving):
Calories 94; Fat 9.4 g; Carbohydrates 3.2 g; Sugar 1.3 g; Protein 0.4 g; Cholesterol 0 mg

Cheese Baked Broccoli

Preparation Time: 10 minutes; Cooking Time: 10 minutes; Serve: 4
Ingredients:
- 1 lb broccoli, cut into florets
- 1/2 cup mozzarella cheese, shredded
- 1/2 cup heavy cream
- 2 garlic cloves, minced
- 1/4 cup parmesan cheese, grated
- 1/2 cup gruyere cheese, shredded
- 1 tbsp butter

Directions:
1. Melt butter in a pan over medium heat.

2. Add broccoli and season with pepper and salt.
3. Cook broccoli over medium heat for 5 minutes or until tender. Add garlic and stir for a minute.
4. Transfer broccoli into the baking dish.
5. Pour heavy cream over broccoli then top with parmesan cheese, gruyere cheese, and mozzarella cheese.
6. Select Bake mode.
7. Set time to 10 minutes and temperature 375 F then press START.
8. The air fryer display will prompt you to ADD FOOD once the temperature is reached then place the baking dish in the air fryer basket.
9. Serve and enjoy.

Nutritional Value (Amount per Serving):
Calories 230; Fat 16.9 g; Carbohydrates 9.2 g; Sugar 2 g; Protein 13.3 g; Cholesterol 55 mg

Cheddar Cheese Broccoli

Preparation Time: 10 minutes; Cooking Time: 30 minutes; Serve: 6

Ingredients:
- 4 cups broccoli florets
- 1/4 cup ranch dressing
- 1/4 cup heavy whipping cream
- 1/2 cup cheddar cheese, shredded
- Pepper
- Salt

Directions:
1. Add all ingredients into the mixing bowl and mix until well coated.
2. Spread broccoli in baking dish.
3. Select Bake mode.
4. Set time to 30 minutes and temperature 375 F then press START.
5. The air fryer display will prompt you to ADD FOOD once the temperature is reached then place the baking dish in the air fryer basket.
6. Serve and enjoy.

Nutritional Value (Amount per Serving):
Calories 79; Fat 5.2 g; Carbohydrates 4.8 g; Sugar 1.4 g; Protein 4.3 g; Cholesterol 17 mg

Stuffed Bell Peppers

Preparation Time: 10 minutes; Cooking Time: 45 minutes; Serve: 4

Ingredients:
- 4 eggs
- 2 medium bell peppers, sliced in half and remove seeds
- 1/2 cup parmesan cheese, grated
- 1/2 cup mozzarella cheese, shredded
- 1/2 cup ricotta cheese
- 1/4 cup baby spinach
- 1/4 tsp dried parsley
- 1 tsp garlic powder

Directions:
1. Add three cheeses, parsley, garlic powder, and eggs in food processor and process until combined.
2. Pour egg mixture into each pepper half and top with baby spinach.
3. Place stuffed peppers in a baking dish. Cover dish with foil.
4. Select Bake mode.
5. Set time to 45 minutes and temperature 375 F then press START.
6. The air fryer display will prompt you to ADD FOOD once the temperature is reached then place the baking dish in the air fryer basket.
7. Serve and enjoy.

Nutritional Value (Amount per Serving):

Calories 232; Fat 13.9 g; Carbohydrates 8.2 g; Sugar 3.6 g; Protein 20.2 g; Cholesterol 196 mg

Baked Artichoke Spinach

Preparation Time: 10 minutes; Cooking Time: 20 minutes; Serve: 3

Ingredients:
- 6 oz artichoke hearts, chopped
- 4 oz cream cheese
- 1/8 tsp red pepper flakes
- 10 oz baby spinach
- 1 garlic clove, minced
- 1 tbsp olive oil
- 2 oz brie cheese
- 1/3 cup black olives
- Pepper
- Salt

Directions:
1. Heat olive oil in a large pan over medium heat.
2. Add garlic and sauté for 1-2 minutes.
3. Add spinach, red pepper flakes, pepper, and salt and cook for 2-3 minutes or until spinach wilted.
4. Add cream cheese and cook until cheese is melted.
5. Add artichoke hearts and reduce heat. Cook for 3-5 minutes more.
6. Stir in olives. Transfer mixture to a baking dish and top with cheese.
7. Select Bake mode.
8. Set time to 20 minutes and temperature 350 F then press START.
9. The air fryer display will prompt you to ADD FOOD once the temperature is reached then place the baking dish in the air fryer basket.
10. Serve and enjoy.

Nutritional Value (Amount per Serving):
Calories 302; Fat 25.2 g; Carbohydrates 11.8 g; Sugar 1.2 g; Protein 11.5 g; Cholesterol 60 mg

Delicious Zucchini Casserole

Preparation Time: 10 minutes; Cooking Time: 30 minutes; Serve: 6

Ingredients:
- 3 medium zucchini, sliced into 1/4-inch thick slices
- 1 tbsp butter
- 2 tbsp unsweetened almond milk
- 1/3 cup heavy cream
- 3 oz brie cheese
- 1/2 tbsp Italian seasoning
- 1 cup Swiss gruyere cheese, shredded
- 2 garlic cloves, minced
- Pepper
- Salt

Directions:
1. Toss zucchini slices with salt and place into a colander and set aside for 45 minutes. Pat dry with a paper towel.
2. In a baking dish, arrange zucchini slices and season with pepper and salt.
3. Combine brie, garlic, butter, almond milk, and cream in a small saucepan and heat for few minutes or until cheese melts.
4. Pour cheese mixture over zucchini and sprinkle with shredded cheese.
5. Top with Italian seasoning.
6. Select Bake mode.
7. Set time to 30 minutes and temperature 400 F then press START.
8. The air fryer display will prompt you to ADD FOOD once the temperature is reached then place the baking dish in the air fryer basket.
9. Serve and enjoy.

Nutritional Value (Amount per Serving):
Calories 180; Fat 14.3 g; Carbohydrates 4 g; Sugar 1.9 g; Protein 9.1 g; Cholesterol 44 mg

Cheesy Baked Zoodle

Preparation Time: 10 minutes; Cooking Time: 35 minutes; Serve: 4
Ingredients:
- 2 medium zucchini, spiralized
- 2 tbsp butter
- 1 tsp fresh thyme, chopped
- 1 small onion, sliced
- 1 cup Fontina cheese, grated
- 2 tsp Worcestershire sauce
- 1/4 cup vegetable broth
- Pepper
- Salt

Directions:
1. Melt butter in a pan over medium heat.
2. Add the onion in a pan and sauté for a few minutes.
3. Add thyme, Worcestershire sauce, pepper, and salt. Stir for minutes.
4. Add broth in the pan and cook onions for 10 minutes.
5. In a large bowl, combine together zucchini noodles and onion mixture and pour into the greased baking dish.
6. Top with grated cheese.
7. Select Bake mode.
8. Set time to 25 minutes and temperature 400 F then press START.
9. The air fryer display will prompt you to ADD FOOD once the temperature is reached then place the baking dish in the air fryer basket.
10. Garnish with thyme and serve.

Nutritional Value (Amount per Serving):
Calories 184; Fat 14.5 g; Carbohydrates 6.1 g; Sugar 3.4 g; Protein 8.7 g; Cholesterol 47 mg

Parmesan Squash Casserole

Preparation Time: 10 minutes; Cooking Time: 45 minutes; Serve: 4
Ingredients:
- 4 medium squash, cut into slices
- 1/4 cup parmesan cheese, shredded
- 3/4 stick butter, cut into cubes
- 1 medium onion, sliced
- Pepper
- Salt

Directions:
1. Layer slices squash, onion, butter, pepper, and salt. Sprinkle with shredded parmesan cheese in a baking dish.
2. Cover dish with foil.
3. Select Bake mode.
4. Set time to 45 minutes and temperature 350 F then press START.
5. The air fryer display will prompt you to ADD FOOD once the temperature is reached then place the baking dish in the air fryer basket.
6. Serve and enjoy.

Nutritional Value (Amount per Serving):
Calories 241; Fat 20.7 g; Carbohydrates 9.7 g; Sugar 4.6 g; Protein 7.5 g; Cholesterol 56 mg

Roasted Cauliflower and Broccoli

Preparation Time: 10 minutes; Cooking Time: 20 minutes; Serve: 6
Ingredients:
- 4 cups broccoli florets
- 4 cups cauliflower florets
- 2/3 cup parmesan cheese, shredded
- 1/3 cup olive oil
- 3 garlic cloves, minced
- Pepper
- Salt

Directions:

1. Add half parmesan cheese, broccoli, cauliflower, garlic, oil, pepper, and salt into the large bowl and toss well.
2. Spread broccoli and cauliflower mixture in a baking dish.
3. Select Bake mode.
4. Set time to 20 minutes and temperature 400 F then press START.
5. The air fryer display will prompt you to ADD FOOD once the temperature is reached then place the baking dish in the air fryer basket.
6. Add remaining cheese and toss well.
7. Serve and enjoy.

Nutritional Value (Amount per Serving):
Calories 220; Fat 17.1 g; Carbohydrates 9 g; Sugar 2.7 g; Protein 11.5 g; Cholesterol 19 mg

Pecan Green Bean Casserole

Preparation Time: 10 minutes; Cooking Time: 20 minutes; Serve: 4
Ingredients:
- 1 lb green beans, trimmed and cut into pieces
- 1/4 cup olive oil
- 2 oz pecans, crushed
- 1 small onion, chopped
- 2 tbsp lemon zest
- 1/4 cup parmesan cheese, shredded

Directions:
1. Add all ingredients into the mixing bowl and toss well.
2. Spread green bean mixture into the baking dish.
3. Select Bake mode.
4. Set time to 20 minutes and temperature 400 F then press START.
5. The air fryer display will prompt you to ADD FOOD once the temperature is reached then place the baking dish in the air fryer basket.
6. Serve and enjoy.

Nutritional Value (Amount per Serving):
Calories 297; Fat 26 g; Carbohydrates 12.9 g; Sugar 3 g; Protein 8.5 g; Cholesterol 10 mg

Delicious Spaghetti Squash

Preparation Time: 10 minutes; Cooking Time: 10 minutes; Serve: 4
Ingredients:
- 2 cups spaghetti squash, cooked and drained
- 4 oz mozzarella cheese, cubed
- 1/4 cup basil pesto
- 1/2 cup ricotta cheese
- 1 tbsp olive oil
- Pepper
- Salt

Directions:
1. In a bowl, combine together olive oil and squash. Season with pepper and salt.
2. Spread squash mixture in a baking dish.
3. Spread mozzarella cheese and ricotta cheese on top.
4. Select Bake mode.
5. Set time to 10 minutes and temperature 375 F then press START.
6. The air fryer display will prompt you to ADD FOOD once the temperature is reached then place the baking dish in the air fryer basket.
7. Drizzle with basil pesto and serve.

Nutritional Value (Amount per Serving):
Calories 169; Fat 11.3 g; Carbohydrates 6.1 g; Sugar 0.1 g; Protein 11.9 g; Cholesterol 25 mg

Brussels Sprouts and Broccoli

Preparation Time: 10 minutes; Cooking Time: 30 minutes; Serve: 6
Ingredients:
- 1 lb broccoli, cut into florets
- 1 lb Brussels sprouts, cut ends
- 1 tsp paprika
- 1/2 onion, chopped
- 1 tsp garlic powder
- 1/2 tsp pepper
- 3 tbsp olive oil
- 3/4 tsp salt

Directions:
1. Add all ingredients into the mixing bowl and toss well.
2. The spread vegetable mixture in a baking dish.
3. Select Bake mode.
4. Set time to 30 minutes and temperature 400 F then press START.
5. The air fryer display will prompt you to ADD FOOD once the temperature is reached then place the baking dish in the air fryer basket.
6. Serve and enjoy.

Nutritional Value (Amount per Serving):
Calories 122; Fat 7.3 g; Carbohydrates 11.9 g; Sugar 2.2 g; Protein 5.5 g; Cholesterol 0 mg

Cauliflower Casserole

Preparation Time: 10 minutes; Cooking Time: 15 minutes; Serve: 6
Ingredients:
- 1 cauliflower head, cut into florets and boil
- 1 cup cheddar cheese, shredded
- 1 cup mozzarella cheese, shredded
- 2 oz cream cheese
- 1 cup heavy cream
- 1/2 tsp pepper
- 1/2 tsp salt

Directions:
1. Add cream in a small saucepan and bring to simmer, stir well. Add cream cheese and stir until thickens.
2. Remove from heat and add 1 cup shredded cheddar cheese and seasoning and stir well.
3. Place boiled cauliflower florets into the greased baking dish.
4. Pour saucepan mixture over cauliflower florets.
5. Sprinkle mozzarella cheese over the cauliflower mixture.
6. Select Bake mode.
7. Set time to 15 minutes and temperature 375 F then press START.
8. The air fryer display will prompt you to ADD FOOD once the temperature is reached then place the baking dish in the air fryer basket.
9. Serve and enjoy.

Nutritional Value (Amount per Serving):
Calories 203; Fat 17.8 g; Carbohydrates 3.7 g; Sugar 1.2 g; Protein 8 g; Cholesterol 60 mg

Basil Eggplant Casserole

Preparation Time: 10 minutes; Cooking Time: 35 minutes; Serve: 6
Ingredients:
- 1 eggplant, sliced
- 3 zucchini, sliced
- 4 tbsp basil, chopped
- 1 tbsp olive oil
- 3 garlic cloves, minced
- 3 oz mozzarella cheese, grated
- 1/4 cup parsley, chopped
- 1 cup grape tomatoes, halved
- 1/4 tsp pepper
- 1/4 tsp salt

Directions:
1. Add all ingredients into the large bowl and toss well to combine.

2. Pour eggplant mixture into the greased baking dish.
3. Select Bake mode.
4. Set time to 35 minutes and temperature 350 F then press START.
5. The air fryer display will prompt you to ADD FOOD once the temperature is reached then place the baking dish in the air fryer basket.
6. Serve and enjoy.

Nutritional Value (Amount per Serving):
Calories 104; Fat 5.3 g; Carbohydrates 10.2 g; Sugar 4.8 g; Protein 6.4 g; Cholesterol 8 mg

Air Fry Green Beans

Preparation Time: 5 minutes; Cooking Time: 10 minutes; Serve: 2
Ingredients:
- 2 cups green beans
- 2 tbsp olive oil
- 1/4 tsp ground coriander
- 1/4 tsp ground cumin
- 1/2 tsp dried oregano
- 1/8 tsp cayenne pepper
- 1/8 tsp ground allspice
- 1/4 tsp ground cinnamon
- 1/2 tsp salt

Directions:
1. Add all ingredients into the mixing bowl and toss well.
2. Select Bake mode.
3. Set time to 10 minutes and temperature 370 F then press START.
4. The air fryer display will prompt you to ADD FOOD once the temperature is reached then add green beans in the air fryer basket. Shake basket halfway through
5. Serve and enjoy.

Nutritional Value (Amount per Serving):
Calories 158; Fat 14.3 g; Carbohydrates 8.6 g; Sugar 1.6 g; Protein 2.1 g; Cholesterol 0 mg

Spicy Okra

Preparation Time: 10 minutes; Cooking Time: 10 minutes; Serve: 2
Ingredients:
- 1/2 lb okra, trimmed and sliced
- 1 tsp olive oil
- 1/8 tsp pepper
- 1/2 tsp chili powder
- 1/2 tsp garlic powder
- 1/4 tsp salt

Directions:
1. Add all ingredients into the bowl and toss well.
2. Select Bake mode.
3. Set time to 10 minutes and temperature 350 F then press START.
4. The air fryer display will prompt you to ADD FOOD once the temperature is reached then add okra in the air fryer basket. Stir halfway through.
5. Serve and enjoy.

Nutritional Value (Amount per Serving):
Calories 70; Fat 2.7 g; Carbohydrates 9.4 g; Sugar 1.9 g; Protein 2.4 g; Cholesterol 0 mg

Lemon Green Beans

Preparation Time: 5 minutes; Cooking Time: 10 minutes; Serve: 2
Ingredients:
- 1 lb green beans, washed and ends trimmed
- 1 fresh lemon juice
- 1/4 tsp olive oil
- Pepper
- Salt

Directions:

1. Place green beans in a baking dish and drizzle with lemon juice and oil. Season with pepper and salt.
2. Select Bake mode.
3. Set time to 10 minutes and temperature 400 F then press START.
4. The air fryer display will prompt you to ADD FOOD once the temperature is reached then place the baking dish in the air fryer basket.
5. Serve and enjoy.

Nutritional Value (Amount per Serving):
Calories 23; Fat 0.8 g; Carbohydrates 3 g; Sugar 1.5 g; Protein 0.7 g; Cholesterol 0 mg

Air Fry Asparagus

Preparation Time: 10 minutes; Cooking Time: 10 minutes; Serve: 4
Ingredients:
- 1 lb asparagus, ends trimmed and cut in half
- 1 1/2 tbsp coconut aminos
- 2 tbsp olive oil
- 1 tbsp vinegar
- Pepper
- Salt

Directions:
1. Add asparagus in a large bowl with remaining ingredients and toss well.
2. Select Air Fry mode.
3. Set time to 10 minutes and temperature 400 F then press START.
4. The air fryer display will prompt you to ADD FOOD once the temperature is reached then place asparagus in the air fryer basket. Stir halfway through.
5. Serve and enjoy.

Nutritional Value (Amount per Serving):
Calories 89; Fat 7.1 g; Carbohydrates 5.6 g; Sugar 2.2 g; Protein 2.5 g; Cholesterol 0 mg

Mixed Vegetables

Preparation Time: 10 minutes; Cooking Time: 10 minutes; Serve: 6
Ingredients:
- 2 cups mushrooms, cut in half
- 3/4 tsp Italian seasoning
- 1/2 onion, sliced
- 1/2 cup olive oil
- 2 yellow squash, sliced
- 2 medium zucchini, sliced
- 1/2 tsp garlic salt

Directions:
1. Add vegetables and remaining ingredients into the mixing bowl and toss well.
2. Select Air Fry mode.
3. Set time to 10 minutes and temperature 400 F then press START.
4. The air fryer display will prompt you to ADD FOOD once the temperature is reached then add vegetables in the air fryer basket.
5. Serve and enjoy.

Nutritional Value (Amount per Serving):
Calories 176; Fat 17.3 g; Carbohydrates 6.2 g; Sugar 3.2 g; Protein 2.5 g; Cholesterol 0 mg

Crisp Brussels Sprouts

Preparation Time: 10 minutes; Cooking Time: 15 minutes; Serve: 4
Ingredients:
- 2 cups Brussels sprouts
- 1/4 cup almonds, crushed
- 1/4 cup parmesan cheese, grated
- 2 tbsp olive oil
- 2 tbsp everything bagel seasoning
- Salt

Directions:
1. Add Brussels sprouts into the saucepan with 2 cups of water.
2. Cover and cook for 8-10 minutes.
3. Drain well and allow to cool completely.
4. Sliced each Brussels sprouts in half.
5. Add Brussels sprouts and remaining ingredients into the mixing bowl and toss to coat.
6. Select Air Fry mode.
7. Set time to 15 minutes and temperature 375 F then press START.
8. The air fryer display will prompt you to ADD FOOD once the temperature is reached then add Brussels sprouts mixture in the air fryer basket.
9. Serve and enjoy.

Nutritional Value (Amount per Serving):
Calories 172; Fat 13.3 g; Carbohydrates 8.3 g; Sugar 1.4 g; Protein 7.8 g; Cholesterol 10 mg

Jicama & Green Beans

Preparation Time: 10 minutes; Cooking Time: 45 minutes; Serve: 6
Ingredients:
- 1 medium jicama, cubed
- 12 oz green beans, sliced in half
- 3 garlic cloves
- 3 tbsp olive oil
- 1 tsp dried thyme
- 1 tsp dried rosemary
- 1/2 tsp salt

Directions:
1. Add green beans, jicama, thyme, rosemary, garlic, oil, and salt into the mixing bowl and toss well.
2. Spread green beans and jicama mixture into a baking dish.
3. Select Air Fry mode.
4. Set time to 45 minutes and temperature 400 F then press START.
5. The air fryer display will prompt you to ADD FOOD once the temperature is reached then place the baking dish in the air fryer basket. Stir halfway through.
6. Serve and enjoy.

Nutritional Value (Amount per Serving):
Calories 107; Fat 7.2 g; Carbohydrates 10.8 g; Sugar 2.1 g; Protein 1 g; Cholesterol 0 mg

Tasty Cauliflower Rice

Preparation Time: 10 minutes; Cooking Time: 40 minutes; Serve: 8
Ingredients:
- 6 cups grated cauliflower
- 1/8 tsp red pepper flakes
- 2 tbsp fresh cilantro, chopped
- 10 oz can tomatoes with green chilis
- 1/2 tsp salt

Directions:
1. Add can tomatoes into the blender and blend well.
2. Add grated cauliflower, cilantro, tomatoes, red pepper flakes, and salt into the prepared baking dish and stir until well combined.
3. Select Bake mode.
4. Set time to 40 minutes and temperature 350 F then press START.
5. The air fryer display will prompt you to ADD FOOD once the temperature is reached then place the baking dish in the air fryer basket.
6. Serve and enjoy.

Nutritional Value (Amount per Serving):
Calories 107; Fat 7.2 g; Carbohydrates 10.8 g; Sugar 2.1 g; Protein 1 g; Cholesterol 0 mg

Squash & Zucchini

Preparation Time: 10 minutes; Cooking Time: 25 minutes; Serve: 4

Ingredients:
- 1 lb yellow squash, cut into 1/2-inch half-moons
- 1 lb zucchini, cut into 1/2-inch half-moons
- 1 tbsp olive oil
- Pepper
- Salt

Directions:
1. In a bowl, add zucchini, squash, oil, pepper, and salt and toss well.
2. Select Bake mode.
3. Set time to 25 minutes and temperature 400 F then press START.
4. The air fryer display will prompt you to ADD FOOD once the temperature is reached then add zucchini and squash mixture in the air fryer basket.
5. Serve and enjoy.

Nutritional Value (Amount per Serving):
Calories 66; Fat 3.9 g; Carbohydrates 7.6 g; Sugar 3.9 g; Protein 2.7 g; Cholesterol 0 mg

Spinach Squares

Preparation Time: 10 minutes; Cooking Time: 35 minutes; Serve: 9

Ingredients:
- 3 eggs
- 1/2 cup ricotta cheese
- 16 oz frozen spinach, cooked and drained
- 8 oz cheddar cheese, grated
- 1/2 tsp paprika
- Pepper
- Salt

Directions:
1. Add eggs, paprika, ricotta cheese, pepper, and salt into the blender and blend until smooth. Stir in spinach and cheese.
2. Pour egg mixture into the greased baking dish.
3. Select Bake mode.
4. Set time to 35 minutes and temperature 350 F then press START.
5. The air fryer display will prompt you to ADD FOOD once the temperature is reached then place the baking dish in the air fryer basket.
6. Slice and serve.

Nutritional Value (Amount per Serving):
Calories 154; Fat 11.1 g; Carbohydrates 3.1 g; Sugar 0.5 g; Protein 11.2 g; Cholesterol 85 mg

Air Fried Cabbage

Preparation Time: 10 minutes; Cooking Time: 10 minutes; Serve: 2

Ingredients:
- 1/2 cabbage head, sliced into 2-inch slices
- 1 tbsp olive oil
- 1/2 tsp garlic powder
- Pepper
- Salt

Directions:
1. Drizzle cabbage with olive oil and season with garlic powder, pepper, and salt.
2. Select Bake mode.
3. Set time to 10 minutes and temperature 375 F then press START.
4. The air fryer display will prompt you to ADD FOOD once the temperature is reached then place Cabbage slices in the air fryer basket. Turn cabbage slices halfway through.
5. Serve and enjoy.

Nutritional Value (Amount per Serving):

Calories 107; Fat 7.2 g; Carbohydrates 10.9 g; Sugar 5.9 g; Protein 2.4 g; Cholesterol 0 mg

Vegetable Kebabs

Preparation Time: 10 minutes; Cooking Time: 10 minutes; Serve: 4

Ingredients:
- 2 bell peppers, cut into 1-inch pieces
- 1 eggplant, cut into 1-inch pieces
- 1/2 onion, cut into 1-inch pieces
- 1 zucchini, cut into 1-inch pieces
- Pepper
- Salt

Directions:
1. Thread vegetables onto the soaked wooden skewers and spray them with cooking spray. Season with pepper and salt.
2. Select Air Fry mode.
3. Set time to 10 minutes and temperature 390 F then press START.
4. The air fryer display will prompt you to ADD FOOD once the temperature is reached then place skewers in the air fryer basket. Turn halfway through.
5. Serve and enjoy.

Nutritional Value (Amount per Serving):
Calories 28; Fat 0.2 g; Carbohydrates 6.2 g; Sugar 3.1 g; Protein 1.3 g; Cholesterol 0 mg

Chapter 7: Seafood Recipes

Old Bay Shrimp

Preparation Time: 10 minutes; Cooking Time: 10 minutes; Serve: 4
Ingredients:
- 12 oz shrimp, peeled
- 3/25 oz pork rind, crushed
- 1 1/2 tsp old bay seasoning
- 1/4 cup mayonnaise

Directions:
1. In a shallow bowl, mix together crushed pork rind and old bay seasoning.
2. Add shrimp and mayonnaise into the mixing bowl and toss well.
3. Place the cooking tray in the air fryer basket.
4. Select Air Fry mode.
5. Set time to 10 minutes and temperature 380 F then press START.
6. The air fryer display will prompt you to ADD FOOD once the temperature is reached then coat shrimp with crushed pork rind and place in the air fryer basket.
7. Serve and enjoy.

Nutritional Value (Amount per Serving):
Calories 163; Fat 6.7 g; Carbohydrates 4.8 g; Sugar 0.9 g; Protein 20.1 g; Cholesterol 184 mg

Crunchy Fish Sticks

Preparation Time: 10 minutes; Cooking Time: 15 minutes; Serve: 5
Ingredients:
- 12 oz tilapia loins, cut into fish sticks
- 1/2 cup parmesan cheese, grated
- 3.25 oz pork rind, crushed
- 1 tsp paprika
- 1 tsp garlic powder
- 1/4 cup mayonnaise

Directions:
1. In a shallow bowl, mix together parmesan cheese, crushed pork rind, paprika, and garlic powder.
2. Add fish pieces and mayonnaise into the mixing bowl and mix well.
3. Place the cooking tray in the air fryer basket.
4. Select Air Fry mode.
5. Set time to 15 minutes and temperature 380 F then press START.
6. The air fryer display will prompt you to ADD FOOD once the temperature is reached then coat fish pieces with parmesan mixture and place in the air fryer basket.
7. Serve and enjoy.

Nutritional Value (Amount per Serving):
Calories 295; Fat 16.8 g; Carbohydrates 4.3 g; Sugar 0.9 g; Protein 33.4 g; Cholesterol 61 mg

Garlic Butter Fish Fillets

Preparation Time: 10 minutes; Cooking Time: 10 minutes; Serve: 2
Ingredients:
- 2 salmon fillets
- 1/4 tsp dried parsley
- 1 tsp garlic, minced
- 2 tbsp butter, melted
- Pepper
- Salt

Directions:
1. In a small bowl, mix together melted butter, garlic, and parsley.
2. Season fish fillets with pepper and salt and brush with melted butter mixture.
3. Place the cooking tray in the air fryer basket.
4. Select Air Fry mode.
5. Set time to 10 minutes and temperature 360 F then press START.

6. The air fryer display will prompt you to ADD FOOD once the temperature is reached then place fish fillets skin side down in the air fryer basket.
7. Serve and enjoy.

Nutritional Value (Amount per Serving):
Calories 340; Fat 22.5 g; Carbohydrates 0.5 g; Sugar 0 g; Protein 34.8 g; Cholesterol 109 mg

Parmesan Shrimp

Preparation Time: 10 minutes; Cooking Time: 12 minutes; Serve: 4

Ingredients:
- 1 lb shrimp, peeled & deveined
- 2 tbsp parsley, minced
- 2 tbsp parmesan cheese, grated
- 1/8 tsp garlic powder
- 2 tbsp olive oil
- 1/2 tsp pepper
- 1/2 tsp salt

Directions:
1. In a mixing bowl, toss shrimp with olive oil. Add remaining ingredients and toss until shrimp is well coated.
2. Place the cooking tray in the air fryer basket.
3. Select Air Fry mode.
4. Set time to 12 minutes and temperature 400 F then press START.
5. The air fryer display will prompt you to ADD FOOD once the temperature is reached then add shrimp in the air fryer basket.
6. Stir shrimp halfway through.
7. Serve and enjoy.

Nutritional Value (Amount per Serving):
Calories 205; Fat 9.5 g; Carbohydrates 2.2 g; Sugar 0 g; Protein 26.8 g; Cholesterol 241 mg

Flavorful Tuna Steaks

Preparation Time: 10 minutes; Cooking Time: 4 minutes; Serve: 2

Ingredients:
- 12 tuna steaks, skinless and boneless
- 1/2 tsp rice vinegar
- 1 tsp sesame oil
- 1 tsp ginger, grated
- 4 tbsp soy sauce

Directions:
1. Add tuna steaks and remaining ingredients in the zip-lock bag. Seal bag and place in the refrigerator for 30 minutes.
2. Select Air Fry mode.
3. Set time to 4 minutes and temperature 380 F then press START.
4. The air fryer display will prompt you to ADD FOOD once the temperature is reached then place marinated tuna steaks in the air fryer basket.
5. Serve and enjoy.

Nutritional Value (Amount per Serving):
Calories 980; Fat 34.4 g; Carbohydrates 3.1 g; Sugar 0.6 g; Protein 154.7 g; Cholesterol 250 mg

Baked Tilapia

Preparation Time: 10 minutes; Cooking Time: 15 minutes; Serve: 6

Ingredients:
- 6 tilapia fillets
- 1/2 cup Asiago cheese, grated
- 1/4 tsp basil
- 1/4 tsp thyme
- 1/4 tsp onion powder
- 1 tsp garlic, minced
- 1/2 cup mayonnaise
- 1/8 tsp pepper

- 1/4 tsp salt

Directions:
1. In a small bowl, mix together the grated cheese, basil, thyme, onion powder, garlic, mayonnaise, pepper, and salt.
2. Place the cooking tray in the air fryer basket. Line air fryer basket with parchment paper.
3. Select Bake mode.
4. Set time to 15 minutes and temperature 350 F then press START.
5. The air fryer display will prompt you to ADD FOOD once the temperature is reached then place fish fillets in the air fryer basket and spread cheese mixture on top of each fish fillet.
6. Serve and enjoy.

Nutritional Value (Amount per Serving):
Calories 287; Fat 13.7 g; Carbohydrates 5 g; Sugar 1.3 g; Protein 36.7 g; Cholesterol 105 mg

Baked Parmesan Tilapia

Preparation Time: 10 minutes; Cooking Time: 10 minutes; Serve: 4

Ingredients:
- 2 lbs tilapia
- 1/4 tsp paprika
- 1/4 tsp dried basil
- 2 garlic cloves, minced
- 1 tsp dried parsley
- 1 tbsp butter, softened
- 2 tbsp fresh lemon juice
- 1/4 cup mayonnaise
- 1/2 cup parmesan cheese, grated
- 1/2 tsp salt

Directions:
1. In a small bowl, mix together parmesan cheese, mayonnaise, lemon juice, butter, parsley, garlic, basil, paprika, and salt.
2. Place the cooking tray in the air fryer basket. Line air fryer basket with parchment paper.
3. Select Bake mode.
4. Set time to 10 minutes and temperature 400 F then press START.
5. The air fryer display will prompt you to ADD FOOD once the temperature is reached then place fish fillets in the air fryer basket and spread the parmesan mixture on top of each fish fillet.
6. Serve and enjoy.

Nutritional Value (Amount per Serving):
Calories 368; Fat 16.2 g; Carbohydrates 5.3 g; Sugar 1.1 g; Protein 51.9 g; Cholesterol 143 mg

Pecan Crusted Fish Fillets

Preparation Time: 10 minutes; Cooking Time: 17 minutes; Serve: 2

Ingredients:
- 2 halibut fillets
- 1/2 lemon juice
- 1 tsp garlic, minced
- 1/4 cup parmesan cheese, grated
- 1/4 cup pecans
- 2 tbsp butter
- Pepper
- Salt

Directions:
1. Add pecans, lemon juice, garlic, parmesan cheese, and butter into the food processor and process until completely blended.
2. Place the cooking tray in the air fryer basket. Line air fryer basket with parchment paper.
3. Select Bake mode.
4. Set time to 5 minutes and temperature 400 F then press START.
5. The air fryer display will prompt you to ADD FOOD once the temperature is reached then season fish fillets with pepper and salt and place in the air fryer basket.

6. Spread pecan mixture on top of fish fillets and bake for 12 minutes more.
7. Serve and enjoy.

Nutritional Value (Amount per Serving):
Calories 606; Fat 33.5 g; Carbohydrates 3.6 g; Sugar 0.7 g; Protein 71.6 g; Cholesterol 144 mg

Bagel Crust Fish Fillets

Preparation Time: 10 minutes; Cooking Time: 10 minutes; Serve: 4

Ingredients:
- 4 white fish fillets
- 1 tbsp mayonnaise
- 1 tsp lemon pepper seasoning
- 2 tbsp almond flour
- 1/4 cup bagel seasoning

Directions:
1. In a small bowl, mix together bagel seasoning, almond flour, and lemon pepper seasoning.
2. Brush mayonnaise over fish fillets. Sprinkle seasoning mixture over fish fillets.
3. Place the cooking tray in the air fryer basket. Line air fryer basket with parchment paper.
4. Select Bake mode.
5. Set time to 10 minutes and temperature 400 F then press START.
6. The air fryer display will prompt you to ADD FOOD once the temperature is reached then place fish fillets in the air fryer basket.
7. Serve and enjoy.

Nutritional Value (Amount per Serving):
Calories 375; Fat 2.5 g; Carbohydrates 7.2 g; Sugar 1 g; Protein 41.3 g; Cholesterol 120 mg

Moist & Juicy Baked Cod

Preparation Time: 10 minutes; Cooking Time: 10 minutes; Serve: 2

Ingredients:
- 1 lb cod fillets
- 1 1/2 tbsp olive oil
- 3 dashes cayenne pepper
- 1 tbsp lemon juice
- 1/4 tsp salt

Directions:
1. In a small bowl, mix together olive oil, cayenne pepper, lemon juice, and salt.
2. Brush fish fillets with oil mixture.
3. Place the cooking tray in the air fryer basket. Line air fryer basket with parchment paper.
4. Select Bake mode.
5. Set time to 10 minutes and temperature 400 F then press START.
6. The air fryer display will prompt you to ADD FOOD once the temperature is reached then place fish fillets in the air fryer basket.
7. Serve and enjoy.

Nutritional Value (Amount per Serving):
Calories 275; Fat 12.7 g; Carbohydrates 0.4 g; Sugar 0.2 g; Protein 40.6 g; Cholesterol 111 mg

Baked Salmon Patties

Preparation Time: 10 minutes; Cooking Time: 20 minutes; Serve: 4

Ingredients:
- 2 eggs, lightly beaten
- 12 oz can salmon, skinless, boneless, and drained
- 1/2 cup almond flour
- 1/2 tsp pepper
- 1 tbsp Dijon mustard
- 1 tsp garlic powder
- 2 tbsp fresh parsley, chopped
- 1/2 cup celery, diced
- 1/2 cup bell pepper, diced

- 1/2 cup onion, diced

Directions:
1. Add salmon and remaining ingredients into the mixing bowl and mix until well combined.
2. Make 8 equal shapes of patties from the mixture.
3. Place the cooking tray in the air fryer basket. Line air fryer basket with parchment paper.
4. Select Bake mode.
5. Set time to 20 minutes and temperature 400 F then press START.
6. The air fryer display will prompt you to ADD FOOD once the temperature is reached then place patties in the air fryer basket.
7. Turn patties halfway through.
8. Serve and enjoy.

Nutritional Value (Amount per Serving):
Calories 182; Fat 6.5 g; Carbohydrates 4.8 g; Sugar 2.1 g; Protein 22.9 g; Cholesterol 105 mg

Easy Air Fryer Scallops

Preparation Time: 10 minutes; Cooking Time: 4 minutes; Serve: 2

Ingredients:
- 8 scallops
- 1 tbsp olive oil
- Pepper
- Salt

Directions:
1. Brush scallops with olive oil and season with pepper and salt.
2. Place the cooking tray in the air fryer basket.
3. Select Air Fry mode.
4. Set time to 2 minutes and temperature 390 F then press START.
5. The air fryer display will prompt you to ADD FOOD once the temperature is reached then add scallops in the air fryer basket.
6. Turn scallops and air fry for 2 minutes more.
7. Serve and enjoy.

Nutritional Value (Amount per Serving):
Calories 166; Fat 7.9 g; Carbohydrates 2.9 g; Sugar 0 g; Protein 20.2 g; Cholesterol 40 mg

Pesto Scallops

Preparation Time: 10 minutes; Cooking Time: 7 minutes; Serve: 4

Ingredients:
- 1 lb sea scallops
- 2 tsp garlic, minced
- 3 tbsp heavy cream
- 1/4 cup basil pesto
- 1 tbsp olive oil
- 1/2 tsp pepper
- 1 tsp salt

Directions:
1. In a small pan, mix together oil, cream, garlic, pesto, pepper, and salt, and simmer for 2-3 minutes.
2. Select Air Fry mode.
3. Set time to 5 minutes and temperature 320 F then press START.
4. The air fryer display will prompt you to ADD FOOD once the temperature is reached then add scallops in the air fryer basket.
5. Turn scallops and after 3 minutes.
6. Transfer scallops into the mixing bowl.
7. Pour pesto sauce over scallops and serve.

Nutritional Value (Amount per Serving):

Calories 172; Fat 8.6 g; Carbohydrates 3.7 g; Sugar 0 g; Protein 19.4 g; Cholesterol 53 mg

Mayo Cheese Crust Salmon

Preparation Time: 10 minutes; Cooking Time: 14 minutes; Serve: 4
Ingredients:
- 4 salmon fillets
- 2 tsp Italian seasoning
- 2 tbsp parmesan cheese, grated
- 2 tbsp crushed pork rind
- 4 tbsp mayonnaise

Directions:
1. Spread mayonnaise on top of fish fillets. Sprinkle with cheese, Italian seasoning, and crushed pork rind.
2. Place the cooking tray in the air fryer basket. Line air fryer basket with parchment paper.
3. Select Bake mode.
4. Set time to 14 minutes and temperature 375 F then press START.
5. The air fryer display will prompt you to ADD FOOD once the temperature is reached then place fish fillets in the air fryer basket.
6. Serve and enjoy.

Nutritional Value (Amount per Serving):
Calories 349; Fat 19.7 g; Carbohydrates 3.9 g; Sugar 1.1 g; Protein 40.1 g; Cholesterol 96 mg

Juicy Baked Halibut

Preparation Time: 10 minutes; Cooking Time: 12 minutes; Serve: 4
Ingredients:
- 1 lb halibut fillets
- 1/4 tsp garlic powder
- 1/4 tsp paprika
- 1/4 tsp pepper
- 1/4 cup olive oil
- 1 lemon juice
- 1/2 tsp salt

Directions:
1. In a small bowl, mix together olive oil, lemon juice, pepper, paprika, garlic powder, and salt.
2. Brush olive oil mixture over fish fillets.
3. Place the cooking tray in the air fryer basket. Line air fryer basket with parchment paper.
4. Select Bake mode.
5. Set time to 12 minutes and temperature 400 F then press START.
6. The air fryer display will prompt you to ADD FOOD once the temperature is reached then place fish fillets in the air fryer basket.
7. Serve and enjoy.

Nutritional Value (Amount per Serving):
Calories 272; Fat 15.4 g; Carbohydrates 0.5 g; Sugar 0.3 g; Protein 30.8 g; Cholesterol 53 mg

Delicious Crab Cakes

Preparation Time: 10 minutes; Cooking Time: 20 minutes; Serve: 4
Ingredients:
- 1 lb lump crab meat
- 1 tbsp butter, melted
- 1/2 tsp old bay seasoning
- 1 tbsp parsley, chopped
- 1 tsp garlic powder
- 1 tsp onion powder
- 1/4 cup parmesan cheese
- 1 egg yolk, lightly beaten
- 1 egg, lightly beaten
- 2 tsp Dijon mustard
- 1/4 cup mayonnaise

Directions:

1. Add all ingredients except melted butter into the mixing bowl and mix until well combined.
2. Make 4 equal shapes of patties from the mixture.
3. Place the cooking tray in the air fryer basket. Line air fryer basket with parchment paper.
4. Select Bake mode.
5. Set time to 20 minutes and temperature 400 F then press START.
6. The air fryer display will prompt you to ADD FOOD once the temperature is reached then place patties in the air fryer basket and drizzle with melted butter.
7. Serve and enjoy.

Nutritional Value (Amount per Serving):
Calories 247; Fat 22.4 g; Carbohydrates 7.3 g; Sugar 1.5 g; Protein 23.7 g; Cholesterol 179 mg

Simple Salmon Patties

Preparation Time: 10 minutes; Cooking Time: 14 minutes; Serve: 4
Ingredients:
- 2 eggs, lightly beaten
- 2 oz salmon, cooked and flaked
- 1/4 tsp paprika
- 1/8 tsp pepper
- 1/3 cup parsley, chopped
- 2 garlic cloves, minced
- 1/4 cup onion, diced
- 2/3 cup almond flour
- Pinch of salt

Directions:
1. Add all ingredients into the mixing bowl and mix until well combined.
2. Make the equal shape of patties from the mixture.
3. Place the cooking tray in the air fryer basket. Line air fryer basket with parchment paper.
4. Select Air Fry mode.
5. Set time to 14 minutes and temperature 380 F then press START.
6. The air fryer display will prompt you to ADD FOOD once the temperature is reached then place patties in the air fryer basket.
7. Turn patties halfway through.
8. Serve and enjoy.

Nutritional Value (Amount per Serving):
Calories 84; Fat 5.5 g; Carbohydrates 2.8 g; Sugar 0.7 g; Protein 6.9 g; Cholesterol 88 mg

Easy Tuna Patties

Preparation Time: 10 minutes; Cooking Time: 10 minutes; Serve: 5
Ingredients:
- 15 oz can albacore tuna, drained
- 1/2 tsp dried mix herbs
- 1/2 tsp garlic powder
- 3 tbsp onion, minced
- 1 celery stalk, chopped
- 3 tbsp parmesan cheese, grated
- 1/2 cup almond flour
- 1 tbsp lemon juice
- 2 large eggs, lightly beaten

Directions:
1. Add all ingredients into the mixing bowl and mix until well combined.
2. Make the equal shape of patties from the mixture.
3. Place the cooking tray in the air fryer basket. Line air fryer basket with parchment paper.
4. Select Air Fry mode.
5. Set time to 10 minutes and temperature 360 F then press START.
6. The air fryer display will prompt you to ADD FOOD once the temperature is reached then place patties in the air fryer basket.
7. Turn patties halfway through.

8. Serve and enjoy.

Nutritional Value (Amount per Serving):
   Calories 138; Fat 4.9 g; Carbohydrates 2.2 g; Sugar 0.7 g; Protein 21.2 g; Cholesterol 107 mg

Baked Mahi Mahi

Preparation Time: 10 minutes; Cooking Time: 30 minutes; Serve: 4

Ingredients:
- 4 Mahi Mahi fillets
- 1 tsp onion powder
- 1 tsp garlic powder
- 1 tsp turmeric
- 1 tbsp dried basil
- 1 tsp pepper
- 1 tsp salt

Directions:
1. In a small bowl, mix together onion powder, garlic powder, turmeric, basil, pepper, and salt.
2. Season fish fillets with spice mixture.
3. Place the cooking tray in the air fryer basket. Line air fryer basket with parchment paper.
4. Select Bake mode.
5. Set time to 30 minutes and temperature 350 F then press START.
6. The air fryer display will prompt you to ADD FOOD once the temperature is reached then place the fish fillet in the air fryer basket.
7. Serve and enjoy.

Nutritional Value (Amount per Serving):
   Calories 108; Fat 1.1 g; Carbohydrates 2.7 g; Sugar 0.4 g; Protein 21.3 g; Cholesterol 80 mg

Baked Basa

Preparation Time: 10 minutes; Cooking Time: 30 minutes; Serve: 2

Ingredients:
- 2 basa fish fillets
- 4 lemon slices
- 1/8 tsp lemon juice
- 1/2 tbsp dried basil
- 1/2 tsp paprika
- 4 tsp butter, melted
- 1/8 tsp salt

Directions:
1. In a small bowl, mix together butter, paprika, basil, lemon juice, and salt.
2. Brush fish fillets with melted butter mixture.
3. Place the cooking tray in the air fryer basket. Line air fryer basket with parchment paper.
4. Select Air Fry mode.
5. Set time to 30 minutes and temperature 350 F then press START.
6. The air fryer display will prompt you to ADD FOOD once the temperature is reached then place fish fillets in the air fryer basket and place lemon slices on fish fillets.
7. Turn fish fillets halfway through.
8. Serve and enjoy.

Nutritional Value (Amount per Serving):
   Calories 293; Fat 19.6 g; Carbohydrates 5.8 g; Sugar 3.2 g; Protein 24 g; Cholesterol 20 mg

Parmesan Cod

Preparation Time: 10 minutes; Cooking Time: 15 minutes; Serve: 4

Ingredients:
- 4 cod fillets
- 1 tbsp olive oil
- 1 tbsp parsley, chopped
- 2 tsp paprika
- 3/4 cup parmesan cheese, grated
- 1/4 tsp sea salt

Directions:
1. In a shallow dish, mix together parmesan cheese, paprika, parsley, and salt.
2. Brush fish fillets with oil and coat with cheese mixture.
3. Place the cooking tray in the air fryer basket. Line air fryer basket with parchment paper.
4. Select Bake mode.
5. Set time to 15 minutes and temperature 400 F then press START.
6. The air fryer display will prompt you to ADD FOOD once the temperature is reached then place the fish fillet in the air fryer basket.
7. Serve and enjoy.

Nutritional Value (Amount per Serving):
Calories 265; Fat 14.1 g; Carbohydrates 2.2 g; Sugar 0.1 g; Protein 34.3 g; Cholesterol 86 mg

Old Bay Baked Cod

Preparation Time: 10 minutes; Cooking Time: 15 minutes; Serve: 4

Ingredients:
- 1 lb cod fillets
- 1/8 tsp dried basil
- 1/8 tsp old bay seasoning
- 1 tbsp lemon juice
- 1 1/2 tbsp mayonnaise
- 2 tbsp butter, melted
- 1/4 cup parmesan cheese, grated

Directions:
1. In a bowl, mix together parmesan cheese, butter, mayonnaise, lemon juice, old bay seasoning, and basil.
2. Spread parmesan cheese mixture on top of fish fillets.
3. Place the cooking tray in the air fryer basket. Line air fryer basket with parchment paper.
4. Select Bake mode.
5. Set time to 15 minutes and temperature 350 F then press START.
6. The air fryer display will prompt you to ADD FOOD once the temperature is reached then place the fish fillet in the air fryer basket.
7. Serve and enjoy.

Nutritional Value (Amount per Serving):
Calories 211; Fat 11.8 g; Carbohydrates 1.9 g; Sugar 0.4 g; Protein 25.1 g; Cholesterol 83 mg

Baked Mayo Cod

Preparation Time: 10 minutes; Cooking Time: 10 minutes; Serve: 4

Ingredients:
- 4 cod fillets
- 1/2 cup almond flour
- 1 tbsp parsley, chopped
- 1/2 tsp old bay seasoning
- 1/2 tsp lemon zest
- 1 tbsp lemon juice
- 1/4 cup parmesan cheese, grated
- 1/4 cup onion, minced
- 2 tbsp butter, melted
- 1/3 cup mayonnaise

Directions:
1. In a bowl, mix together mayonnaise, butter, onion, cheese, lemon juice, lemon zest, old bay seasoning, and parsley.
2. Spread mayonnaise mixture on top of fish fillets. Sprinkle with almond flour.
3. Place the cooking tray in the air fryer basket. Line air fryer basket with parchment paper.
4. Select Bake mode.
5. Set time to 10 minutes and temperature 400 F then press START.
6. The air fryer display will prompt you to ADD FOOD once the temperature is reached then place the fish fillet in the air fryer basket.
7. Serve and enjoy.

Nutritional Value (Amount per Serving):
Calories 288; Fat 18.2 g; Carbohydrates 6.8 g; Sugar 1.8 g; Protein 25.8 g; Cholesterol 86 mg

Blackened Tilapia

Preparation Time: 10 minutes; Cooking Time: 14 minutes; Serve: 3

Ingredients:
- 3 tilapia fillets
- 1 tbsp dried parsley flakes
- 1/4 tsp cayenne pepper
- 1 tsp garlic powder
- 1 tsp onion powder
- 2 1/2 tbsp paprika
- 1/2 tsp pepper
- 1 tsp salt

Directions:
1. In a small bowl, mix together paprika, pepper, onion powder, garlic powder, cayenne, parsley, pepper, and salt.
2. Spray fish fillets with cooking spray.
3. Rub the paprika mixture on both sides of fish fillets.
4. Place the cooking tray in the air fryer basket. Line air fryer basket with parchment paper.
5. Select Bake mode.
6. Set time to 14 minutes and temperature 400 F then press START.
7. The air fryer display will prompt you to ADD FOOD once the temperature is reached then place the fish fillet in the air fryer basket.
8. Serve and enjoy.

Nutritional Value (Amount per Serving):
Calories 117; Fat 1.8 g; Carbohydrates 4.9 g; Sugar 1.1 g; Protein 22.2 g; Cholesterol 55 mg

Lemon Pepper Tilapia

Preparation Time: 10 minutes; Cooking Time: 15 minutes; Serve: 4

Ingredients:
- 4 tilapia fillets, thawed
- 4 tbsp lemon pepper seasoning

Directions:
1. Spray fish fillets with cooking spray.
2. Sprinkle lemon pepper seasoning over fish fillets.
3. Place the cooking tray in the air fryer basket. Line air fryer basket with parchment paper.
4. Select Bake mode.
5. Set time to 15 minutes and temperature 350 F then press START.
6. The air fryer display will prompt you to ADD FOOD once the temperature is reached then place the fish fillet in the air fryer basket.
7. Serve and enjoy.

Nutritional Value (Amount per Serving):
Calories 109; Fat 1.2 g; Carbohydrates 4.2 g; Sugar 0 g; Protein 21.7 g; Cholesterol 55 mg

Garlic Butter Baked Shrimp

Preparation Time: 10 minutes; Cooking Time: 8 minutes; Serve: 4

Ingredients:
- 1 1/2 lbs shrimp, peeled & deveined
- 1/4 cup parmesan cheese, grated
- 1/2 tsp paprika
- 1 tsp garlic powder
- 1/4 tsp pepper
- 1/4 cup butter, melted
- 1 tsp kosher salt

Directions:
1. Add shrimp and remaining ingredients into the large bowl and toss well.
2. Place the cooking tray in the air fryer basket. Line air fryer basket with parchment paper.

3. Select Bake mode.
4. Set time to 8 minutes and temperature 400 F then press START.
5. The air fryer display will prompt you to ADD FOOD once the temperature is reached then add shrimp in the air fryer basket.
6. Serve and enjoy.

Nutritional Value (Amount per Serving):
Calories 354; Fat 17.5 g; Carbohydrates 3.8 g; Sugar 0.2 g; Protein 43.7 g; Cholesterol 399 mg

Cajun Salmon Cakes

Preparation Time: 10 minutes; Cooking Time: 15 minutes; Serve: 4
Ingredients:
- 2 eggs, lightly beaten
- 12 oz can salmon, boneless & skinless
- 3/4 cup almond flour
- 2 1/2 tsp Cajun seasoning
- 1/2 onion, chopped
- 1/2 bell pepper, chopped
- 2 tbsp mayonnaise
- Pepper
- Salt

Directions:
1. Add all ingredients into the mixing bowl and mix until well combined.
2. Make 8 equal shapes of patties from the mixture.
3. Place the cooking tray in the air fryer basket. Line air fryer basket with parchment paper.
4. Select Bake mode.
5. Set time to 10 minutes and temperature 375 F then press START.
6. The air fryer display will prompt you to ADD FOOD once the temperature is reached then add patties in the air fryer basket.
7. Broil patties for 5 minutes.
8. Serve and enjoy.

Nutritional Value (Amount per Serving):
Calories 212; Fat 9.6 g; Carbohydrates 5.5 g; Sugar 2.2 g; Protein 22.9 g; Cholesterol 107 mg

Cajun Catfish Fillets

Preparation Time: 10 minutes; Cooking Time: 25 minutes; Serve: 2
Ingredients:
- 2 catfish fillets
- 1/2 tbsp olive oil
- 1/2 tsp red pepper flakes, crushed
- 1/2 tsp oregano
- 1/2 tsp paprika
- 1/2 tsp cayenne pepper
- 1/2 tsp onion powder
- 1/2 tsp garlic powder
- Pepper
- Salt

Directions:
1. In a small bowl, mix together garlic powder, onion powder, cayenne pepper, paprika, oregano, red pepper flakes, pepper, and salt.
2. Brush fish fillets with olive oil and rub with spice mixture.
3. Place the cooking tray in the air fryer basket. Line air fryer basket with parchment paper.
4. Select Bake mode.
5. Set time to 25 minutes and temperature 350 F then press START.
6. The air fryer display will prompt you to ADD FOOD once the temperature is reached then place fish fillets in the air fryer basket.
7. Serve and enjoy.

Nutritional Value (Amount per Serving):
Calories 256; Fat 15.9 g; Carbohydrates 2.1 g; Sugar 0.6 g; Protein 25.3 g; Cholesterol 75 mg

Old Bay Shrimp

Preparation Time: 10 minutes; Cooking Time: 10 minutes; Serve: 4
Ingredients:
- 1 lb shrimp, peeled & deveined
- 1 tbsp old bay seasoning
- 1/2 tbsp garlic, minced
- 1/2 tbsp lemon juice
- 1/2 tbsp olive oil

Directions:
1. Add shrimp and remaining ingredients into the mixing bowl and toss well.
2. Place the cooking tray in the air fryer basket.
3. Select Air Fry mode.
4. Set time to 10 minutes and temperature 390 F then press START.
5. The air fryer display will prompt you to ADD FOOD once the temperature is reached then add shrimp in the air fryer basket.
6. Serve and enjoy.

Nutritional Value (Amount per Serving):
Calories 152; Fat 3.7 g; Carbohydrates 2.1 g; Sugar 0.1 g; Protein 25.9 g; Cholesterol 239 mg

Lemon Garlic Shrimp

Preparation Time: 10 minutes; Cooking Time: 14 minutes; Serve: 3
Ingredients:
- 1 lb shrimp, peeled & deveined
- 1/4 tsp garlic powder
- 1 tbsp olive oil
- 1/2 lemon
- Pepper
- Salt

Directions:
1. In a mixing bowl, toss shrimp with garlic powder, olive oil, pepper, and salt.
2. Place the cooking tray in the air fryer basket.
3. Select Air Fry mode.
4. Set time to 14 minutes and temperature 400 F then press START.
5. The air fryer display will prompt you to ADD FOOD once the temperature is reached then add shrimp in the air fryer basket. Shake basket halfway through.
6. Squeeze lemon juice over shrimp and serve.

Nutritional Value (Amount per Serving):
Calories 223; Fat 7.3 g; Carbohydrates 3.4 g; Sugar 0.3 g; Protein 34.6 g; Cholesterol 318 mg

Healthy Lemon Pepper Shrimp

Preparation Time: 10 minutes; Cooking Time: 8 minutes; Serve: 2
Ingredients:
- 12 oz shrimp, peeled and deveined
- 1 lemon, sliced
- 1/4 tsp garlic powder
- 1/4 tsp paprika
- 1 tsp lemon pepper
- 1 lemon juice
- 1/2 tbsp olive oil

Directions:
1. Toss shrimp with garlic powder, paprika, lemon pepper, lemon juice, and olive oil.
2. Place the cooking tray in the air fryer basket.
3. Select Air Fry mode.
4. Set time to 8 minutes and temperature 400 F then press START.
5. The air fryer display will prompt you to ADD FOOD once the temperature is reached then add shrimp in the air fryer basket. Shake basket halfway through.
6. Serve shrimp with lemon slices.

Nutritional Value (Amount per Serving):

Calories 251; Fat 6.7 g; Carbohydrates 6.8 g; Sugar 1.4 g; Protein 39.5 g; Cholesterol 358 mg

Cod with Vegetables

Preparation Time: 10 minutes; Cooking Time: 15 minutes; Serve: 4
Ingredients:
- 1 lb cod fillets
- 1/2 tsp paprika
- 1/4 cup olive oil
- 1/4 cup lemon juice
- 8 oz asparagus, chopped
- 3 cups broccoli, chopped
- 1/2 tsp lemon pepper seasoning
- 1 tsp salt

Directions:
1. In a small bowl, mix together lemon juice, paprika, olive oil, lemon pepper seasoning, and salt.
2. Place the cooking tray in the air fryer basket. Line air fryer basket with parchment paper.
3. Select Bake mode.
4. Set time to 15 minutes and temperature 400 F then press START.
5. The air fryer display will prompt you to ADD FOOD once the temperature is reached.
6. Then place fish fillets in the middle of the parchment paper in the air fryer basket. Place broccoli and asparagus around the fish fillets.
7. Pour lemon juice mixture over the fish fillets.
8. Serve and enjoy.

Nutritional Value (Amount per Serving):
Calories 239; Fat 14.1 g; Carbohydrates 7.4 g; Sugar 2.6 g; Protein 23.6 g; Cholesterol 56 mg

Baked Mahi-Mahi

Preparation Time: 10 minutes; Cooking Time: 12 minutes; Serve: 4
Ingredients:
- 4 Mahi Mahi fillets
- 1 tsp oregano
- 1 tsp garlic powder
- 3 tbsp olive oil
- 1 tsp cumin
- 1 tsp onion powder
- 1 tsp paprika
- 1/2 cayenne
- 1/2 tsp pepper
- 1/2 tsp salt

Directions:
1. Place fish fillets on the baking sheet and drizzle with oil.
2. In a small bowl, mix together cumin, onion powder, paprika, cayenne, oregano, garlic powder, pepper, and salt.
3. Rub fish fillets with a spice mixture.
4. Place the cooking tray in the air fryer basket. Line air fryer basket with parchment paper.
5. Select Bake mode.
6. Set time to 12 minutes and temperature 400 F then press START.
7. The air fryer display will prompt you to ADD FOOD once the temperature is reached then place fish fillets onto the parchment paper in the air fryer basket.
8. Serve and enjoy.

Nutritional Value (Amount per Serving):
Calories 189; Fat 11.7 g; Carbohydrates 2.1 g; Sugar 0.5 g; Protein 19.4 g; Cholesterol 86 mg

Healthy Swordfish Fillets

Preparation Time: 10 minutes; Cooking Time: 20 minutes; Serve: 2
Ingredients:
- 12 oz swordfish fillets
- 1 garlic clove, minced
- 2 tsp fresh parsley, chopped
- 3 tbsp olive oil

- 1/2 tsp lemon zest, grated
- 1/2 tsp ginger, grated
- 1/8 tsp crushed red pepper

Directions:
1. In a small bowl, mix together 2 tablespoon oil, lemon zest, red pepper, ginger, garlic, and parsley.
2. Season fish fillets with salt.
3. Heat remaining oil in a pan over medium-high heat.
4. Place fish fillets in the pan and cook until lightly browned 2-3 minutes.
5. Select Bake mode.
6. Set time to 10 minutes and temperature 400 F then press START.
7. The air fryer display will prompt you to ADD FOOD once the temperature is reached then place fish fillets in the air fryer basket.
8. Pour oil mixture over fish fillets and serve.

Nutritional Value (Amount per Serving):
Calories 449; Fat 29.8 g; Carbohydrates 1.1 g; Sugar 0.1 g; Protein 43.4 g; Cholesterol 85 mg

Flavorful Prawns

Preparation Time: 10 minutes; Cooking Time: 6 minutes; Serve: 4

Ingredients:
- 12 prawns
- 1 tsp chili powder
- 1 tsp red chili flakes
- 1 tbsp vinegar
- 1 tbsp ketchup
- 3 tbsp mayonnaise
- 1/2 tsp sea salt

Directions:
1. In a bowl, toss prawns with chili flakes, chili powder, and salt.
2. Select Air Fry mode.
3. Set time to 6 minutes and temperature 350 F then press START.
4. The air fryer display will prompt you to ADD FOOD once the temperature is reached then place prawns in the air fryer basket.
5. In a small bowl, mix together mayonnaise, vinegar, and ketchup and serve with prawns.

Nutritional Value (Amount per Serving):
Calories 128; Fat 4.9 g; Carbohydrates 5 g; Sugar 1.6 g; Protein 15.3 g; Cholesterol 142 mg

Air Fry Fish Patties

Preparation Time: 10 minutes; Cooking Time: 6 minutes; Serve: 4

Ingredients:
- 1 egg, lightly beaten
- 1/4 cup almond flour
- 8 oz can tuna, drained
- 1 tbsp mustard
- Pepper
- Salt

Directions:
1. Add all ingredients into the large bowl and mix until well combined.
2. Make four equal shapes of patties from the mixture.
3. Select Air Fry mode.
4. Set time to 6 minutes and temperature 400 F then press START.
5. The air fryer display will prompt you to ADD FOOD once the temperature is reached then place patties in the air fryer basket. Turn patties halfway through.
6. Serve and enjoy.

Nutritional Value (Amount per Serving):
Calories 105; Fat 3.2 g; Carbohydrates 1.5 g; Sugar 0.3 g; Protein 16.9 g; Cholesterol 58 mg

Air Fry Blackened Shrimp

Preparation Time: 10 minutes; Cooking Time: 6 minutes; Serve: 4
Ingredients:
- 1 lb shrimp, peeled and deveined
- 1 tsp garlic powder
- 1 tsp onion powder
- 2 tbsp olive oil
- 2 tsp paprika
- 1/4 tsp cayenne
- 1 tsp dried oregano
- Pepper
- Salt

Directions:
1. In a bowl, toss shrimp with remaining ingredients.
2. Select Air Fry mode.
3. Set time to 6 minutes and temperature 400 F then press START.
4. The air fryer display will prompt you to ADD FOOD once the temperature is reached then place shrimp in the air fryer basket.
5. Serve and enjoy.

Nutritional Value (Amount per Serving):
Calories 204; Fat 9.1 g; Carbohydrates 3.6 g; Sugar 0.5 g; Protein 26.2 g; Cholesterol 239 mg

Delicious Shrimp Fajitas

Preparation Time: 10 minutes; Cooking Time: 22 minutes; Serve: 12
Ingredients:
- 1 lb shrimp
- 1/2 cup onion, diced
- 2 bell pepper, diced
- 1 tbsp olive oil
- 2 tbsp taco seasoning

Directions:
1. Add shrimp and remaining ingredients into the bowl and toss well.
2. Select Air Fry mode.
3. Set time to 22 minutes and temperature 390 F then press START.
4. The air fryer display will prompt you to ADD FOOD once the temperature is reached then place shrimp mixture in the air fryer basket. Stir halfway through.
5. Serve and enjoy.

Nutritional Value (Amount per Serving):
Calories 67; Fat 2.1 g; Carbohydrates 2.8 g; Sugar 1.2 g; Protein 9.1 g; Cholesterol 80 mg

Jumbo Shrimp

Preparation Time: 10 minutes; Cooking Time: 6 minutes; Serve: 4
Ingredients:
- 1 lb jumbo shrimp
- 1 tsp steak seasoning
- 1/4 tsp crushed red pepper flakes
- 2 garlic cloves, minced
- 2 tsp olive oil
- 1 tbsp parsley, chopped
- 2 tsp lemon juice
- 1 tsp lemon zest

Directions:
1. In a bowl, toss shrimp with parsley, lemon juice, lemon zest, steak seasoning, red pepper flakes, garlic, and olive oil.
2. Select Air Fry mode.
3. Set time to 6 minutes and temperature 400 F then press START.
4. The air fryer display will prompt you to ADD FOOD once the temperature is reached then add shrimp in the air fryer basket.
5. Serve and enjoy.

Nutritional Value (Amount per Serving):

Calories 105; Fat 2.4 g; Carbohydrates 0.8 g; Sugar 2.2 g; Protein 20.4 g; Cholesterol 233 mg

Tasty Crab Patties

Preparation Time: 10 minutes; Cooking Time: 10 minutes; Serve: 4
Ingredients:
- 8 oz crab meat
- 2 tbsp mayonnaise
- 2 green onion, chopped
- 1/4 cup bell pepper, chopped
- 1 tsp old bay seasoning
- 1 tbsp Dijon mustard
- 2 tbsp almond flour
- Pepper
- Salt

Directions:
1. Add all ingredients into the mixing bowl and mix until well combined.
2. Make 4 equal shapes of patties from the mixture.
3. Select Air Fry mode.
4. Set time to 10 minutes and temperature 370 F then press START.
5. The air fryer display will prompt you to ADD FOOD once the temperature is reached then place patties in the air fryer basket.
6. Serve and enjoy.

Nutritional Value (Amount per Serving):
Calories 167; Fat 10.7 g; Carbohydrates 7.1 g; Sugar 1.6 g; Protein 10.6 g; Cholesterol 32 mg

Lemon Pepper White Fish

Preparation Time: 10 minutes; Cooking Time: 12 minutes; Serve: 2
Ingredients:
- 12 oz white fish fillets
- 1/2 tsp garlic powder
- 1/2 tsp onion powder
- 1/2 tsp lemon pepper seasoning
- Pepper
- Salt

Directions:
1. Spray fish fillets with cooking spray and season with onion powder, lemon pepper seasoning, garlic powder, pepper, and salt.
2. Select Air Fry mode.
3. Set time to 12 minutes and temperature 360 F then press START.
4. The air fryer display will prompt you to ADD FOOD once the temperature is reached then place fish fillets in the air fryer basket.
5. Serve and enjoy.

Nutritional Value (Amount per Serving):
Calories 298; Fat 12.8 g; Carbohydrates 1.4 g; Sugar 0.4 g; Protein 41.9 g; Cholesterol 131 mg

Cajun Scallops

Preparation Time: 10 minutes; Cooking Time: 6 minutes; Serve: 1
Ingredients:
- 4 scallops, rinsed and pat dry
- 1/2 tsp Cajun seasoning
- Pepper
- Salt

Directions:
1. Spray scallops with cooking spray and season with Cajun seasoning, pepper, and salt.
2. Select Air Fry mode.
3. Set time to 6 minutes and temperature 400 F then press START.
4. The air fryer display will prompt you to ADD FOOD once the temperature is reached then place scallops in the air fryer basket. Turn scallops halfway through.
5. Serve and enjoy.

Nutritional Value (Amount per Serving):
Calories 106; Fat 0.9 g; Carbohydrates 2.9 g; Sugar 0 g; Protein 20.2 g; Cholesterol 40 mg

Italian Tilapia Fillets

Preparation Time: 10 minutes; Cooking Time: 17 minutes; Serve: 2

Ingredients:
- 1/2 lb tilapia fillets, remove bones
- 1/3 cup fresh parsley, chopped
- 1 tsp olive oil
- 1 tbsp garlic, minced
- 2 oz feta cheese, crumbled
- 2/3 cup tomatoes, chopped
- Pepper
- Salt

Directions:
1. In a medium bowl, mix together tomatoes, garlic, feta, parsley, and olive oil.
2. Spray tilapia fillets with cooking spray and season with pepper and salt.
3. Select Bake mode.
4. Set time to 17 minutes and temperature 400 F then press START.
5. The air fryer display will prompt you to ADD FOOD once the temperature is reached then place fish fillets in the air fryer basket and top with tomato mixture.
6. Serve and enjoy.

Nutritional Value (Amount per Serving):
Calories 209; Fat 9.6 g; Carbohydrates 5.5 g; Sugar 2.9 g; Protein 26.2 g; Cholesterol 80 mg

Greek Baked Salmon

Preparation Time: 10 minutes; Cooking Time: 20 minutes; Serve: 5

Ingredients:
- 1 3/4 lbs salmon fillet
- 1/3 cup artichoke hearts
- 1/4 cup sun-dried tomatoes, drained
- 1/4 cup olives, pitted and chopped
- 1/3 cup basil pesto
- 1 tbsp fresh dill, chopped
- 1/4 cup capers
- 1 tsp paprika
- 1/4 tsp salt

Directions:
1. Season salmon with paprika and salt.
2. Place the cooking tray in the air fryer basket. Place piece of parchment paper into the air fryer basket.
3. Select Bake mode.
4. Set time to 20 minutes and temperature 400 F then press START.
5. The air fryer display will prompt you to ADD FOOD once the temperature is reached then place salmon in the air fryer basket and top with remaining ingredients.
6. Serve and enjoy.

Nutritional Value (Amount per Serving):
Calories 228; Fat 10.7 g; Carbohydrates 2.6 g; Sugar 0.4 g; Protein 31.6 g; Cholesterol 70 mg

Greek Style Fish Fillets

Preparation Time: 10 minutes; Cooking Time: 10 minutes; Serve: 4

Ingredients:
- 24 oz salmon, cut into 4 pieces
- 1 tsp lemon zest
- 2 tbsp lemon juice
- 2 tbsp olive oil
- 1 tsp oregano
- 1 garlic clove, grated
- 1 tbsp yogurt
- 1/4 tsp pepper
- 1/4 tsp salt

Directions:

1. Add all ingredients except salmon in a baking dish and mix well.
2. Add salmon and coat well and let it sit for 30 minutes.
3. Select Bake mode.
4. Set time to 10 minutes and temperature 400 F then press START.
5. The air fryer display will prompt you to ADD FOOD once the temperature is reached then place the baking dish in the air fryer basket.
6. Serve and enjoy.

Nutritional Value (Amount per Serving):
Calories 292; Fat 17.7 g; Carbohydrates 1.1 g; Sugar 0.5 g; Protein 33.4 g; Cholesterol 75 mg

White Fish Fillet with Roasted Pepper

Preparation Time: 10 minutes; Cooking Time: 30 minutes; Serve: 1
Ingredients:
- 8 oz frozen white fish fillet
- 1/2 tsp Italian seasoning
- 1 1/2 tbsp butter, melted
- 1 tbsp lemon juice
- 1 tbsp fresh parsley, chopped
- 1 tbsp roasted red bell pepper, diced

Directions:
1. Place the fish fillet in a baking dish.
2. Drizzle butter and lemon juice over fish. Sprinkle with Italian seasoning.
3. Top with roasted bell pepper and parsley.
4. Select Bake mode.
5. Set time to 30 minutes and temperature 400 F then press START.
6. The air fryer display will prompt you to ADD FOOD once the temperature is reached then place the baking dish in the air fryer basket.
7. Serve and enjoy.

Nutritional Value (Amount per Serving):
Calories 357; Fat 18.8 g; Carbohydrates 1.3 g; Sugar 0.8 g; Protein 46.8 g; Cholesterol 47 mg

Roasted Fish Fillets

Preparation Time: 10 minutes; Cooking Time: 15 minutes; Serve: 2
Ingredients:
- 1 lb red snapper fillet
- 1/4 tsp herb de Provence
- 1 garlic clove, crushed
- 2 tbsp olive oil
- 3/4 cup white wine
- 2 fresh rosemary sprigs
- Pepper
- Salt

Directions:
1. Season fish fillet with pepper and salt and place in baking dish.
2. Drizzle oil over fish. Place rosemary, garlic, and herb de Provence on top of fish.
3. Select Roast mode.
4. Set time to 10 minutes and temperature 400 F then press START.
5. The air fryer display will prompt you to ADD FOOD once the temperature is reached then place the baking dish in the air fryer basket.
6. Pour wine over fish fillet and continue roast for 5 minutes.
7. Serve and enjoy.

Nutritional Value (Amount per Serving):
Calories 494; Fat 18.3 g; Carbohydrates 3.7 g; Sugar 0.7 g; Protein 60.4 g; Cholesterol 107 mg

Rosemary Basil Salmon

Preparation Time: 10 minutes; Cooking Time: 15 minutes; Serve: 4
Ingredients:

- 1 lbs salmon, cut into 4 pieces
- 1 tbsp olive oil
- 1/2 tbsp dried rosemary
- 1/4 tsp dried basil
- 1 tbsp dried chives
- Pepper
- Salt

Directions:
1. Mix together olive oil, basil, chives, and rosemary. Brush salmon with oil mixture.
2. Select Air Fry mode.
3. Set time to 15 minutes and temperature 400 F then press START.
4. The air fryer display will prompt you to ADD FOOD once the temperature is reached then place salmon pieces in the air fryer basket.
5. Serve and enjoy.

Nutritional Value (Amount per Serving):
Calories 182; Fat 10.6 g; Carbohydrates 0.3 g; Sugar 0 g; Protein 22 g; Cholesterol 50 mg

Shrimp with Cherry Tomatoes

Preparation Time: 10 minutes; Cooking Time: 25 minutes; Serve: 4
Ingredients:
- 1 lb shrimp, peeled
- 1 tbsp garlic, sliced
- 2 cups cherry tomatoes
- 1 tbsp olive oil
- Pepper
- Salt

Directions:
1. Add shrimp, oil, garlic, tomatoes, pepper, and salt into the large bowl and toss well.
2. Transfer shrimp mixture into the baking dish.
3. Select Bake mode.
4. Set time to 25 minutes and temperature 400 F then press START.
5. The air fryer display will prompt you to ADD FOOD once the temperature is reached then place the baking dish in the air fryer basket.
6. Serve and enjoy.

Nutritional Value (Amount per Serving):
Calories 184; Fat 5.6 g; Carbohydrates 5.9 g; Sugar 2.4 g; Protein 26.8 g; Cholesterol 239 mg

Tomato Basil Fish Fillets

Preparation Time: 10 minutes; Cooking Time: 20 minutes; Serve: 2
Ingredients:
- 2 salmon fillets
- 1 tomato, sliced
- 1 tbsp dried basil
- 2 tbsp parmesan cheese, grated
- 1 tbsp olive oil

Directions:
1. Place salmon fillets in the baking dish.
2. Sprinkle basil on top of salmon fillets.
3. Arrange tomato slices on top of salmon fillets.
4. Drizzle with oil and sprinkle cheese on top.
5. Select Bake mode.
6. Set time to 20 minutes and temperature 375 F then press START.
7. The air fryer display will prompt you to ADD FOOD once the temperature is reached then place the baking dish in the air fryer basket.
8. Serve and enjoy.

Nutritional Value (Amount per Serving):
Calories 333; Fat 20.2 g; Carbohydrates 1.6 g; Sugar 0.8 g; Protein 38.1 g; Cholesterol 173 mg

Cod with Asparagus

Preparation Time: 10 minutes; Cooking Time: 20 minutes; Serve: 4
Ingredients:
- 1 lb cod, cut into 4 pieces
- 1 leek, sliced
- 1 onion, quartered
- 2 tomatoes, halved
- 2 tbsp olive oil
- 1/2 tsp oregano
- 1/2 tsp red chili flakes
- 1/2 cup olives, chopped
- 8 asparagus spears
- 1/4 tsp pepper
- 1/4 tsp salt

Directions:
1. In a baking dish, place fish pieces, olives, asparagus, leek, onion, and tomatoes.
2. Season with oregano, chili flakes, pepper, and salt and drizzle with olive oil.
3. Select Bake mode.
4. Set time to 20 minutes and temperature 400 F then press START.
5. The air fryer display will prompt you to ADD FOOD once the temperature is reached then place the baking dish in the air fryer basket.
6. Serve and enjoy.

Nutritional Value (Amount per Serving):
Calories 245; Fat 10.1 g; Carbohydrates 11.2 g; Sugar 4.6 g; Protein 28.3 g; Cholesterol 62 mg

Baked Salmon & Carrots

Preparation Time: 10 minutes; Cooking Time: 20 minutes; Serve: 4
Ingredients:
- 1 lb salmon, cut into four pieces
- 2 tbsp olive oil
- 2 cups baby carrots
- Salt

Directions:
1. Place salmon pieces in the baking dish.
2. In a mixing bowl, toss together baby carrots and olive oil.
3. Arrange carrot around the salmon.
4. Select Bake mode.
5. Set time to 20 minutes and temperature 400 F then press START.
6. The air fryer display will prompt you to ADD FOOD once the temperature is reached then place the baking dish in the air fryer basket.
7. Serve and enjoy.

Nutritional Value (Amount per Serving):
Calories 212; Fat 14 g; Carbohydrates 0.4 g; Sugar 0.2 g; Protein 22 g; Cholesterol 50 mg

Pesto Fish Fillets

Preparation Time: 10 minutes; Cooking Time: 20 minutes; Serve: 2
Ingredients:
- 2 salmon fillets

For pesto:
- 1/4 cup parmesan cheese, grated
- 1/4 cup pine nuts
- 1/4 cup olive oil
- 1 1/2 cups fresh basil leaves
- 1/4 cup parmesan cheese, grated
- 2 garlic cloves, peeled and chopped
- 1/2 tsp pepper
- 1/2 tsp salt

Directions:
1. Add all pesto ingredients into the food processor and process until smooth.
2. Place salmon fillet in a baking dish and spread 2 tablespoons of the pesto on each salmon fillet.

3. Sprinkle grated cheese on top of the pesto.
4. Select Bake mode.
5. Set time to 20 minutes and temperature 400 F then press START.
6. The air fryer display will prompt you to ADD FOOD once the temperature is reached then place the baking dish in the air fryer basket.
7. Serve and enjoy.

Nutritional Value (Amount per Serving):
Calories 762; Fat 60.4 g; Carbohydrates 6.1 g; Sugar 0.7 g; Protein 56.3 g; Cholesterol 120 mg

Baked Shrimp Scampi

Preparation Time: 10 minutes; Cooking Time: 13 minutes; Serve: 4

Ingredients:
- 1 lb shrimp, peeled and deveined
- 1/4 cup parmesan cheese, grated
- 8 garlic cloves, peeled
- 2 tbsp olive oil
- 1 fresh lemon, cut into wedges

Directions:
1. Add all ingredients except parmesan cheese into the mixing bowl and toss well.
2. Transfer shrimp mixture into the baking dish.
3. Select Bake mode.
4. Set time to 13 minutes and temperature 400 F then press START.
5. The air fryer display will prompt you to ADD FOOD once the temperature is reached then place the baking dish in the air fryer basket.
6. Sprinkle with parmesan cheese and serve.

Nutritional Value (Amount per Serving):
Calories 255; Fat 12.1 g; Carbohydrates 5.6 g; Sugar 0.4 g; Protein 31 g; Cholesterol 249 mg

Mediterranean Salmon

Preparation Time: 10 minutes; Cooking Time: 20 minutes; Serve: 1

Ingredients:
- 4 oz salmon fillet
- 1/2 lemon juice
- 1 garlic clove, sliced
- 1/4 onion, diced
- 5 grape tomatoes
- 1 tbsp fresh parsley, chopped
- 1 tbsp olive oil
- Pepper
- Salt

Directions:
1. Add all ingredients except lemon juice into the mixing bowl and let sit for one hour.
2. Select Bake mode.
3. Set time to 20 minutes and temperature 350 F then press START.
4. The air fryer display will prompt you to ADD FOOD once the temperature is reached then transfer bowl mixture in the air fryer basket. Drizzle with lemon juice.
5. Serve and enjoy.

Nutritional Value (Amount per Serving):
Calories 210; Fat 17.6 g; Carbohydrates 4.4 g; Sugar 1.7 g; Protein 8.8 g; Cholesterol 23 mg

Tangy Salmon

Preparation Time: 10 minutes; Cooking Time: 22 minutes; Serve: 4

Ingredients:
- 2 lbs salmon fillet, skinless and boneless
- 1 tbsp olive oil
- 1/4 cup fresh dill
- 1 chili, sliced
- 2 fresh lemon juice

- 1 orange juice
- Pepper
- Salt

Directions:
1. Place salmon fillet in a baking dish and drizzle with olive oil, lemon juice, and orange juice.
2. Sprinkle chili over the salmon and season with pepper and salt.
3. Select Bake mode.
4. Set time to 22 minutes and temperature 350 F then press START.
5. The air fryer display will prompt you to ADD FOOD once the temperature is reached then place the baking dish in the air fryer basket.
6. Garnish with dill.
7. Serve and enjoy.

Nutritional Value (Amount per Serving):
Calories 358; Fat 18.1 g; Carbohydrates 4.9 g; Sugar 2.3 g; Protein 45.2 g; Cholesterol 101 mg

Salsa Fish Fillets

Preparation Time: 10 minutes; Cooking Time: 15 minutes; Serve: 4
Ingredients:
- 4 halibut fish fillets
- 2 tsp olive oil
- 3 tbsp fresh basil, chopped
- 2 tomatoes, chopped
- 2 garlic cloves, minced
- 1 tsp oregano, chopped

Directions:
1. In a bowl, mix together chopped tomatoes, garlic, oregano, and basil.
2. Arrange fish fillets in the baking dish and top with tomato mixture.
3. Select Bake mode.
4. Set time to 15 minutes and temperature 350 F then press START.
5. The air fryer display will prompt you to ADD FOOD once the temperature is reached then place the baking dish in the air fryer basket.
6. Serve and enjoy.

Nutritional Value (Amount per Serving):
Calories 145; Fat 4.5 g; Carbohydrates 3.2 g; Sugar 1.7 g; Protein 23.7 g; Cholesterol 35 mg

Cheese Herb Salmon

Preparation Time: 10 minutes; Cooking Time: 10 minutes; Serve: 5
Ingredients:
- 5 salmon fillets
- 1/4 cup fresh parsley, chopped
- 3 garlic cloves, minced
- 3/4 cup parmesan cheese, shredded
- 1 tsp McCormick's BBQ seasoning
- 1 tsp paprika
- 1 tbsp olive oil
- Pepper
- Salt

Directions:
1. Add salmon, seasoning, and olive oil to the bowl and mix well.
2. Place salmon fillet into the baking dish.
3. In a bowl, mix together cheese, garlic, and parsley.
4. Sprinkle cheese mixture on top of salmon.
5. Select Air Fry mode.
6. Set time to 10 minutes and temperature 400 F then press START.
7. The air fryer display will prompt you to ADD FOOD once the temperature is reached then place the baking dish in the air fryer basket.
8. Serve and enjoy.

Nutritional Value (Amount per Serving):
Calories 381; Fat 21.4 g; Carbohydrates 2.9 g; Sugar 0.5 g; Protein 46.1 g; Cholesterol 104 mg

Easy Bacon Shrimp

Preparation Time: 10 minutes; Cooking Time: 7 minutes; Serve: 2

Ingredients:
- 8 shrimp, deveined
- 8 bacon slices
- Pepper

Directions:
1. Wrap shrimp with bacon slices.
2. Select Air Fry mode.
3. Set time to 7 minutes and temperature 390 F then press START.
4. The air fryer display will prompt you to ADD FOOD once the temperature is reached then place shrimp in the air fryer basket.
5. Season shrimp with pepper and serve.

Nutritional Value (Amount per Serving):
Calories 516; Fat 33.2 g; Carbohydrates 2.5 g; Sugar 0 g; Protein 48.2 g; Cholesterol 269 mg

Crispy Coconut Shrimp

Preparation Time: 10 minutes; Cooking Time: 5 minutes; Serve: 4

Ingredients:
- 2 egg whites
- 16 oz shrimp, peeled
- 1/2 cup shredded coconut
- 1/2 cup almond flour
- 1/2 tsp salt

Directions:
1. Whisk egg whites in a shallow dish.
2. In a bowl, mix together shredded coconut and almond flour.
3. Dip shrimp into the egg then coat with coconut mixture.
4. Select Air Fry mode.
5. Set time to 5 minutes and temperature 400 F then press START.
6. The air fryer display will prompt you to ADD FOOD once the temperature is reached then place coated shrimp in the air fryer basket.
7. Serve and enjoy.

Nutritional Value (Amount per Serving):
Calories 199; Fat 7 g; Carbohydrates 4.1 g; Sugar 0.9 g; Protein 28.7 g; Cholesterol 239 mg

Chapter 8: Snacks & Appetizers

Green Bean Fries

Preparation Time: 10 minutes; Cooking Time: 10 minutes; Serve: 6

Ingredients:
- 1 egg, lightly beaten
- 1 lb green beans, ends trimmed
- 1/2 cup parmesan cheese, grated
- 1/2 tsp garlic powder
- 1 cup almond flour
- 1 tbsp mayonnaise
- 1/2 tsp garlic salt

Directions:
1. In a shallow bowl, whisk together egg and mayonnaise.
2. In a separate shallow bowl, mix together almond flour, parmesan cheese, garlic powder, and garlic salt.
3. Place the cooking tray in the air fryer basket.
4. Select Air Fry mode.
5. Set time to 10 minutes and temperature 390 F then press START.
6. Roll green beans in egg then coat with almond flour mixture. Spray breaded green beans with cooking spray.
7. The air fryer display will prompt you to ADD FOOD once the temperature is reached then add breaded green beans in the air fryer basket. Turn beans halfway through.
8. Serve and enjoy.

Nutritional Value (Amount per Serving):
Calories 134; Fat 8.2 g; Carbohydrates 7.9 g; Sugar 1.5 g; Protein 9.6 g; Cholesterol 42 mg

Quick & Delicious Biscuits

Preparation Time: 10 minutes; Cooking Time: 10 minutes; Serve: 5

Ingredients:
- 2 eggs
- 2 tbsp sour cream
- 2 tbsp butter, melted
- 1 cup cheddar cheese, shredded
- 1/2 tsp baking powder
- 1 cup almond flour
- 1/4 tsp pink Himalayan salt

Directions:
1. In a large bowl, mix together almond flour, cheddar cheese, baking powder, and salt until well combined.
2. Add sour cream, butter, and egg and mix until a sticky batter is formed.
3. Place the cooking tray in the air fryer basket. Place piece of parchment paper into the air fryer basket.
4. Select Air Fry mode.
5. Set time to 10 minutes and temperature 400 F then press START.
6. The air fryer display will prompt you to ADD FOOD once the temperature is reached then drop 1/4 cup sized of batter onto the parchment paper in the air fryer basket.
7. Serve and enjoy.

Nutritional Value (Amount per Serving):
Calories 200; Fat 17.7 g; Carbohydrates 2.1 g; Sugar 0.5 g; Protein 9.2 g; Cholesterol 104 mg

Easy Sausage Balls

Preparation Time: 10 minutes; Cooking Time: 16 minutes; Serve: 10

Ingredients:
- 1 cup almond flour
- 1 lb ground sausage
- 1 cup cheddar cheese, shredded

Directions:
1. Add all ingredients into the mixing bowl and mix until well combined.
2. Make 1-inch balls from meat mixture.
3. Place the cooking tray in the air fryer basket. Place piece of aluminum foil into the air fryer basket.
4. Select Air Fry mode.
5. Set time to 16 minutes and temperature 375 F then press START.
6. The air fryer display will prompt you to ADD FOOD once the temperature is reached then place meatballs onto the aluminum foil in the air fryer basket.
7. Serve and enjoy.

Nutritional Value (Amount per Serving):
Calories 215; Fat 18 g; Carbohydrates 0.7 g; Sugar 0.2 g; Protein 12.2 g; Cholesterol 50 mg

Tasty Zucchini Chips

Preparation Time: 10 minutes; Cooking Time: 12 minutes; Serve: 3
Ingredients:
- 1 egg, lightly beaten
- 1 large zucchini, cut into slices
- 3 tbsp roasted pecans, chopped
- 3 tbsp almond flour
- 1 tbsp Bagel seasoning

Directions:
1. In a small bowl, add egg and whisk lightly.
2. In a shallow dish, mix together almond flour, chopped pecans, and bagel seasoning.
3. Dip zucchini slices into the egg then coat with almond flour mixture.
4. Place the cooking tray in the air fryer basket. Place piece of parchment paper into the air fryer basket.
5. Select Air Fry mode.
6. Set time to 12 minutes and temperature 350 F then press START.
7. The air fryer display will prompt you to ADD FOOD once the temperature is reached then place zucchini slices onto the parchment paper in the air fryer basket.
8. Turn zucchini slices halfway through.
9. Serve and enjoy.

Nutritional Value (Amount per Serving):
Calories 264; Fat 22.5 g; Carbohydrates 10.5 g; Sugar 2.2 g; Protein 9.4 g; Cholesterol 55 mg

Healthy Onion Rings

Preparation Time: 10 minutes; Cooking Time: 10 minutes; Serve: 3
Ingredients:
- 2 eggs, lightly beaten
- 2 large onions, peel & cut into 1-inch slices
- 1/2 tsp garlic powder
- 1 tsp paprika
- 2 tsp Italian seasoning
- 1 1/2 cups almond flour
- 1/2 tsp sea salt

Directions:
1. In a small bowl, add eggs and whisk well.
2. In a shallow bowl, mix together almond flour, Italian seasoning, paprika, garlic powder, and sea salt.
3. Dip onion slice into the egg then coat with almond flour mixture.
4. Place breaded onion slices onto the parchment-lined plate and place it in the refrigerator for 30 minutes.
5. Place the cooking tray in the air fryer basket. Place piece of parchment paper into the air fryer basket.

6. Select Air Fry mode.
7. Set time to 10 minutes and temperature 380 F then press START.
8. The air fryer display will prompt you to ADD FOOD once the temperature is reached then place onion slices onto the parchment paper in the air fryer basket. Spray onion slices with cooking spray.
9. Turn onion slices halfway through.
10. Serve and enjoy.

Nutritional Value (Amount per Serving):
Calories 146; Fat 9.7 g; Carbohydrates 9.7 g; Sugar 3 g; Protein 6.5 g; Cholesterol 92 mg

Perfect Cauliflower Tots

Preparation Time: 10 minutes; Cooking Time: 12 minutes; Serve: 4
Ingredients:
- 1 large cauliflower head, cut into florets
- 3 tbsp hot sauce
- 1/4 cup butter, melted
- 2 tbsp arrowroot
- 1 tbsp olive oil

Directions:
1. Toss cauliflower florets with olive oil and coat with arrowroot.
2. Place the cooking tray in the air fryer basket. Place piece of parchment paper into the air fryer basket.
3. Select Air Fry mode.
4. Set time to 6 minutes and temperature 380 F then press START.
5. The air fryer display will prompt you to ADD FOOD once the temperature is reached then place cauliflower florets onto the parchment paper in the air fryer basket.
6. Meanwhile, in a mixing bowl, mix together hot sauce and melted butter.
7. Once cauliflower florets are done then transfer them into the sauce and toss well.
8. Return cauliflower florets into the air fryer basket and air fry for 6 minutes more.
9. Serve and enjoy.

Nutritional Value (Amount per Serving):
Calories 406; Fat 39.6 g; Carbohydrates 11.2 g; Sugar 4.3 g; Protein 4.4 g; Cholesterol 0 mg

Crispy Parmesan Asparagus Fries

Preparation Time: 10 minutes; Cooking Time: 12 minutes; Serve: 4
Ingredients:
- 3 eggs, lightly beaten
- 16 asparagus, trim 2-inches of bottom
- 1/2 cup parmesan cheese, grated
- 1 tbsp garlic powder
- 1/2 tbsp paprika
- 2 cups pork rinds, crushed
- 1 tbsp olive oil
- 2 tbsp heavy cream
- 1 tsp pepper

Directions:
1. In a shallow dish, whisk eggs with olive oil, and heavy cream.
2. On a plate, mix together crushed pork rinds, pepper, paprika, garlic powder, and parmesan cheese.
3. Dip asparagus in egg then coat with pork rind mixture.
4. Place the cooking tray in the air fryer basket. Place piece of parchment paper into the air fryer basket.
5. Select Bake mode.
6. Set time to 12 minutes and temperature 400 F then press START.
7. The air fryer display will prompt you to ADD FOOD once the temperature is reached then place coated asparagus onto the parchment paper in the air fryer basket.

8. Serve and enjoy.

Nutritional Value (Amount per Serving):
Calories 264; Fat 18.7 g; Carbohydrates 6.3 g; Sugar 2.1 g; Protein 20.5 g; Cholesterol 165 mg

Crispy Air Fried Pickles

Preparation Time: 10 minutes; Cooking Time: 6 minutes; Serve: 4

Ingredients:
- 1 egg, lightly beaten
- 1/3 cup almond flour
- 16 dill pickle slices
- 1/4 cup parmesan cheese, grated
- 1/2 cup pork rinds, crushed

Directions:
1. In a small bowl, add egg and whisk well.
2. In a separate bowl, add the almond flour.
3. In a shallow dish, mix together pork rinds and parmesan cheese.
4. Dredge pickle slices in almond flour mixture then egg and finally coat with crushed pork rind mixture.
5. Place the cooking tray in the air fryer basket. Place piece of parchment paper into the air fryer basket.
6. Select Air Fry mode.
7. Set time to 6 minutes and temperature 370 F then press START.
8. The air fryer display will prompt you to ADD FOOD once the temperature is reached then place breaded pickle slices onto the parchment paper in the air fryer basket.
9. Serve and enjoy.

Nutritional Value (Amount per Serving):
Calories 164; Fat 10.8 g; Carbohydrates 1.7 g; Sugar 0.5 g; Protein 16.3 g; Cholesterol 73 mg

Crab Stuffed Jalapenos

Preparation Time: 10 minutes; Cooking Time: 20 minutes; Serve: 10

Ingredients:
- 8 oz lump crab meat
- 10 jalapenos, cut in half & remove seeds
- 2 green onions, sliced
- 3 bacon slices, cooked and crumbled
- 3/4 cup cheddar cheese, shredded
- 1/4 tsp garlic powder
- 1/2 tsp Cajun seasoning
- 4 oz cream cheese, softened

Directions:
1. In a bowl, mix together crab meat, green onions, bacon, cheese, garlic powder, cajun seasoning, and cream cheese.
2. Stuff crab meat mixture into each jalapeno half.
3. Place the cooking tray in the air fryer basket.
4. Select Bake mode.
5. Set time to 20 minutes and temperature 375 F then press START.
6. The air fryer display will prompt you to ADD FOOD once the temperature is reached then place stuff jalapenos in the air fryer basket.
7. Serve and enjoy.

Nutritional Value (Amount per Serving):
Calories 126; Fat 11.1 g; Carbohydrates 2 g; Sugar 0.6 g; Protein 8.6 g; Cholesterol 40 mg

Asiago Asparagus Fries

Preparation Time: 10 minutes; Cooking Time: 10 minutes; Serve: 4

Ingredients:

- 1 lb asparagus spears, trim & cut in half
- 2 tbsp mayonnaise
- 2 oz asiago cheese, grated

Directions:
1. Add grated cheese in a shallow dish.
2. Add asparagus and mayonnaise into the mixing bowl and mix well.
3. Coat asparagus spears with grated cheese.
4. Place the cooking tray in the air fryer basket. Line air fryer basket with parchment paper.
5. Select Air Fry mode.
6. Set time to 10 minutes and temperature 380 F then press START.
7. The air fryer display will prompt you to ADD FOOD once the temperature is reached then arrange asparagus spears onto the parchment paper in the air fryer basket.
8. Serve and enjoy.

Nutritional Value (Amount per Serving):
Calories 102; Fat 6.6 g; Carbohydrates 6.2 g; Sugar 2.6 g; Protein 6.1 g; Cholesterol 15 mg

Chicken Stuffed Poblanos

Preparation Time: 10 minutes; Cooking Time: 15 minutes; Serve: 6
Ingredients:
- 3 poblano pepper, cut in half & remove seeds
- 2 oz cheddar cheese, grated
- 1 1/2 cups spinach artichoke dip
- 1 cup chicken breast, cooked & chopped

Directions:
1. In a bowl, mix together chicken, spinach artichoke dip, and half cheddar cheese.
2. Stuff chicken mixture into each poblano pepper half.
3. Place the cooking tray in the air fryer basket. Line air fryer basket with parchment paper.
4. Select Air Fry mode.
5. Set time to 15 minutes and temperature 350 F then press START.
6. The air fryer display will prompt you to ADD FOOD once the temperature is reached then place stuff poblano pepper onto the parchment paper in the air fryer basket. Sprinkle remaining cheese on top of stuff peppers.
7. Serve and enjoy.

Nutritional Value (Amount per Serving):
Calories 91; Fat 5.6 g; Carbohydrates 3 g; Sugar 1.5 g; Protein 7.1 g; Cholesterol 24 mg

Crispy Air Fried Zucchini

Preparation Time: 10 minutes; Cooking Time: 15 minutes; Serve: 10
Ingredients:
- 1 medium zucchini, sliced thinly lengthwise
- 1/4 cup mayonnaise
- 1 garlic clove, crushed
- 1/2 cup parmesan cheese, grated
- 1 cup pork rinds, crushed

Directions:
1. In a shallow dish, mix together crushed pork rinds and grated cheese.
2. In a mixing bowl, mix together zucchini slices, mayonnaise, and garlic.
3. Coat each zucchini slice with crushed pork rind mixture.
4. Place the cooking tray in the air fryer basket. Line air fryer basket with parchment paper.
5. Select Air Fry mode.
6. Set time to 15 minutes and temperature 350 F then press START.
7. The air fryer display will prompt you to ADD FOOD once the temperature is reached then place breaded zucchini slices onto the parchment paper in the air fryer basket.
8. Serve and enjoy.

Nutritional Value (Amount per Serving):
Calories 129; Fat 8.6 g; Carbohydrates 2.6 g; Sugar 0.7 g; Protein 11.4 g; Cholesterol 26 mg

Thai Meatballs

Preparation Time: 10 minutes; Cooking Time: 20 minutes; Serve: 6

Ingredients:
- 2 eggs, lightly beaten
- 2 lbs ground turkey
- 1 tsp crushed red pepper
- 2 tbsp lemongrass, chopped
- 3 tbsp fish sauce
- 3 garlic cloves, minced
- 1/2 cup fresh basil, chopped
- 3/4 cup scallions, chopped
- 1 cup almond flour

Directions:
1. Add ground turkey in the mixing bowl. Add remaining ingredients and mix until well combined.
2. Make small balls from the turkey mixture.
3. Place the cooking tray in the air fryer basket. Line air fryer basket with parchment paper.
4. Select Bake mode.
5. Set time to 20 minutes and temperature 400 F then press START.
6. The air fryer display will prompt you to ADD FOOD once the temperature is reached then place meatballs onto the parchment paper in the air fryer basket. Turn meatballs halfway through.
7. Serve and enjoy.

Nutritional Value (Amount per Serving):
Calories 355; Fat 20.5 g; Carbohydrates 3.5 g; Sugar 1 g; Protein 45 g; Cholesterol 209 mg

Cheese Balls

Preparation Time: 10 minutes; Cooking Time: 12 minutes; Serve: 8

Ingredients:
- 2 eggs
- 1/2 tsp baking powder
- 1/2 cup almond flour
- 1/4 cup parmesan cheese, shredded
- 1/4 cup mozzarella cheese, shredded
- 1/2 cup cheddar cheese, shredded

Directions:
1. In a bowl, whisk eggs. Add remaining ingredients and mix until well combined.
2. Divide mixture into 8 equal portions. Roll each portion into a ball.
3. Place the cooking tray in the air fryer basket. Line air fryer basket with parchment paper.
4. Select Bake mode.
5. Set time to 12 minutes and temperature 400 F then press START.
6. The air fryer display will prompt you to ADD FOOD once the temperature is reached then place cheese balls onto the parchment paper in the air fryer basket.
7. Serve and enjoy.

Nutritional Value (Amount per Serving):
Calories 80; Fat 6 g; Carbohydrates 1 g; Sugar 0.2 g; Protein 6.1 g; Cholesterol 54 mg

Cheese Herb Zucchini

Preparation Time: 10 minutes; Cooking Time: 15 minutes; Serve: 4

Ingredients:
- 4 zucchini, quartered lengthwise
- 2 tbsp fresh parsley, chopped
- 1/2 tsp dried oregano
- 1/2 tsp dried thyme
- 1/2 cup parmesan cheese, grated
- 2 tbsp olive oil
- 1/4 tsp garlic powder
- 1/2 tsp dried basil

- Pepper
- Salt

Directions:
1. In a small bowl, mix together parmesan cheese, garlic powder, basil, oregano, thyme, pepper, and salt.
2. Place the cooking tray in the air fryer basket. Line air fryer basket with parchment paper.
3. Select Bake mode.
4. Set time to 15 minutes and temperature 350 F then press START.
5. The air fryer display will prompt you to ADD FOOD once the temperature is reached then arrange zucchini onto the parchment paper in the air fryer basket. Drizzle with oil and sprinkle with parmesan cheese mixture.
6. Garnish with parsley and serve.

Nutritional Value (Amount per Serving):
Calories 188; Fat 13.7 g; Carbohydrates 8.1 g; Sugar 3.5 g; Protein 11.9 g; Cholesterol 21 mg

Meatballs

Preparation Time: 10 minutes; Cooking Time: 25 minutes; Serve: 4
Ingredients:
- 1 lb ground chicken
- 1/2 cup almond flour
- 1/2 cup parmesan cheese, grated
- 1/4 tsp red pepper flakes
- 1/2 tsp dried oregano
- 1 tsp dried onion flakes
- 1 garlic clove, minced
- 1 egg, lightly beaten
- 2 tbsp olive oil
- 1 tbsp parsley, chopped
- 1/4 tsp pepper
- 1/2 tsp sea salt

Directions:
1. Add all ingredients into the bowl and mix until just combined.
2. Make small balls from the meat mixture.
3. Place the cooking tray in the air fryer basket. Line air fryer basket with parchment paper.
4. Select Bake mode.
5. Set time to 25 minutes and temperature 400 F then press START.
6. The air fryer display will prompt you to ADD FOOD once the temperature is reached then place meatballs onto the parchment paper in the air fryer basket.
7. Serve and enjoy.

Nutritional Value (Amount per Serving):
Calories 443; Fat 23.5 g; Carbohydrates 11.8 g; Sugar 1.1 g; Protein 45.6 g; Cholesterol 163 mg

Chicken Meatballs

Preparation Time: 10 minutes; Cooking Time: 10 minutes; Serve: 6
Ingredients:
- 2 eggs
- 2 lbs ground chicken breast
- 1/2 cup almond flour
- 1/2 cup ricotta cheese
- 1/4 cup fresh parsley, chopped
- 1 tsp pepper
- 2 tsp salt

Directions:
1. Add all ingredients into the large bowl and mix until just combined.
2. Make small balls from the meat mixture.
3. Place the cooking tray in the air fryer basket. Line air fryer basket with parchment paper.
4. Select Air Fry mode.
5. Set time to 10 minutes and temperature 375 F then press START.
6. The air fryer display will prompt you to ADD FOOD once the temperature is reached then place meatballs onto the parchment paper in the air fryer basket.

7. Serve and enjoy.

Nutritional Value (Amount per Serving):
Calories 227; Fat 5.6 g; Carbohydrates 2.1 g; Sugar 0.3 g; Protein 42.6 g; Cholesterol 155 mg

Delicious Spinach Dip

Preparation Time: 10 minutes; Cooking Time: 20 minutes; Serve: 12

Ingredients:
- 3 oz frozen spinach, defrosted & chopped
- 1 cup cheddar cheese, shredded
- 8 oz cream cheese
- 1 cup Asiago cheese, shredded
- 1 cup sour cream
- 1 tsp salt

Directions:
1. Add all ingredients into the mixing bowl and mix until well combined. Transfer mixture into the baking dish.
2. Cover dish with foil.
3. Select Bake mode.
4. Set time to 20 minutes and temperature 350 F then press START.
5. The air fryer display will prompt you to ADD FOOD once the temperature is reached then baking dish in the air fryer basket.
6. Serve and enjoy.

Nutritional Value (Amount per Serving):
Calories 155; Fat 14.4 g; Carbohydrates 1.7 g; Sugar 0.2 g; Protein 5.2 g; Cholesterol 41 mg

Garlic Dip

Preparation Time: 10 minutes; Cooking Time: 20 minutes; Serve: 12

Ingredients:
- 3 garlic cloves, minced
- 5 oz Asiago cheese, shredded
- 1 cup sour cream
- 1 cup mozzarella cheese, shredded
- 8 oz cream cheese, softened

Directions:
1. Add all ingredients into the mixing bowl and mix until well combined.
2. Pour mixture into the greased baking dish.
3. Select Bake mode.
4. Set time to 20 minutes and temperature 350 F then press START.
5. The air fryer display will prompt you to ADD FOOD once the temperature is reached then place the baking dish in the air fryer basket.
6. Serve and enjoy.

Nutritional Value (Amount per Serving):
Calories 157; Fat 14.4 g; Carbohydrates 1.7 g; Sugar 0.1 g; Protein 5.7 g; Cholesterol 41 mg

Cauliflower Hummus

Preparation Time: 10 minutes; Cooking Time: 35 minutes; Serve: 8

Ingredients:
- 1 cauliflower head, cut into florets
- 3 tbsp olive oil
- 1/2 tsp ground cumin
- 1 tsp garlic, chopped
- 2 tbsp fresh lemon juice
- 1/3 cup tahini
- Pepper
- Salt

Directions:
1. Place the cooking tray in the air fryer basket. Line air fryer basket with parchment paper.
2. Select Bake mode.

3. Set time to 35 minutes and temperature 400 F then press START.
4. The air fryer display will prompt you to ADD FOOD once the temperature is reached then spread cauliflower onto the parchment paper in the air fryer basket.
5. Transfer roasted cauliflower into the food processor along with remaining ingredients and process until smooth.
6. Serve and enjoy.

Nutritional Value (Amount per Serving):
Calories 115; Fat 10.7 g; Carbohydrates 4.2 g; Sugar 0.9 g; Protein 2.4 g; Cholesterol 0 mg

Crispy Tofu

Preparation Time: 10 minutes; Cooking Time: 15 minutes; Serve: 4
Ingredients:
- 15 oz extra-firm tofu, pressed and cut into cubes
- 1 tsp sesame oil
- 1 tbsp rice vinegar
- 2 tbsp soy sauce

Directions:
1. In a large bowl, mix together tofu, sesame oil, vinegar, and soy sauce. Let it sit for 15 minutes.
2. Place the cooking tray in the air fryer basket. Line air fryer basket with parchment paper.
3. Select Bake mode.
4. Set time to 15 minutes and temperature 400 F then press START.
5. The air fryer display will prompt you to ADD FOOD once the temperature is reached then place tofu onto the parchment paper in the air fryer basket. Stir halfway through.
6. Serve and enjoy.

Nutritional Value (Amount per Serving):
Calories 113; Fat 7.3 g; Carbohydrates 2.7 g; Sugar 0.7 g; Protein 11 g; Cholesterol 0 mg

Spicy Mixed Nuts

Preparation Time: 10 minutes; Cooking Time: 4 minutes; Serve: 2
Ingredients:
- 2 cup mixed nuts
- 1 tsp chili powder
- 1 tsp ground cumin
- 1 tbsp olive oil
- 1 tsp pepper
- 1 tsp salt

Directions:
1. In a bowl, add all ingredients and toss well.
2. Place the cooking tray in the air fryer basket. Line air fryer basket with parchment paper.
3. Select Air Fry mode.
4. Set time to 4 minutes and temperature 350 F then press START.
5. The air fryer display will prompt you to ADD FOOD once the temperature is reached then place mixed nuts onto the parchment paper in the air fryer basket.
6. Serve and enjoy.

Nutritional Value (Amount per Serving):
Calories 374; Fat 34.3 g; Carbohydrates 10.8 g; Sugar 1.9 g; Protein 11.2 g; Cholesterol 0 mg

Air Fried Walnuts

Preparation Time: 10 minutes; Cooking Time: 5 minutes; Serve: 6
Ingredients:
- 2 cups walnuts
- 1 tsp olive oil
- 1/4 tsp garlic powder
- 1/4 tsp chili powder
- Pepper
- Salt

Directions:
1. Add walnuts, garlic powder, chili powder, oil, pepper, and salt into the bowl and toss well.
2. Place the cooking tray in the air fryer basket. Line air fryer basket with parchment paper.
3. Select Air Fry mode.
4. Set time to 5 minutes and temperature 320 F then press START.
5. The air fryer display will prompt you to ADD FOOD once the temperature is reached then place walnuts onto the parchment paper in the air fryer basket.
6. Serve and enjoy.

Nutritional Value (Amount per Serving):
Calories 265; Fat 25.4 g; Carbohydrates 4.3 g; Sugar 0.5 g; Protein 10.1 g; Cholesterol 0 mg

Tasty Cauliflower Bites

Preparation Time: 10 minutes; Cooking Time: 15 minutes; Serve: 4

Ingredients:
- 1 lb cauliflower florets
- 1/2 tsp dried rosemary
- 1 1/2 tsp garlic powder
- 1 tbsp olive oil
- 1 tsp sesame seeds
- 1 tsp ground coriander
- Pepper
- Salt

Directions:
1. Place the cooking tray in the air fryer basket. Line air fryer basket with parchment paper.
2. Select Bake mode.
3. Set time to 15 minutes and temperature 400 F then press START.
4. The air fryer display will prompt you to ADD FOOD once the temperature is reached then spread cauliflower florets onto the parchment paper in the air fryer basket.
5. Serve and enjoy.

Nutritional Value (Amount per Serving):
Calories 67; Fat 4 g; Carbohydrates 7.1 g; Sugar 3 g; Protein 2.6 g; Cholesterol 0 mg

Meatballs

Preparation Time: 10 minutes; Cooking Time: 15 minutes; Serve: 4

Ingredients:
- 1 lb ground lamb
- 1 tsp onion powder
- 1 tbsp garlic, minced
- 1 tsp ground coriander
- 1 tsp ground cumin
- Pepper
- Salt

Directions:
1. Add all ingredients into the large bowl and mix until well combined.
2. Make small balls from the meat mixture.
3. Place the cooking tray in the air fryer basket. Line air fryer basket with parchment paper.
4. Select Bake mode.
5. Set time to 15 minutes and temperature 400 F then press START.
6. The air fryer display will prompt you to ADD FOOD once the temperature is reached then place meatballs onto the parchment paper in the air fryer basket.
7. Serve and enjoy.

Nutritional Value (Amount per Serving):
Calories 218; Fat 8.5 g; Carbohydrates 1.4 g; Sugar 0.2 g; Protein 32.1 g; Cholesterol 102 mg

Parmesan Brussels Sprouts

Preparation Time: 10 minutes; Cooking Time: 12 minutes; Serve: 4

Ingredients:

- 1 lb Brussels sprouts, cut stems and halved
- 1 1/2 tbsp olive oil
- 1/4 cup parmesan cheese, grated
- 1/4 tsp garlic powder
- 1/4 tsp onion powder
- Pepper
- Salt

Directions:
1. In a bowl, toss Brussels sprouts with oil, garlic powder, onion powder, pepper, and salt.
2. Place the cooking tray in the air fryer basket. Line air fryer basket with parchment paper.
3. Select Air Fry mode.
4. Set time to 12 minutes and temperature 350 F then press START.
5. The air fryer display will prompt you to ADD FOOD once the temperature is reached then spread brussels sprouts onto the parchment paper in the air fryer basket.
6. Top with grated parmesan cheese and serve.

Nutritional Value (Amount per Serving):
Calories 142; Fat 8.8 g; Carbohydrates 11.1 g; Sugar 2.5 g; Protein 8.6 g; Cholesterol 10 mg

Crab Dip

Preparation Time: 10 minutes; Cooking Time: 7 minutes; Serve: 4

Ingredients:
- 1 cup crab, cooked
- 2 tbsp fresh parsley, chopped
- 2 tbsp fresh lemon juice
- 2 tbsp hot sauce
- 2 cups Jalapeno jack cheese, grated
- 1/2 cup green onions, sliced
- 1/4 cup mayonnaise
- 1 tsp pepper
- 1/2 tsp salt

Directions:
1. Add all ingredients except parsley and lemon juice in the 6-inch baking dish and mix well.
2. Select Air Fry mode.
3. Set time to 7 minutes and temperature 400 F then press START.
4. The air fryer display will prompt you to ADD FOOD once the temperature is reached then place the baking dish in the air fryer basket.
5. Remove dish from air fryer. Add parsley and lemon juice. Mix well.
6. Serve and enjoy.

Nutritional Value (Amount per Serving):
Calories 307; Fat 22.7 g; Carbohydrates 5.6 g; Sugar 1.8 g; Protein 20.4 g; Cholesterol 84 mg

Stuffed Chicken Jalapenos

Preparation Time: 10 minutes; Cooking Time: 25 minutes; Serve: 12

Ingredients:
- 6 jalapenos, halved
- 1/2 cup chicken, cooked and shredded
- 1/4 tsp garlic powder
- 4 oz cream cheese
- 1/4 tsp dried oregano
- 1/4 cup green onion, sliced
- 1/4 cup Monterey jack cheese, shredded
- 1/4 tsp dried basil
- 1/4 tsp salt

Directions:
1. Mix all ingredients in a bowl except jalapenos.
2. Spoon 1 tablespoon mixture into each jalapeno half.
3. Place the cooking tray in the air fryer basket. Line air fryer basket with parchment paper.
4. Select Bake mode.
5. Set time to 25 minutes and temperature 390 F then press START.

6. The air fryer display will prompt you to ADD FOOD once the temperature is reached then place jalapeno halves onto the parchment paper in the air fryer basket.
7. Serve and enjoy.

Nutritional Value (Amount per Serving):
Calories 54; Fat 4.2 g; Carbohydrates 0.9 g; Sugar 0.3 g; Protein 3.1 g; Cholesterol 17 mg

Broccoli Cheese Balls

Preparation Time: 10 minutes; Cooking Time: 30 minutes; Serve: 20

Ingredients:
- 2 eggs
- 1/4 cup onion, minced
- 1/2 cup almond flour
- 2 cups broccoli florets
- 1 tsp Italian seasoning
- 1 garlic clove, minced
- 1 cup cheddar cheese, shredded
- Pepper
- Salt

Directions:
1. Steam broccoli florets in boiling water until tender. Drain well and chopped.
2. In a large bowl, mix together broccoli, eggs, cheese, almond flour, onion, garlic, and spices until well combined.
3. Make small balls from the mixture.
4. Place the cooking tray in the air fryer basket. Line air fryer basket with parchment paper.
5. Select Bake mode.
6. Set time to 30 minutes and temperature 400 F then press START.
7. The air fryer display will prompt you to ADD FOOD once the temperature is reached then place broccoli balls onto the parchment paper in the air fryer basket.
8. Serve and enjoy.

Nutritional Value (Amount per Serving):
Calories 38; Fat 2.8 g; Carbohydrates 1.1 g; Sugar 0.3 g; Protein 2.4 g; Cholesterol 22 mg

Spinach Sausage Balls

Preparation Time: 10 minutes; Cooking Time: 20 minutes; Serve: 10

Ingredients:
- 1 egg
- 1/2 cup parmesan cheese, grated
- 1/2 cup mozzarella cheese, shredded
- 1 lb sausage
- 1 garlic clove, chopped
- 1/2 onion, chopped
- 1 cup spinach, chopped
- 1 tsp salt

Directions:
1. Add all ingredients in mixing bowl and mix until well combined.
2. Make balls from the mixture.
3. Place the cooking tray in the air fryer basket. Line air fryer basket with parchment paper.
4. Select Bake mode.
5. Set time to 20 minutes and temperature 400 F then press START.
6. The air fryer display will prompt you to ADD FOOD once the temperature is reached then place sausage balls onto the parchment paper in the air fryer basket.
7. Serve and enjoy.

Nutritional Value (Amount per Serving):
Calories 205; Fat 16.1 g; Carbohydrates 1.2 g; Sugar 0.3 g; Protein 13.7 g; Cholesterol 64 mg

Pepperoni Chips

Preparation Time: 10 minutes; Cooking Time: 10 minutes; Serve: 2

Ingredients:

- 1 oz pepperoni
- 4 tbsp mozzarella cheese, shredded
- 2 tbsp parmesan cheese, grated
- 1/2 tsp Italian seasoning

Directions:
1. Place the cooking tray in the air fryer basket. Line air fryer basket with parchment paper.
2. Select Bake mode.
3. Set time to 10 minutes and temperature 400 F then press START.
4. The air fryer display will prompt you to ADD FOOD once the temperature is reached then arrange pepperoni onto the parchment paper in the air fryer basket. Sprinkle parmesan cheese, Italian seasoning, and mozzarella cheese over pepperoni.
5. Serve and enjoy.

Nutritional Value (Amount per Serving):
Calories 266; Fat 18.7 g; Carbohydrates 2.5 g; Sugar 0.1 g; Protein 22.4 g; Cholesterol 53 mg

Crispy Zucchini Fries

Preparation Time: 10 minutes; Cooking Time: 20 minutes; Serve: 4
Ingredients:
- 2 eggs
- 2 medium zucchini, peel and cut into matchsticks
- 1/4 tsp onion powder
- 1 cup pork rinds, crushed
- 1 tbsp heavy cream
- 1/2 cup parmesan cheese, grated
- 1/4 tsp garlic powder

Directions:
1. In a bowl, whisk together cream and eggs.
2. In a shallow dish, mix together crushed pork rinds, parmesan cheese, onion powder, and garlic powder.
3. Dip each zucchini piece into the egg mixture then coat with pork rind mixture.
4. Place the cooking tray in the air fryer basket. Line air fryer basket with parchment paper.
5. Select Bake mode.
6. Set time to 20 minutes and temperature 400 F then press START.
7. The air fryer display will prompt you to ADD FOOD once the temperature is reached then place breaded zucchini fries onto the parchment paper in the air fryer basket.
8. Serve and enjoy.

Nutritional Value (Amount per Serving):
Calories 201; Fat 12.9 g; Carbohydrates 4.9 g; Sugar 2 g; Protein 18.6 g; Cholesterol 119 mg

Simple Parmesan Zucchini Bites

Preparation Time: 10 minutes; Cooking Time: 15 minutes; Serve: 4
Ingredients:
- 1 egg
- 1/2 cup parmesan cheese, grated
- 2 cups zucchini, grated
- 1/4 cup cilantro, chopped
- Pepper
- Salt

Directions:
1. In a bowl, mix together zucchini, cilantro, cheese, egg, pepper, and salt.
2. Pour mixture into the small baking dish.
3. Select Bake mode.
4. Set time to 15 minutes and temperature 400 F then press START.
5. The air fryer display will prompt you to ADD FOOD once the temperature is reached then place the baking dish in the air fryer basket.
6. Serve and enjoy.

Nutritional Value (Amount per Serving):
Calories 119; Fat 7.5 g; Carbohydrates 3.1 g; Sugar 1.1 g; Protein 11.5 g; Cholesterol 62 mg

Cheesy Jalapeno Poppers

Preparation Time: 10 minutes; Cooking Time: 20 minutes; Serve: 24
Ingredients:
- 12 jalapeno peppers, cut in half and remove seeds
- 2 oz feta cheese
- 1/4 tsp garlic powder
- 1/2 tsp onion powder
- 1/4 cup cilantro, chopped
- 4 oz cheddar cheese, shredded
- 4 oz cream cheese

Directions:
1. Add all ingredients except jalapeno peppers into the bowl and mix well to combine.
2. Stuff cheese mixture into each jalapeno half.
3. Place the cooking tray in the air fryer basket. Line air fryer basket with parchment paper.
4. Select Bake mode.
5. Set time to 20 minutes and temperature 400 F then press START.
6. The air fryer display will prompt you to ADD FOOD once the temperature is reached then place jalapeno halves onto the parchment paper in the air fryer basket.
7. Serve and enjoy.

Nutritional Value (Amount per Serving):
Calories 45; Fat 3.8 g; Carbohydrates 0.9 g; Sugar 0.4 g; Protein 2 g; Cholesterol 12 mg

Yummy Chicken Dip

Preparation Time: 10 minutes; Cooking Time: 25 minutes; Serve: 6
Ingredients:
- 2 cups chicken, cooked and shredded
- 1/2 cup sour cream
- 8 oz cream cheese, softened
- 4 tbsp hot sauce

Directions:
1. Add all ingredients in a large bowl and mix until well combined.
2. Transfer mixture in a baking dish. Cover dish with foil.
3. Select Bake mode.
4. Set time to 25 minutes and temperature 350 F then press START.
5. The air fryer display will prompt you to ADD FOOD once the temperature is reached then place the baking dish in the air fryer basket.
6. Serve and enjoy.

Nutritional Value (Amount per Serving):
Calories 244; Fat 18.7 g; Carbohydrates 2 g; Sugar 0.2 g; Protein 17 g; Cholesterol 86 mg

Roasted Cashew

Preparation Time: 5 minutes; Cooking Time: 10 minutes; Serve: 3
Ingredients:
- 3/4 cups cashews
- 1/2 tsp olive oil
- 1/2 tsp chili powder
- 1/4 tsp salt

Directions
1. Add all ingredients into the bowl and toss well.
2. Place the cooking tray in the air fryer basket. Line air fryer basket with parchment paper.
3. Select Bake mode.
4. Set time to 10 minutes and temperature 250 F then press START.
5. The air fryer display will prompt you to ADD FOOD once the temperature is reached then place cashews onto the parchment paper in the air fryer basket.
6. Serve and enjoy.

Nutritional Value (Amount per Serving):
Calories 205; Fat 16.7 g; Carbohydrates 11.4 g; Sugar 1.8 g; Protein 5.3 g; Cholesterol 0 mg

Roasted Cauliflower Florets

Preparation Time: 10 minutes; Cooking Time: 20 minutes; Serve: 4
Ingredients:
- 5 cups cauliflower florets
- 1/2 tsp cumin powder
- 1/2 tsp garlic powder
- 1/4 tsp onion powder
- 1/4 tsp chili powder
- 1/2 tsp coriander powder
- 4 tablespoons olive oil
- 1/2 tsp salt

Directions:
1. Add all ingredients into the large bowl and toss well.
2. Place the cooking tray in the air fryer basket. Line air fryer basket with parchment paper.
3. Select Air Fry mode.
4. Set time to 20 minutes and temperature 400 F then press START.
5. The air fryer display will prompt you to ADD FOOD once the temperature is reached then place cauliflower florets onto the parchment paper in the air fryer basket.
6. Serve and enjoy.

Nutritional Value (Amount per Serving):
Calories 154; Fat 14.2 g; Carbohydrates 7.2 g; Sugar 3.2 g; Protein 2.6 g; Cholesterol 0 mg

Tasty Zucchini Chips

Preparation Time: 10 minutes; Cooking Time: 10 minutes; Serve: 3
Ingredients:
- 1 egg, lightly beaten
- 3 tbsp pecans, roasted and chopped
- 1/4 cup almond flour
- 1 large zucchini, thinly sliced
- 1 tbsp herb seasoning

Directions:
1. In a shallow bowl, whisk the egg.
2. In another shallow bowl, mix together almond flour, seasoning, and pecans.
3. Dip each zucchini slice into the egg mixture then coat with almond mixture.
4. Place the cooking tray in the air fryer basket. Line air fryer basket with parchment paper.
5. Select Bake mode.
6. Set time to 10 minutes and temperature 350 F then press START.
7. The air fryer display will prompt you to ADD FOOD once the temperature is reached then place coated zucchini slices onto the parchment paper in the air fryer basket.
8. Serve and enjoy.

Nutritional Value (Amount per Serving):
Calories 121; Fat 10 g; Carbohydrates 5.7 g; Sugar 2.4 g; Protein 4.7 g; Cholesterol 55 mg

Healthy Carrots Chips

Preparation Time: 10 minutes; Cooking Time: 12 minutes; Serve: 4
Ingredients:
- 12 oz carrot chips
- 1 tbsp olive oil
- 1/4 tsp paprika
- 1/4 tsp pepper
- 1/2 tsp garlic powder
- 1/2 tsp salt

Directions:
1. Add all ingredients into the bowl and toss well.
2. Place the cooking tray in the air fryer basket. Line air fryer basket with parchment paper.
3. Select Air Fry mode.
4. Set time to 12 minutes and temperature 375 F then press START.
5. The air fryer display will prompt you to ADD FOOD once the temperature is reached then place carrot chips onto the parchment paper in the air fryer basket.

6. Serve and enjoy.

Nutritional Value (Amount per Serving):
Calories 35; Fat 3.5 g; Carbohydrates 1.2 g; Sugar 0.5 g; Protein 0.2 g; Cholesterol 0 mg

Lamb Patties

Preparation Time: 10 minutes; Cooking Time: 8 minutes; Serve: 4

Ingredients:
- 1 lb ground lamb
- 1/4 cup fresh parsley, chopped
- 1 tsp dried oregano
- 1 cup feta cheese, crumbled
- 1 tbsp garlic, minced
- 5 basil leaves, minced
- 10 mint leaves, minced
- 1 jalapeno pepper, minced
- 1/4 tsp pepper
- 1/2 tsp kosher salt

Directions:
1. Add all ingredients into the mixing bowl and mix until well combined.
2. Make four equal shape patties from the meat mixture.
3. Place the cooking tray in the air fryer basket. Line air fryer basket with parchment paper.
4. Select Bake mode.
5. Set time to 8 minutes and temperature 390 F then press START.
6. The air fryer display will prompt you to ADD FOOD once the temperature is reached then place patties onto the parchment paper in the air fryer basket.
7. Serve and enjoy.

Nutritional Value (Amount per Serving):
Calories 330; Fat 16.6 g; Carbohydrates 5.4 g; Sugar 1.7 g; Protein 38.5 g; Cholesterol 135 mg

Herb Olives

Preparation Time: 10 minutes; Cooking Time: 5 minutes; Serve: 4

Ingredients:
- 2 cups olives
- 1/2 tsp crushed red pepper
- 2 tsp garlic, minced
- 2 tbsp olive oil
- 1/2 tsp dried fennel seeds
- 1/2 tsp dried oregano
- Pepper
- Salt

Directions:
1. Add olives and remaining ingredients into the mixing bowl and toss to coat well.
2. Place the cooking tray in the air fryer basket. Line air fryer basket with parchment paper.
3. Select Air Fry mode.
4. Set time to 5 minutes and temperature 300 F then press START.
5. The air fryer display will prompt you to ADD FOOD once the temperature is reached then place olives onto the parchment paper in the air fryer basket.
6. Serve and enjoy.

Nutritional Value (Amount per Serving):
Calories 142; Fat 14.3 g; Carbohydrates 5.1 g; Sugar 0 g; Protein 0.7 g; Cholesterol 0 mg

Buffalo Chicken Dip

Preparation Time: 10 minutes; Cooking Time: 25 minutes; Serve: 8

Ingredients:
- 2 chicken breasts, skinless, boneless, cooked and shredded
- 1 cup Monterey jack cheese, shredded
- 1/2 cup ranch dressing
- 1/2 cup buffalo wing sauce
- 8 oz cream cheese, softened
- 1 cup cheddar cheese, shredded
- 1/4 cup blue cheese, crumbled

Directions:

1. Add cream cheese into the baking dish and top with shredded chicken, ranch dressing, and buffalo sauce.
2. Sprinkle cheddar cheese, Monterey jack cheese, and blue cheese on top of chicken mixture. Cover dish with foil.
3. Select Bake mode.
4. Set time to 25 minutes and temperature 350 F then press START.
5. The air fryer display will prompt you to ADD FOOD once the temperature is reached then place the baking dish in the air fryer basket.
6. Serve and enjoy.

Nutritional Value (Amount per Serving):
Calories 298; Fat 22.8 g; Carbohydrates 2 g; Sugar 0.6 g; Protein 20.8 g; Cholesterol 94 mg

Healthy Mixed Nuts

Preparation Time: 5 minutes; Cooking Time: 20 minutes; Serve: 20

Ingredients:
- 5 cups mixed nuts
- 1 tsp paprika
- 1 tsp onion powder
- 1 tsp garlic powder
- 1/4 cup olive oil
- 1 tsp salt

Directions:
1. Add mixed nuts and remaining ingredients into the mixing bowl and mix well.
2. Place the cooking tray in the air fryer basket. Line air fryer basket with parchment paper.
3. Select Bake mode.
4. Set time to 20 minutes and temperature 325 F then press START.
5. The air fryer display will prompt you to ADD FOOD once the temperature is reached then spread nuts onto the parchment paper in the air fryer basket.
6. Serve and enjoy.

Nutritional Value (Amount per Serving):
Calories 244; Fat 22.8 g; Carbohydrates 8.3 g; Sugar 1.7 g; Protein 5.6 g; Cholesterol 0 mg

Ricotta Dip

Preparation Time: 10 minutes; Cooking Time: 15 minutes; Serve: 8

Ingredients:
- 1 cup ricotta cheese
- 1/2 tbsp fresh rosemary
- 1 tbsp lemon juice
- 2 tbsp olive oil
- 2 garlic cloves, minced
- 1/4 cup parmesan cheese
- 1/2 cup mozzarella cheese
- Pepper
- Salt

Directions:
1. Add ricotta cheese, garlic, oil, lemon juice, rosemary, pepper, and salt into the baking dish and mix until well combined.
2. Sprinkle mozzarella cheese and parmesan cheese on top. Cover dish with foil.
3. Select Bake mode.
4. Set time to 15 minutes and temperature 400 F then press START.
5. The air fryer display will prompt you to ADD FOOD once the temperature is reached then place the baking dish in the air fryer basket.
6. Serve and enjoy.

Nutritional Value (Amount per Serving):
Calories 103; Fat 7.9 g; Carbohydrates 2.3 g; Sugar 0.2 g; Protein 6.4 g; Cholesterol 16 mg

Chicken Cheese Dip

Preparation Time: 10 minutes; Cooking Time: 10 minutes; Serve: 8
Ingredients:
- 2 cups cheddar cheese, shredded
- 1 cup ranch dressing
- 2 can chunk chicken, drained
- 1 package cream cheese
- 3/4 cup hot sauce

Directions:
1. Add chicken and hot sauce to the pan and cook for 2 minutes.
2. Add cream and ranch dressing and stir well. Add half cheese and stir until well blended.
3. Transfer chicken mixture to the baking dish and sprinkle the remaining cheese on top. Cover dish with foil.
4. Select Bake mode.
5. Set time to 10 minutes and temperature 370 F then press START.
6. The air fryer display will prompt you to ADD FOOD once the temperature is reached then place the baking dish in the air fryer basket.
7. Serve and enjoy.

Nutritional Value (Amount per Serving):
Calories 192; Fat 14.2 g; Carbohydrates 2.7 g; Sugar 1.2 g; Protein 13.3 g; Cholesterol 51 mg

Spicy Artichoke Dip

Preparation Time: 10 minutes; Cooking Time: 30 minutes; Serve: 12
Ingredients:
- 7 oz can green chiles, diced
- 15 oz can artichoke hearts, drained and chopped
- 2 cups mayonnaise
- 8 oz parmesan cheese, grated

Directions:
1. Add all ingredients into the mixing bowl and mix until well combined.
2. Pour mixture into the 2-quart baking dish. Cover dish with foil.
3. Select Bake mode.
4. Set time to 30 minutes and temperature 325 F then press START.
5. The air fryer display will prompt you to ADD FOOD once the temperature is reached then place the baking dish in the air fryer basket.
6. Serve and enjoy.

Nutritional Value (Amount per Serving):
Calories 227; Fat 17.1 g; Carbohydrates 12.4 g; Sugar 3.4 g; Protein 7 g; Cholesterol 24 mg

Crispy Cauliflower Florets

Preparation Time: 10 minutes; Cooking Time: 15 minutes; Serve: 4
Ingredients:
- 1 medium cauliflower head, cut into florets
- 1/2 tsp Italian seasoning
- 1/4 tsp paprika
- 1/4 tsp onion powder
- 1 tbsp garlic, minced
- 3 tbsp olive oil
- Pepper
- Salt

Directions:
1. In a large bowl, toss cauliflower with remaining ingredients.
2. Place the cooking tray in the air fryer basket. Line air fryer basket with parchment paper.
3. Select Bake mode.
4. Set time to 15 minutes and temperature 400 F then press START.

5. The air fryer display will prompt you to ADD FOOD once the temperature is reached then spread cauliflower florets onto the parchment paper in the air fryer basket.
   6. Serve and enjoy.

Nutritional Value (Amount per Serving):
Calories 132; Fat 10.8 g; Carbohydrates 8.6 g; Sugar 3.6 g; Protein 3 g; Cholesterol 0 mg

Fresh Herb Mushrooms

Preparation Time: 10 minutes; Cooking Time: 14 minutes; Serve: 4
Ingredients:
- 1 lb mushrooms
- 1 tbsp basil, minced
- 1 garlic clove, minced
- 1/2 tbsp vinegar
- 1/2 tsp ground coriander
- 1 tsp rosemary, chopped
- Pepper
- Salt

Directions:
1. Add all ingredients into the large bowl and toss well.
2. Place the cooking tray in the air fryer basket. Line air fryer basket with parchment paper.
3. Select Bake mode.
4. Set time to 14 minutes and temperature 350 F then press START.
5. The air fryer display will prompt you to ADD FOOD once the temperature is reached then spread mushrooms onto the parchment paper in the air fryer basket.
6. Serve and enjoy.

Nutritional Value (Amount per Serving):
Calories 27; Fat 0.4 g; Carbohydrates 4.2 g; Sugar 2 g; Protein 3.6 g; Cholesterol 0 mg

Goat Cheese Dip

Preparation Time: 10 minutes; Cooking Time: 10 minutes; Serve: 4
Ingredients:
- 10 oz goat cheese
- 2 garlic cloves, minced
- 1/4 tsp sage
- 1/4 tsp thyme
- 2 tbsp olive oil
- 1/4 cup parmesan cheese
- Pepper
- Salt

Directions:
1. Add all ingredients into the food processor and process until just combined.
2. Pour mixture into the prepared baking dish and spread well. Select Bake mode.
3. Set time to 10 minutes and temperature 400 F then press START.
4. The air fryer display will prompt you to ADD FOOD once the temperature is reached then place the baking dish in the air fryer basket.
5. Serve and enjoy.

Nutritional Value (Amount per Serving):
Calories 430; Fat 35.4 g; Carbohydrates 2.6 g; Sugar 1.6 g; Protein 26.4 g; Cholesterol 85 mg

Zucchini Dill Dip

Preparation Time: 10 minutes; Cooking Time: 15 minutes; Serve: 6
Ingredients:
- 1 lb zucchini, grated & squeeze out all liquid
- 1 tsp garlic, minced
- 1 tsp dill, chopped
- 1 tbsp lime juice
- 1 tbsp olive oil
- 1 cup heavy cream
- Pepper
- Salt

Directions:

1. Add all ingredients into the large bowl and mix until well combined.
2. Pour zucchini mixture into the prepared baking dish.
3. Select Bake mode.
4. Set time to 15 minutes and temperature 375 F then press START.
5. The air fryer display will prompt you to ADD FOOD once the temperature is reached then place the baking dish in the air fryer basket.
6. Serve and enjoy.

Nutritional Value (Amount per Serving):
Calories 104; Fat 9.9 g; Carbohydrates 4 g; Sugar 1.5 g; Protein 1.4 g; Cholesterol 27 mg

Meatballs

Preparation Time: 10 minutes; Cooking Time: 25 minutes; Serve: 4
Ingredients:
- 1 lb ground chicken
- 1/2 cup cilantro, chopped
- 1 jalapeno pepper, minced
- 1/2 tsp garlic powder
- Salt

Directions:
1. Add all ingredients into the large bowl and mix until well combined.
2. Make small balls from the meat mixture.
3. Place the cooking tray in the air fryer basket. Line air fryer basket with parchment paper.
4. Select Bake mode.
5. Set time to 25 minutes and temperature 400 F then press START.
6. The air fryer display will prompt you to ADD FOOD once the temperature is reached then place meatballs onto the parchment paper in the air fryer basket.
7. Serve and enjoy.

Nutritional Value (Amount per Serving):
Calories 218; Fat 8.4 g; Carbohydrates 0.5 g; Sugar 0.2 g; Protein 33 g; Cholesterol 101 mg

Mexican Cheese Dip

Preparation Time: 10 minutes; Cooking Time: 30 minutes; Serve: 10
Ingredients:
- 1/2 cup hot salsa
- 3 cups cheddar cheese, shredded
- 16 oz cream cheese, softened
- 1 cup sour cream

Directions:
1. In a bowl, mix together all ingredients until well combined and pour into the baking dish. Cover dish with foil.
2. Select Bake mode.
3. Set time to 30 minutes and temperature 350 F then press START.
4. The air fryer display will prompt you to ADD FOOD once the temperature is reached then place the baking dish in the air fryer basket.
5. Serve and enjoy.

Nutritional Value (Amount per Serving):
Calories 348; Fat 31.9 g; Carbohydrates 3.4 g; Sugar 0.7 g; Protein 12.8 g; Cholesterol 96 mg

Cheddar Cheese Garlic Dip

Preparation Time: 10 minutes; Cooking Time: 8 minutes; Serve: 6
Ingredients:
- 13 oz cheddar cheese, remove the rind and cubed
- 3 garlic cloves, chopped
- 1 tbsp dried thyme
- 2 tsp rosemary, chopped
- Pepper

- Salt

Directions:
1. Add all ingredients into the mixing bowl and mix well.
2. Pour mixture into the baking dish and cover dish with foil.
3. Select Bake mode.
4. Set time to 8 minutes and temperature 375 F then press START.
5. The air fryer display will prompt you to ADD FOOD once the temperature is reached then place the baking dish in the air fryer basket.
6. Serve and enjoy.

Nutritional Value (Amount per Serving):
Calories 252; Fat 20.5 g; Carbohydrates 1.9 g; Sugar 0.4 g; Protein 15.5 g; Cholesterol 64 mg

Air Fry Pecans

Preparation Time: 5 minutes; Cooking Time: 6 minutes; Serve: 6
Ingredients:
- 2 cups pecan halves
- 1 tbsp butter, melted
- 1/4 tsp chili powder
- Salt

Directions:
1. Add pecans, chili powder, butter, and salt in a mixing bowl and toss well.
2. Place the cooking tray in the air fryer basket. Line air fryer basket with parchment paper.
3. Select Bake mode.
4. Set time to 6 minutes and temperature 400 F then press START.
5. The air fryer display will prompt you to ADD FOOD once the temperature is reached then place pecans onto the parchment paper in the air fryer basket.
6. Serve and enjoy.

Nutritional Value (Amount per Serving):
Calories 249; Fat 25.8 g; Carbohydrates 4.8 g; Sugar 1.2 g; Protein 3.6 g; Cholesterol 5 mg

Air Fry Taro Fries

Preparation Time: 10 minutes; Cooking Time: 20 minutes; Serve: 2
Ingredients:
- 8 small taro, peel and cut into fries shape
- 1 tbsp olive oil
- 1/2 tsp chili powder
- 1/4 tsp garlic powder
- 1/4 tsp pepper
- 1/2 tsp salt

Directions:
1. Add taro fries in a bowl and drizzle with olive oil. Season with chili powder, garlic powder, pepper, and salt.
2. Place the cooking tray in the air fryer basket. Line air fryer basket with parchment paper.
3. Select Bake mode.
4. Set time to 20 minutes and temperature 375 F then press START.
5. The air fryer display will prompt you to ADD FOOD once the temperature is reached then place taro fries onto the parchment paper in the air fryer basket.
6. Serve and enjoy.

Nutritional Value (Amount per Serving):
Calories 355; Fat 20.5 g; Carbohydrates 3.5 g; Sugar 1 g; Protein 4.5 g; Cholesterol 18 mg

Stuffed Mushrooms

Preparation Time: 10 minutes; Cooking Time: 5 minutes; Serve: 3
Ingredients:

- 12 baby mushrooms
- 4 bacon slices, cooked and crumbled
- 4 oz cream cheese
- 2 tbsp butter, melted
- Pepper
- Salt

Directions:
1. In a small bowl, mix together cream cheese, butter, bacon, pepper, and salt.
2. Stuff cream cheese mixture into the mushrooms.
3. Place the cooking tray in the air fryer basket. Line air fryer basket with parchment paper.
4. Select Bake mode.
5. Set time to 5 minutes and temperature 350 F then press START.
6. The air fryer display will prompt you to ADD FOOD once the temperature is reached then place stuffed mushrooms onto the parchment paper in the air fryer basket.
7. Serve and enjoy.

Nutritional Value (Amount per Serving):
Calories 352; Fat 31.7 g; Carbohydrates 3.8 g; Sugar 1.3 g; Protein 14.6 g; Cholesterol 90 mg

Crispy Zucchini Chips

Preparation Time: 10 minutes; Cooking Time: 30 minutes; Serve: 2

Ingredients:
- 2 medium zucchini, cut into 1/4-inch thick slices
- 1/2 cup parmesan cheese, grated
- 1/4 cup olive oil
- Pepper
- Salt

Directions:
1. In a mixing bowl, toss zucchini slices with cheese, oil, pepper, and salt.
2. Place the cooking tray in the air fryer basket. Line air fryer basket with parchment paper.
3. Select Bake mode.
4. Set time to 30 minutes and temperature 300 F then press START.
5. The air fryer display will prompt you to ADD FOOD once the temperature is reached then arrange zucchini slices onto the parchment paper in the air fryer basket. Turn halfway through.
6. Serve and enjoy.

Nutritional Value (Amount per Serving):
Calories 436; Fat 38.1 g; Carbohydrates 8.7 g; Sugar 3.4 g; Protein 21.2 g; Cholesterol 42 mg

Roasted Nuts

Preparation Time: 10 minutes; Cooking Time: 15 minutes; Serve: 6

Ingredients:
- 1 cup cashew nuts
- 1 cup almonds
- 1/2 tsp chili powder
- 1 tbsp olive oil
- 1/2 tsp salt

Directions
1. In a bowl, toss almonds and cashew with oil, chili powder, and salt.
2. Place the cooking tray in the air fryer basket. Line air fryer basket with parchment paper.
3. Select Bake mode.
4. Set time to 15 minutes and temperature 300 F then press START.
5. The air fryer display will prompt you to ADD FOOD once the temperature is reached then place cashew and almonds onto the parchment paper in the air fryer basket.
6. Serve and enjoy.

Nutritional Value (Amount per Serving):
Calories 243; Fat 20.9 g; Carbohydrates 11 g; Sugar 1.8 g; Protein 6.9 g; Cholesterol 0 mg

Cinnamon Apple Chips

Preparation Time: 10 minutes; Cooking Time: 8 minutes; Serve: 4

Ingredients :
- 1 large apple, sliced thinly
- 1/4 tsp ground nutmeg
- 1/4 tsp ground cinnamon

Directions:
1. Season apple slices with nutmeg and cinnamon.
2. Place the cooking tray in the air fryer basket. Line air fryer basket with parchment paper.
3. Select Air Fry mode.
4. Set time to 8 minutes and temperature 375 F then press START.
5. The air fryer display will prompt you to ADD FOOD once the temperature is reached then place apple slices onto the parchment paper in the air fryer basket.
6. Serve and enjoy.

Nutritional Value (Amount per Serving):
Calories 30; Fat 0.2 g; Carbohydrates 7.9 g; Sugar 5.8 g; Protein 0.2 g; Cholesterol 0 mg

Cheese Pesto Jalapeno Poppers

Preparation Time: 10 minutes; Cooking Time: 15 minutes; Serve: 6

Ingredients:
- 3 jalapeno peppers, halved and remove seeds
- 3 tbsp basil pesto
- 1/4 cup cream cheese
- 1/2 cup mozzarella cheese, shredded

Directions:
1. In a bowl, mix together pesto, shredded cheese, and cream cheese.
2. Stuff pesto cheese mixture into each jalapeno half.
3. Place the cooking tray in the air fryer basket. Line air fryer basket with parchment paper.
4. Select Bake mode.
5. Set time to 15 minutes and temperature 400 F then press START.
6. The air fryer display will prompt you to ADD FOOD once the temperature is reached then place stuffed jalapeno halves onto the parchment paper in the air fryer basket.
7. Serve and enjoy.

Nutritional Value (Amount per Serving):
Calories 44; Fat 3.9 g; Carbohydrates 0.9 g; Sugar 0.3 g; Protein 1.5 g; Cholesterol 12 mg

Chapter 9: Dehydrated Recipes

Spicy Cauliflower Popcorn

Preparation Time: 10 minutes; Cooking Time: 12 hours; Serve: 4
Ingredients:
- 1 cauliflower head, cut into bite-size pieces
- 1/2 tsp ground cumin
- 1 tsp cayenne
- 1 tbsp paprika
- 1/4 cup hot sauce
- 3 tbsp coconut oil

Directions:
1. Add cauliflower pieces into the large mixing bowl. Add remaining ingredients and toss until well coated.
2. Place the cooking tray in the air fryer basket.
3. Arrange coated cauliflower pieces in the air fryer basket.
4. Select Dehydrate mode.
5. Set time to 12 hours and temperature 130 F then press START.
6. Store in an airtight container.

Nutritional Value (Amount per Serving):
Calories 113; Fat 10.7 g; Carbohydrates 5.1 g; Sugar 2 g; Protein 1.7 g; Cholesterol 0 mg

Carrot Cake Cookies

Preparation Time: 10 minutes; Cooking Time: 4 hours; Serve: 20
Ingredients:
- 2 cups carrots, grated
- 2 cups almond flour
- 1/8 tsp nutmeg
- 1/8 tsp allspice
- 1/8 tsp cloves
- 1/2 tsp cinnamon
- 6 tbsp unsweetened coconut milk
- 15 drops liquid stevia
- 1 tsp vanilla

Directions:
1. In a bowl, mix together almond flour, nutmeg, allspice, cloves, and cinnamon.
2. Add grated carrots, coconut milk, vanilla, and stevia and mix until well combined.
3. Place the cooking tray in the air fryer basket. Place piece of parchment paper into the air fryer basket.
4. Make small cookies from mixture and place in the air fryer basket.
5. Select Dehydrate mode.
6. Set time to 4 hours and temperature 125 F then press START.
7. Store in an airtight container.

Nutritional Value (Amount per Serving):
Calories 32; Fat 2.5 g; Carbohydrates 2 g; Sugar 0.8 g; Protein 0.8 g; Cholesterol 0 mg

Easy Kiwi Chips

Preparation Time: 10 minutes; Cooking Time: 6 hours; Serve: 4
Ingredients:
- 4 kiwis, peel and cut into 1/4-inch slices

Directions:
1. Place the cooking tray in the air fryer basket.
2. Arrange kiwi slices into the air fryer basket.
3. Select Dehydrate mode.
4. Set time to 6 hours and temperature 135 F then press START.
5. Store in an airtight container.

Nutritional Value (Amount per Serving):
Calories 46; Fat 0.4 g; Carbohydrates 11.1 g; Sugar 6.8 g; Protein 0.9 g; Cholesterol 0 mg

Sun-Dried Tomatoes

Preparation Time: 10 minutes; Cooking Time: 12 hours; Serve: 4
Ingredients:
- 2 lbs fresh tomatoes, cut into 1/4-inch slices
- Salt

Directions:
1. Place the cooking tray in the air fryer basket.
2. Arrange tomato slices into the air fryer basket.
3. Select Dehydrate mode.
4. Set time to 6-12 hours and temperature 145 F then press START.
5. Store in an airtight container.

Nutritional Value (Amount per Serving):
Calories 41; Fat 0.5 g; Carbohydrates 8.8 g; Sugar 6 g; Protein 2 g; Cholesterol 0 mg

Crunchy Broccoli Chips

Preparation Time: 10 minutes; Cooking Time: 12 hours; Serve: 4
Ingredients:
- 1 lb broccoli florets
- 1 tsp onion powder
- 1 garlic clove
- 1/2 cup vegetable broth
- 1/4 cup hemp seeds
- 2 tbsp nutritional yeast
- 2 tbsp low-sodium tamari sauce

Directions:
1. Add hemp seeds, tamari sauce, nutritional yeast, broth, garlic, and onion powder into the blender and blend until smooth.
2. Pour sauce over broccoli florets in a mixing bowl and toss until well coated.
3. Place the cooking tray in the air fryer basket. Place piece of parchment paper into the air fryer basket.
4. Arrange broccoli florets in the air fryer basket.
5. Select Dehydrate mode.
6. Set time to 10-12 hours and temperature 115 F then press START.
7. Store in an airtight container.

Nutritional Value (Amount per Serving):
Calories 65; Fat 1.5 g; Carbohydrates 9.2 g; Sugar 2.2 g; Protein 5.3 g; Cholesterol 0 mg

Easy Apple Chips

Preparation Time: 10 minutes; Cooking Time: 12 hours; Serve: 4
Ingredients:
- 3 apples, washed and cut into 3/8-inch slices
- 1 tbsp ground cinnamon
- 2 tbsp fresh lemon juice
- 2 cups of water

Directions:
1. In a bowl, mix together water, lemon juice, and cinnamon.
2. Add apple slices into the water and soak for 8 hours.
3. Place the cooking tray in the air fryer basket.
4. Arrange soaked apple slices in the air fryer basket.
5. Select Dehydrate mode.
6. Set time to 10-12 hours and temperature 145 F then press START.

7. Store in an airtight container.

Nutritional Value (Amount per Serving):
Calories 26; Fat 0.1 g; Carbohydrates 7 g; Sugar 4.4 g; Protein 0.1 g; Cholesterol 0 mg

Cabbage Chips

Preparation Time: 10 minutes; Cooking Time: 12 hours; Serve: 4

Ingredients:
- 1/2 lb napa cabbage, cut stem, wash & dry leaves
- 1/2 tsp ground pepper
- 1 tbsp olive oil
- 1/2 tsp salt

Directions:
1. Cut cabbage leaves in a triangle shape.
2. Toss cabbage leaves with olive oil, pepper, and salt.
3. Place the cooking tray in the air fryer basket.
4. Arrange cabbage leaves in the air fryer basket.
5. Select Dehydrate mode.
6. Set time to 12 hours and temperature 135 F then press START.
7. Store in an airtight container.

Nutritional Value (Amount per Serving):
Calories 38; Fat 3.6 g; Carbohydrates 1.4 g; Sugar 0.7 g; Protein 0.9 g; Cholesterol 0 mg

Green Bean Chips

Preparation Time: 10 minutes; Cooking Time: 12 hours; Serve: 4

Ingredients:
- 2 lbs frozen green beans, thawed
- 2 tbsp nutritional yeast
- 2 tbsp coconut oil, melted
- 1 1/2 tsp salt

Directions:
1. Toss green beans with oil, nutritional yeast, and salt.
2. Place the cooking tray in the air fryer basket.
3. Arrange green beans in the air fryer basket.
4. Select Dehydrate mode.
5. Set time to 12 hours and temperature 125 F then press START.
6. Store in an airtight container.

Nutritional Value (Amount per Serving):
Calories 68; Fat 3.5 g; Carbohydrates 8.5 g; Sugar 1.4 g; Protein 3.1 g; Cholesterol 0 mg

Healthy Cucumber Chips

Preparation Time: 10 minutes; Cooking Time: 12 hours; Serve: 6

Ingredients:
- 2 medium cucumbers, thinly sliced
- 2 tsp apple cider vinegar
- 1 tbsp olive oil
- 1/2 tsp sea salt

Directions:
1. Toss cucumber slices with vinegar, oil, and salt.
2. Place the cooking tray in the air fryer basket.
3. Arrange cucumber slices in the air fryer basket.
4. Select Dehydrate mode.
5. Set time to 12 hours and temperature 125 F then press START.
6. Store in an airtight container.

Nutritional Value (Amount per Serving):
Calories 25; Fat 2.3 g; Carbohydrates 1 g; Sugar 0.3 g; Protein 0.3 g; Cholesterol 0 mg

Snap Pea Chips

Preparation Time: 10 minutes; Cooking Time: 8 hours; Serve: 6
Ingredients:
- 3 cups snap peas
- 2 tbsp olive oil
- 1/2 tsp garlic powder
- 2 tbsp nutritional yeast
- 1/2 tsp sea salt

Directions:
1. Toss snap peas with oil, garlic powder, nutritional yeast, and salt.
2. Place the cooking tray in the air fryer basket.
3. Arrange snap peas in the air fryer basket.
4. Select Dehydrate mode.
5. Set time to 8 hours and temperature 135 F then press START.
6. Store in an airtight container.

Nutritional Value (Amount per Serving):
Calories 12; Fat 0.4 g; Carbohydrates 1.5 g; Sugar 0.7 g; Protein 0.5 g; Cholesterol 0 mg

Beet Chips

Preparation Time: 10 minutes; Cooking Time: 8 hours; Serve: 4
Ingredients:
- 3 medium beets, peel & thinly sliced
- 1 tsp olive oil
- Pepper
- Salt

Directions:
1. Toss beet slices with olive oil, pepper, and salt.
2. Place the cooking tray in the air fryer basket.
3. Arrange beet slices in the air fryer basket.
4. Select Dehydrate mode.
5. Set time to 8 hours and temperature 130 F then press START.
6. Store in an airtight container.

Nutritional Value (Amount per Serving):
Calories 18; Fat 1.2 g; Carbohydrates 1.5 g; Sugar 0 g; Protein 0.4 g; Cholesterol 0 mg

Crunchy Kale Chips

Preparation Time: 10 minutes; Cooking Time: 2 hours; Serve: 4
Ingredients:
- 2 bunches kale, remove stem and cut into bite-size pieces
- 3 tbsp nutritional yeast
- 2 tsp garlic powder
- 1 tbsp olive oil
- 1 tsp salt

Directions:
1. Add kale pieces into the mixing bowl. Add garlic powder, oil, and salt over kale and massage into the leaves.
2. Sprinkle nutritional yeast over kale and toss well.
3. Place the cooking tray in the air fryer basket.
4. Arrange kale in the air fryer basket.
5. Select Dehydrate mode.
6. Set time to 2 hours and temperature 160 F then press START.
7. Store in an airtight container.

Nutritional Value (Amount per Serving):
Calories 58; Fat 3.5 g; Carbohydrates 5.8 g; Sugar 0.3 g; Protein 1.9 g; Cholesterol 0 mg

Tasty Tomato Chips

Preparation Time: 10 minutes; Cooking Time: 8 hours; Serve: 4
Ingredients:
- 3 large tomatoes, cut into 1.5 mm slices

For sauce:
- 1/2 cup cashews, soaked for 2 hours and drain
- 1/2 tsp red pepper flakes
- 1 tsp paprika
- 1 tsp dried oregano
- 2 tbsp nutritional yeast
- 2 tbsp lemon juice
- 2 cups red bell pepper, chopped
- 1/4 cup water
- 1/4 tsp salt

Directions:
1. Add all sauce ingredients into the blender and blend until smooth.
2. Place the cooking tray in the air fryer basket. Place piece of parchment paper into the air fryer basket.
3. Dredge tomato slices into the sauce. Drip off excess sauce and arrange tomato slices onto the parchment paper in the air fryer basket.
4. Select Dehydrate mode.
5. Set time to 8 hours and temperature 115 F then press START.
6. Store in an airtight container.

Nutritional Value (Amount per Serving):
Calories 40; Fat 0.8 g; Carbohydrates 6.8 g; Sugar 1.3 g; Protein 3.2 g; Cholesterol 0 mg

Dehydrated Okra

Preparation Time: 10 minutes; Cooking Time: 24 hours; Serve: 4
Ingredients:
- 12 pods okra, slice into rounds

Directions:
1. Place the cooking tray in the air fryer basket.
2. Arrange okra in the air fryer basket.
3. Select Dehydrate mode.
4. Set time to 24 hours and temperature 130 F then press START.
5. Store in an airtight container.

Nutritional Value (Amount per Serving):
Calories 10; Fat 0.1 g; Carbohydrates 2.2 g; Sugar 0 g; Protein 0.8 g; Cholesterol 0 mg

Strawberry Chips

Preparation Time: 10 minutes; Cooking Time: 3 hours; Serve: 4
Ingredients:
- 8 fresh strawberries, cut into 1/8-inch slices

Directions:
1. Place the cooking tray in the air fryer basket.
2. Arrange strawberry slices in the air fryer basket.
3. Select Dehydrate mode.
4. Set time to 3 hours and temperature 125 F then press START.
5. Store in an airtight container.

Nutritional Value (Amount per Serving):
Calories 8; Fat 0.1 g; Carbohydrates 1.8 g; Sugar 1.2 g; Protein 0.2 g; Cholesterol 0 mg

Lemon Slices

Preparation Time: 10 minutes; Cooking Time: 5 hours; Serve: 6

Ingredients:
- 4 lemons, cut into 1/4-inch thick slices

Directions:
1. Place the cooking tray in the air fryer basket.
2. Arrange lemon slices in the air fryer basket.
3. Select Dehydrate mode.
4. Set time to 5 hours and temperature 170 F then press START.
5. Store in an airtight container.

Nutritional Value (Amount per Serving):
Calories 11; Fat 0.1 g; Carbohydrates 3.6 g; Sugar 1 g; Protein 0.4 g; Cholesterol 0 mg

Smoky Eggplant Chips

Preparation Time: 10 minutes; Cooking Time: 10 hours; Serve: 4

Ingredients:
- 2 eggplants, cut into thin slices

For seasoning:
- 1/4 tsp dried ground sage
- 1/2 tsp onion powder
- 1/2 tsp pepper
- 1/2 tsp turmeric
- 1/2 tsp dried thyme
- 1 tsp dried oregano
- 1/2 tbsp garlic powder
- 1/2 tbsp smoked paprika
- 1/4 tsp sea salt

Directions:
1. In a small bowl, mix together all seasoning ingredients.
2. Spray eggplant slices with cooking spray and sprinkle with seasoning.
3. Place the cooking tray in the air fryer basket.
4. Arrange eggplant slices in the air fryer basket.
5. Select Dehydrate mode.
6. Set time to 10 hours and temperature 115 F then press START.
7. Store in an airtight container.

Nutritional Value (Amount per Serving):
Calories 20; Fat 0.2 g; Carbohydrates 4.7 g; Sugar 2 g; Protein 0.9 g; Cholesterol 0 mg

Eggplant Jerky

Preparation Time: 10 minutes; Cooking Time: 10 hours; Serve: 3

Ingredients:
- 2 medium eggplant, cut into 1/4-inch thick slices
- 1/2 tsp red chili flakes
- 3 tbsp soy sauce
- 2 tbsp water

Directions:
1. In a small bowl, mix together soy sauce, water, and red chili flakes.
2. Brush eggplant slices with soy sauce mixture. Place eggplant slices into the dish, cover, and place in the refrigerator for 2 hours.
3. Place the cooking tray in the air fryer basket. Place piece of parchment paper into the air fryer basket.
4. Arrange eggplant slices onto the parchment paper in the air fryer basket.
5. Select Dehydrate mode.
6. Set time to 10 hours and temperature 115 F then press START.
7. Store in an airtight container.

Nutritional Value (Amount per Serving):
Calories 22; Fat 0 g; Carbohydrates 4.6 g; Sugar 2.3 g; Protein 1.7 g; Cholesterol 0 mg

Pear Chips

Preparation Time: 10 minutes; Cooking Time: 10 hours; Serve: 4
Ingredients:
- 3 pears, cut into slices

Directions:
1. Place the cooking tray in the air fryer basket.
2. Arrange pear slices in the air fryer basket.
3. Select Dehydrate mode.
4. Set time to 8 hours and temperature 130 F then press START.
5. Store in an airtight container.

Nutritional Value (Amount per Serving):
Calories 25; Fat 0.3 g; Carbohydrates 5.1 g; Sugar 2 g; Protein 1.7 g; Cholesterol 0 mg

Curried Apple Chips

Preparation Time: 10 minutes; Cooking Time: 8 hours; Serve: 2
Ingredients:
- 1 apple, cut into 1/5-inch thick slices
- 1 tsp water
- 1 tsp cinnamon
- 1 tsp curry powder

Directions:
1. In a small bowl, mix together curry powder, cinnamon, and water.
2. Brush apple slices with curry powder mixture.
3. Arrange apple slices in the air fryer basket.
4. Select Dehydrate mode.
5. Set time to 8 hours and temperature 135 F then press START.
6. Store in an airtight container.

Nutritional Value (Amount per Serving):
Calories 37; Fat 0.2 g; Carbohydrates 9.7 g; Sugar 6.5 g; Protein 0.4 g; Cholesterol 0 mg

Broccoli Bites

Preparation Time: 10 minutes; Cooking Time: 18 hours; Serve: 3
Ingredients:
- 1 1/2 broccoli heads, cut into bite-size pieces

For sauce:
- 2 sun-dried tomatoes
- 1 tbsp tahini
- 1/2 tbsp paprika
- 2 tbsp onion, chopped
- 1 garlic clove
- 1/2 tbsp dried oregano
- 1/2 tbsp dried basil
- 1/2 tomato
- Pinch of cayenne

Directions:
1. Add all sauce ingredients into the blender and blend until smooth.
2. Add broccoli pieces into the mixing bowl. Pour sauce over broccoli and toss until well coated.
3. Place the cooking tray in the air fryer basket.
4. Arrange broccoli in the air fryer basket.
5. Select Dehydrate mode.
6. Set time to 18 hours and temperature 110 F then press START.
7. Store in an airtight container.

Nutritional Value (Amount per Serving):
Calories 70; Fat 3.3 g; Carbohydrates 9.4 g; Sugar 3.4 g; Protein 3.2 g; Cholesterol 0 mg

Delicious Cauliflower Popcorn

Preparation Time: 10 minutes; Cooking Time: 12 hours; Serve: 2
Ingredients:
- 2 cups cauliflower florets
- 1 tbsp nutritional yeast
- 1 tbsp olive oil
- Pinch of cayenne pepper
- Salt

Directions:
1. Add cauliflower florets into the mixing bowl. Add remaining ingredients over the cauliflower and toss well.
2. Place the cooking tray in the air fryer basket.
3. Arrange cauliflower florets in the air fryer basket.
4. Select Dehydrate mode.
5. Set time to 12 hours and temperature 115 F then press START.
6. Store in an airtight container.

Nutritional Value (Amount per Serving):
Calories 103; Fat 7.7 g; Carbohydrates 7.7 g; Sugar 2.4 g; Protein 4.3 g; Cholesterol 0 mg

Chili Lime Cauliflower Popcorn

Preparation Time: 10 minutes; Cooking Time: 12 hours; Serve: 4
Ingredients:
- 1 large cauliflower head, cut into florets
- 1 tbsp chili powder
- 1 tbsp olive oil
- 1 lime juice
- 1 tsp sea salt

Directions:
1. Add cauliflower florets into the mixing bowl. Add remaining ingredients and toss well.
2. Place the cooking tray in the air fryer basket.
3. Arrange cauliflower florets in the air fryer basket.
4. Select Dehydrate mode.
5. Set time to 12 hours and temperature 135 F then press START.
6. Store in an airtight container.

Nutritional Value (Amount per Serving):
Calories 39; Fat 3.8 g; Carbohydrates 2 g; Sugar 0.3 g; Protein 0.3 g; Cholesterol 0 mg

Healthy Dehydrated Almonds

Preparation Time: 10 minutes; Cooking Time: 18 hours; Serve: 4
Ingredients:
- 1 cup of raw almonds
- 2 cups of water
- 1 tbsp salt

Directions:
1. Add almonds, water, and salt into the bowl. Cover and soak almonds for 24 hours. Drain well.
2. Place the cooking tray in the air fryer basket.
3. Arrange almonds in the air fryer basket.
4. Select Dehydrate mode.
5. Set time to 18 hours and temperature 115 F then press START.
6. Store in an airtight container.

Nutritional Value (Amount per Serving):
Calories 137; Fat 11.9 g; Carbohydrates 5.1 g; Sugar 1 g; Protein 5 g; Cholesterol 0 mg

Radish Chips

Preparation Time: 10 minutes; Cooking Time: 5 hours; Serve: 4
Ingredients:
- 3 radishes, cut into 1/8-inch thick slices
- Salt

Directions:
1. Place the cooking tray in the air fryer basket.
2. Arrange radish slices in the air fryer basket. Sprinkle salt over radish slices.
3. Select Dehydrate mode.
4. Set time to 5 hours and temperature 125 F then press START.
5. Store in an airtight container.

Nutritional Value (Amount per Serving):
Calories 1; Fat 0 g; Carbohydrates 0.1 g; Sugar 0.1 g; Protein 0.1 g; Cholesterol 0 mg

Orange Slices

Preparation Time: 10 minutes; Cooking Time: 7 hours; Serve: 2
Ingredients:
- 2 oranges, cut into 1/4-inch thick slices

Directions:
1. Place the cooking tray in the air fryer basket.
2. Arrange orange slices in the air fryer basket.
3. Select Dehydrate mode.
4. Set time to 7 hours and temperature 135 F then press START.
5. Store in an airtight container.

Nutritional Value (Amount per Serving):
Calories 50; Fat 0.2 g; Carbohydrates 12.3 g; Sugar 0 g; Protein 1 g; Cholesterol 0 mg

Dehydrated Bell Peppers

Preparation Time: 10 minutes; Cooking Time: 8 hours; Serve: 3
Ingredients:
- 3 bell peppers, remove seeds & cut into slices

Directions:
1. Place the cooking tray in the air fryer basket.
2. Arrange bell pepper slices in the air fryer basket.
3. Select Dehydrate mode.
4. Set time to 8 hours and temperature 125 F then press START.
5. Store in an airtight container.

Nutritional Value (Amount per Serving):
Calories 38; Fat 0.3 g; Carbohydrates 9 g; Sugar 6 g; Protein 1.2 g; Cholesterol 0 mg

Dried Raspberries

Preparation Time: 10 minutes; Cooking Time: 8 hours; Serve: 4
Ingredients:
- 2 cups raspberries, cut in half

Directions:
1. Place the cooking tray in the air fryer basket.
2. Arrange raspberries in the air fryer basket.
3. Select Dehydrate mode.
4. Set time to 8 hours and temperature 135 F then press START.
5. Store in an airtight container.

Nutritional Value (Amount per Serving):
Calories 32; Fat 0.4 g; Carbohydrates 7.3 g; Sugar 2.7 g; Protein 0.7 g; Cholesterol 0 mg

Brussels Sprout Chips

Preparation Time: 10 minutes; Cooking Time: 10 hours; Serve: 4

Ingredients:
- 1 lb Brussel sprouts, cut the stem and separate leaves
- 1 tsp soy sauce
- 2 tbsp sriracha
- Pinch of salt

Directions:
1. In a mixing bowl, toss Brussel sprouts with soy sauce, sriracha, and salt.
2. Place the cooking tray in the air fryer basket.
3. Arrange Brussels sprouts in the air fryer basket.
4. Select Dehydrate mode.
5. Set time to 10 hours and temperature 115 F then press START.
6. Store in airtight container.

Nutritional Value (Amount per Serving):
Calories 78; Fat 1 g; Carbohydrates 11.6 g; Sugar 4 g; Protein 4.1 g; Cholesterol 5 mg

Dehydrated Carrot Slices

Preparation Time: 10 minutes; Cooking Time: 6 hours; Serve: 4

Ingredients:
- 2 carrots, peel & 1/8-inch thick slices

Directions:
1. Place the cooking tray in the air fryer basket.
2. Arrange carrot slices in the air fryer basket.
3. Select Dehydrate mode.
4. Set time to 6 hours and temperature 125 F then press START.
5. Store in an airtight container.

Nutritional Value (Amount per Serving):
Calories 13; Fat 0 g; Carbohydrates 3 g; Sugar 1.5 g; Protein 0.3 g; Cholesterol 0 mg

Dried Apricots

Preparation Time: 10 minutes; Cooking Time: 20 hours; Serve: 12

Ingredients:
- 12 apricots, cut in half & remove pits
- 4 cups of water
- 1 cup lemon juice

Directions:
1. In a large bowl, add water and lemon juice. Add apricots.
2. Remove apricots from water and pat dry.
3. Arrange apricots in the air fryer basket.
4. Select Dehydrate mode.
5. Set time to 20 hours and temperature 135 F then press START.
6. Store in an airtight container.

Nutritional Value (Amount per Serving):
Calories 22; Fat 0.4 g; Carbohydrates 4.3 g; Sugar 3.6 g; Protein 0.6 g; Cholesterol 0 mg

Coconut Peanut Butter Balls

Preparation Time: 10 minutes; Cooking Time: 12 hours; Serve: 5

Ingredients:

- 2/3 cups peanut butter
- 1 tsp vanilla
- 2 cups dried apples, chopped
- 2 cups shredded coconut

Directions:
1. Add all ingredients into the large bowl and mix until well combined.
2. Place the cooking tray in the air fryer basket.
3. Make 1-inch balls from mixture and place in the air fryer basket.
4. Select Dehydrate mode.
5. Set time to 12 hours and temperature 135 F then press START.
6. Store in an airtight container.

Nutritional Value (Amount per Serving):
Calories 113; Fat 10.7 g; Carbohydrates 5.1 g; Sugar 2 g; Protein 1.7 g; Cholesterol 0 mg

Parmesan Tomato Chips

Preparation Time: 10 minutes; Cooking Time: 8 hours; Serve: 6

Ingredients:
- 8 tomatoes, cut into 1/4-inch thick slices
- 1/2 tsp oregano
- 1/2 tsp pepper
- 1/2 tsp basil
- 1/4 cup parmesan cheese, grated
- 1/2 tsp salt

Directions:
1. Place the cooking tray in the air fryer basket.
2. Arrange tomato slices in the air fryer basket. Sprinkle cheese over tomato slices and season with oregano, pepper, basil, and salt.
3. Select Dehydrate mode.
4. Set time to 8 hours and temperature 155 F then press START.
5. Store in an airtight container.

Nutritional Value (Amount per Serving):
Calories 61; Fat 2.4 g; Carbohydrates 6.9 g; Sugar 4.3 g; Protein 4.6 g; Cholesterol 7 mg

Spicy Rosemary Almonds

Preparation Time: 10 minutes; Cooking Time: 24 hours; Serve: 6

Ingredients:
- 2 cups almonds, soak in water for overnight
- 1 tbsp fresh rosemary, chopped
- 1 tsp chili powder
- 1 tbsp olive oil
- 3/4 tsp kosher salt

Directions:
1. Add all ingredients into the mixing bowl and toss well.
2. Place the cooking tray in the air fryer basket.
3. Spread almonds in the air fryer basket.
4. Select Dehydrate mode.
5. Set time to 24 hours and temperature 125 F then press START.
6. Store in an airtight container.

Nutritional Value (Amount per Serving):
Calories 206; Fat 18.3 g; Carbohydrates 7.4 g; Sugar 1.4 g; Protein 6.8 g; Cholesterol 0 mg

Dehydrated Raspberries

Preparation Time: 10 minutes; Cooking Time: 18 hours; Serve: 4

Ingredients:
- 4 cups raspberries, wash and dry
- 1/4 cup fresh lemon juice

Directions:

1. Add raspberries and lemon juice in a bowl and mix well.
2. Place the cooking tray in the air fryer basket.
3. Arrange raspberries in the air fryer basket.
4. Select Dehydrate mode.
5. Set time to 18 hours and temperature 135 F then press START.
6. Store in an airtight container.

Nutritional Value (Amount per Serving):
Calories 12.3; Fat 0.1 g; Carbohydrates 12.3 g; Sugar 6.3 g; Protein 2.1 g; Cholesterol 0 mg

Lemon Avocado Chips

Preparation Time: 10 minutes; Cooking Time: 10 hours; Serve: 4

Ingredients:
- 4 avocados, halved and pitted
- 1/4 tsp cayenne pepper
- 1/2 lemon juice
- 1/4 tsp sea salt

Directions:
1. Cut avocado into the slices.
2. Drizzle lemon juice over avocado slices.
3. Place the cooking tray in the air fryer basket.
4. Arrange avocado slices in the air fryer basket. Sprinkle cayenne pepper and salt over avocado slices.
5. Select Dehydrate mode.
6. Set time to 10 hours and temperature 160 F then press START.
7. Store in an airtight container.

Nutritional Value (Amount per Serving):
Calories 62; Fat 5.1 g; Carbohydrates 3.2 g; Sugar 0.1 g; Protein 1.1 g; Cholesterol 0 mg

Squash Chips

Preparation Time: 10 minutes; Cooking Time: 12 hours; Serve: 8

Ingredients:
- 1 yellow squash, cut into 1/8-inch thick slices
- 2 tsp olive oil
- 2 tbsp vinegar
- Salt

Directions:
1. Add all ingredients into the bowl and toss well.
2. Place the cooking tray in the air fryer basket.
3. Arrange squash slices in the air fryer basket.
4. Select Dehydrate mode.
5. Set time to 12 hours and temperature 115 F then press START.
6. Store in an airtight container.

Nutritional Value (Amount per Serving):
Calories 15; Fat 1.2 g; Carbohydrates 0.9 g; Sugar 0.4 g; Protein 0.3 g; Cholesterol 0 mg

Smokey Tofu Jerky

Preparation Time: 10 minutes; Cooking Time: 4 hours; Serve: 4

Ingredients:
- 1 block tofu, pressed & Cut in half then cut into the slices
- 2 tbsp Worcestershire sauce
- 2 tbsp sriracha
- 4 drops liquid smoke

Directions:

1. In a bowl, mix together liquid smoke, sriracha, and Worcestershire sauce. Add tofu slices in a bowl and mix until well coated.
2. Cover bowl and place in the refrigerator overnight.
3. Place the cooking tray in the air fryer basket.
4. Arrange marinated tofu slices in the air fryer basket.
5. Select Dehydrate mode.
6. Set time to 4 hours and temperature 145 F then press START.
7. Store in an airtight container.

Nutritional Value (Amount per Serving):
Calories 31; Fat 1 g; Carbohydrates 3.4 g; Sugar 1.6 g; Protein 1.9 g; Cholesterol 0 mg

Lemon Chicken Jerky

Preparation Time: 10 minutes; Cooking Time: 7 hours; Serve: 4
Ingredients:
- 1 1/2 lb chicken tenders, boneless, skinless and cut into 1/4-inch slices
- 1/4 tsp ground ginger
- 1/4 tsp black pepper
- 1/2 tsp garlic powder
- 1 tsp lemon juice
- 1/2 cup soy sauce

Directions:
1. Mix all ingredients except chicken into the zip-lock bag.
2. Add chicken slices, seal bag and place in the refrigerator for 30 minutes.
3. Place the cooking tray in the air fryer basket.
4. Arrange marinated chicken slices in the air fryer basket.
5. Select Dehydrate mode.
6. Set time to 7 hours and temperature 145 F then press START.
7. Store in an airtight container.

Nutritional Value (Amount per Serving):
Calories 342; Fat 12.6 g; Carbohydrates 2.9 g; Sugar 0.7 g; Protein 51.3 g; Cholesterol 151 mg

Parmesan Zucchini Chips

Preparation Time: 10 minutes; Cooking Time: 10 hours; Serve: 2
Ingredients:
- 1 zucchini, sliced thinly
- 2 tbsp parmesan cheese, grated
- 1 tsp vinegar
- 1/8 tsp garlic powder
- Salt

Directions:
1. Add zucchini slices, parmesan cheese, vinegar, garlic powder, and salt into the bowl and toss well.
2. Place the cooking tray in the air fryer basket.
3. Arrange zucchini slices in the air fryer basket.
4. Select Dehydrate mode.
5. Set time to 10 hours and temperature 135 F then press START.
6. Store in an airtight container.

Nutritional Value (Amount per Serving):
Calories 35; Fat 1.4 g; Carbohydrates 3.6 g; Sugar 1.8 g; Protein 3 g; Cholesterol 4 mg

Chapter 10: Desserts Recipes

Protein Donut Balls

Preparation Time: 10 minutes; Cooking Time: 6 minutes; Serve: 16
Ingredients:
- 3 eggs
- 2 tbsp coconut oil
- 1/2 tsp lemon zest, grated
- 1 1/2 tsp apple pie spice
- 1 tsp baking powder
- 1 tbsp coconut flour
- 3 scoops vanilla protein powder

Directions:
1. In a large bowl, mix together protein powder, apple pie spice, baking powder, and coconut flour.
2. Add lemon zest, eggs, and coconut oil and mix until kneadable dough is forms.
3. Place the dough onto a clean surface and knead for 10 seconds.
4. Divide dough into the sixteen pieces and roll into balls.
5. Place the cooking tray in the air fryer basket. Place piece of parchment paper into the air fryer basket.
6. Select Air Fry mode.
7. Set time to 6 minutes and temperature 350 F then press START.
8. The air fryer display will prompt you to ADD FOOD once the temperature is reached then place dough balls onto the parchment paper in the air fryer basket.
9. Serve and enjoy.

Nutritional Value (Amount per Serving):
Calories 50; Fat 2.6 g; Carbohydrates 0.7 g; Sugar 0.1 g; Protein 6.2 g; Cholesterol 31 mg

Delicious Brownie Cupcake

Preparation Time: 10 minutes; Cooking Time: 15 minutes; Serve: 6
Ingredients:
- 3 eggs
- 1/3 cup butter, melted
- 1/3 cup unsweetened cocoa powder
- 1/2 cup erythritol
- 1 cup almond flour
- 1 tbsp gelatin

Directions:
1. Add all ingredients into the bowl and stir until just combined.
2. Pour batter into the silicone muffin molds.
3. Select Bake mode.
4. Set time to 15 minutes and temperature 350 F then press START.
5. The air fryer display will prompt you to ADD FOOD once the temperature is reached then place muffin molds in the air fryer basket.
6. Serve and enjoy.

Nutritional Value (Amount per Serving):
Calories 163; Fat 15.4 g; Carbohydrates 3.8 g; Sugar 0.4 g; Protein 5.8 g; Cholesterol 109 mg

Vanilla Cranberry Muffins

Preparation Time: 10 minutes; Cooking Time: 30 minutes; Serve: 6
Ingredients:
- 2 eggs
- 1 tsp vanilla
- 1/4 cup sour cream
- 1/2 cup cranberries
- 1/4 tsp cinnamon
- 1 tsp baking powder
- 1/4 cup Swerve
- 1 1/2 cups almond flour
- Pinch of salt

Directions:
1. In a bowl, whisk sour cream, vanilla, and eggs.
2. Add remaining ingredients except for cranberries and beat until smooth. Add cranberries and fold well.
3. Pour batter into the silicone muffin molds.
4. Select Bake mode.
5. Set time to 30 minutes and temperature 325 F then press START.
6. The air fryer display will prompt you to ADD FOOD once the temperature is reached then place muffin molds in the air fryer basket.
7. Serve and enjoy.

Nutritional Value (Amount per Serving):
Calories 90; Fat 7 g; Carbohydrates 3.5 g; Sugar 0.8 g; Protein 3.7 g; Cholesterol 59 mg

Blueberry Almond Muffins

Preparation Time: 10 minutes; Cooking Time: 30 minutes; Serve: 12
Ingredients:
- 3 eggs
- 1/2 cup fresh blueberries
- 2 tsp baking powder
- 1/4 cup Erythritol
- 2 1/2 cups almond flour
- 5.5 oz Greek yogurt
- 1/2 tsp vanilla
- Pinch of salt

Directions:
1. In a bowl, whisk together yogurt, vanilla, eggs, and salt until smooth.
2. Add almond flour, baking powder, and sweetener and blend again until smooth.
3. Add blueberries and stir well.
4. Pour batter into the silicone muffin molds.
5. Select Bake mode.
6. Set time to 30 minutes and temperature 325 F then press START.
7. The air fryer display will prompt you to ADD FOOD once the temperature is reached then place muffin molds in the air fryer basket.
8. Serve and enjoy.

Nutritional Value (Amount per Serving):
Calories 64; Fat 4.3 g; Carbohydrates 3.1 g; Sugar 1.4 g; Protein 4 g; Cholesterol 42 mg

Lemon Cupcakes

Preparation Time: 10 minutes; Cooking Time: 15 minutes; Serve: 12
Ingredients:
- 2 eggs
- 1 cup almond flour
- 1/3 cup Erythritol
- 1 fresh lemon juice
- 1 tbsp lemon zest
- 1/3 cup butter, melted
- 1/2 cup yogurt
- 2 tbsp poppy seeds
- 1 tsp baking powder
- 1/4 cup coconut flour

Directions:
1. Add all ingredients into the mixing bowl and mix until well combined.
2. Pour batter into the silicone muffin molds.
3. Select Bake mode.
4. Set time to 15 minutes and temperature 350 F then press START.
5. The air fryer display will prompt you to ADD FOOD once the temperature is reached then place muffin molds in the air fryer basket.
6. Serve and enjoy.

Nutritional Value (Amount per Serving):

Calories 87; Fat 7.9 g; Carbohydrates 2.2 g; Sugar 1.2 g; Protein 2.4 g; Cholesterol 41 mg

Almond Lemon Bars

Preparation Time: 10 minutes; Cooking Time: 40 minutes; Serve: 8

Ingredients:
- 4 eggs
- 1/3 cup Swerve
- 1 lemon zest
- 1/4 cup fresh lemon juice
- 1/2 cup butter softened
- 1/2 cup sour cream
- 2 tsp baking powder
- 2 cups almond flour

Directions:
1. In a bowl, beat eggs until frothy.
2. Add butter and sour cream and beat until well combined.
3. Add sweetener, lemon zest, and lemon juice and blend well.
4. Add baking powder and almond flour and stir until well combined.
5. Pour batter into the parchment-lined baking dish.
6. Select Bake mode.
7. Set time to 40 minutes and temperature 350 F then press START.
8. The air fryer display will prompt you to ADD FOOD once the temperature is reached then place the baking dish in the air fryer basket.
9. Slice and serve.

Nutritional Value (Amount per Serving):
Calories 206; Fat 19.9 g; Carbohydrates 3.8 g; Sugar 0.8 g; Protein 5 g; Cholesterol 118 mg

Egg Custard

Preparation Time: 10 minutes; Cooking Time: 40 minutes; Serve: 6

Ingredients:
- 3 eggs
- 2 egg yolks
- 1 tsp vanilla
- 1/2 cup Swerve
- 2 cups heavy whipping cream

Directions:
1. Add all ingredients into the large bowl and beat until just well combined.
2. Pour custard mixture into the greased pie dish.
3. Select Bake mode.
4. Set time to 40 minutes and temperature 350 F then press START.
5. The air fryer display will prompt you to ADD FOOD once the temperature is reached then place the pie dish in the air fryer basket.
6. Place custard in the refrigerator for 2 hours.
7. Slice and serve.

Nutritional Value (Amount per Serving):
Calories 190; Fat 18.5 g; Carbohydrates 1.8 g; Sugar 0.3 g; Protein 4.5 g; Cholesterol 207 mg

Coconut Pumpkin Custard

Preparation Time: 10 minutes; Cooking Time: 40 minutes; Serve: 6

Ingredients:
- 4 egg yolks
- 1/2 tsp cinnamon
- 1 tsp liquid stevia
- 15 oz pumpkin puree
- 3/4 cup coconut cream
- 1/8 tsp cloves
- 1/8 tsp ginger

Directions:
1. In a large bowl, mix pumpkin puree, cloves, ginger, cinnamon, and sweetener.

2. Add egg yolks and beat until well combined. Add coconut cream and stir well.
3. Pour mixture into the six ramekins.
4. Select Bake mode.
5. Set time to 40 minutes and temperature 350 F then press START.
6. The air fryer display will prompt you to ADD FOOD once the temperature is reached then place ramekins in the air fryer basket.
7. Allow cooling completely then place in the refrigerator.
8. Serve and enjoy.

Nutritional Value (Amount per Serving):
Calories 130; Fat 10.4 g; Carbohydrates 8 g; Sugar 3.4 g; Protein 3.3 g; Cholesterol 140 mg

Vanilla Peanut Butter Cookies

Preparation Time: 10 minutes; Cooking Time: 12 minutes; Serve: 15
Ingredients:
- 1 egg
- 1 cup peanut butter
- 1 tsp vanilla
- 1/2 cup Swerve
- Pinch of salt

Directions:
1. Add all ingredients into the large bowl and mix until well combined.
2. Make cookies from the mixture.
3. Place the cooking tray in the air fryer basket. Line air fryer basket with parchment paper.
4. Select Bake mode.
5. Set time to 12 minutes and temperature 350 F then press START.
6. The air fryer display will prompt you to ADD FOOD once the temperature is reached then place cookies onto the parchment paper in the air fryer basket.
7. Serve and enjoy.

Nutritional Value (Amount per Serving):
Calories 106; Fat 8.9 g; Carbohydrates 3.5 g; Sugar 1.7 g; Protein 4.7 g; Cholesterol 11 mg

Pumpkin Cookies

Preparation Time: 10 minutes; Cooking Time: 25 minutes; Serve: 30
Ingredients:
- 1 egg
- 2 cups almond flour
- 1/2 tsp baking powder
- 1 tsp vanilla
- 1/2 cup butter
- 1 tsp liquid stevia
- 1/2 tsp pumpkin pie spice
- 1/2 cup pumpkin puree

Directions:
1. In a large bowl, add all ingredients and mix until well combined.
2. Make cookies from the mixture.
3. Place the cooking tray in the air fryer basket. Line air fryer basket with parchment paper.
4. Select Bake mode.
5. Set time to 25 minutes and temperature 300 F then press START.
6. The air fryer display will prompt you to ADD FOOD once the temperature is reached then place some cookies onto the parchment paper in the air fryer basket. Bake cookies in batches.
7. Serve and enjoy.

Nutritional Value (Amount per Serving):
Calories 42; Fat 4.2 g; Carbohydrates 0.8 g; Sugar 0.2 g; Protein 0.7 g; Cholesterol 14 mg

Almond Pecan Cookies

Preparation Time: 10 minutes; Cooking Time: 20 minutes; Serve: 16
Ingredients:
- 1 1/3 cup almond flour
- 1 cup pecans
- 1/2 cup butter
- 2/3 cup erythritol
- 1 tsp vanilla
- 2 tsp gelatin

Directions:
1. Add butter, vanilla, gelatin, sweetener, and almond flour into the food processor and process until crumbs form.
2. Add pecans and process until chopped.
3. Make cookies from the mixture.
4. Place the cooking tray in the air fryer basket. Line air fryer basket with parchment paper.
5. Select Bake mode.
6. Set time to 20 minutes and temperature 350 F then press START.
7. The air fryer display will prompt you to ADD FOOD once the temperature is reached then place cookies onto the parchment paper in the air fryer basket.
8. Serve and enjoy.

Nutritional Value (Amount per Serving):
Calories 115; Fat 11.8 g; Carbohydrates 1.5 g; Sugar 0.4 g; Protein 2 g; Cholesterol 15 mg

Vanilla Coconut Cake

Preparation Time: 10 minutes; Cooking Time: 20 minutes; Serve: 8
Ingredients:
- 5 eggs, separated
- 1/2 cup Swerve
- 1/4 cup unsweetened coconut milk
- 1/2 cup coconut flour
- 1/2 tsp baking powder
- 1/2 tsp vanilla
- 1/2 cup butter softened
- Pinch of salt

Directions:
1. In a bowl, beat sweetener and butter until combined.
2. Add egg yolks, coconut milk, and vanilla and mix well.
3. Add baking powder, coconut flour, and salt and stir well.
4. In a separate bowl, beat egg whites until stiff peak forms. Slowly fold egg whites into the cake mixture.
5. Pour batter into the greased baking dish.
6. Select Bake mode.
7. Set time to 20 minutes and temperature 400 F then press START.
8. The air fryer display will prompt you to ADD FOOD once the temperature is reached then place the baking dish in the air fryer basket.
9. Slice and serve.

Nutritional Value (Amount per Serving):
Calories 190; Fat 17 g; Carbohydrates 5 g; Sugar 1 g; Protein 4.8 g; Cholesterol 133 mg

Choco Almond Cake

Preparation Time: 10 minutes; Cooking Time: 20 minutes; Serve: 8
Ingredients:
- 2 eggs
- 1/2 cup almond flour
- 1/2 cup butter, melted
- 1 tsp vanilla
- 1/4 cup unsweetened cocoa powder
- 3/4 cup Erythritol
- Pinch of salt

Directions:

1. In a bowl, mix together almond flour, cocoa powder, and salt.
2. In a separate bowl, whisk eggs, vanilla extract, and sweetener until creamy.
3. Slowly fold the almond flour mixture into the egg mixture and stir to combine. Add melted butter and stir well.
4. Pour batter into the greased 8-inch baking dish.
5. Select Bake mode.
6. Set time to 20 minutes and temperature 350 F then press START.
7. The air fryer display will prompt you to ADD FOOD once the temperature is reached then place the baking dish in the air fryer basket.
8. Slice and serve.

Nutritional Value (Amount per Serving):
Calories 135; Fat 13.9 g; Carbohydrates 2 g; Sugar 0.3 g; Protein 2.4 g; Cholesterol 71 mg

Butter Cake

Preparation Time: 10 minutes; Cooking Time: 35 minutes; Serve: 8
Ingredients:
- 5 eggs
- 6.5 oz almond flour
- 1/2 cup butter, softened
- 4 oz cream cheese, softened
- 1 tsp baking powder
- 1 tsp vanilla extract
- 1 cup Erythritol

Directions:
1. Add all ingredients into the mixing bowl and whisk until batter is smooth.
2. Pour batter into the greased 9-inch baking dish.
3. Select Bake mode.
4. Set time to 35 minutes and temperature 350 F then press START.
5. The air fryer display will prompt you to ADD FOOD once the temperature is reached then place the baking dish in the air fryer basket.
6. Slices and serve.

Nutritional Value (Amount per Serving):
Calories 323; Fat 30.6 g; Carbohydrates 5.9 g; Sugar 1.1 g; Protein 9.5 g; Cholesterol 148 mg

Walnut Carrot Cake

Preparation Time: 10 minutes; Cooking Time: 35 minutes; Serve: 16
Ingredients:
- 2 eggs
- 1/2 cup carrots, grated
- 1/8 tsp ground cloves
- 1 tsp cinnamon
- 1 tsp baking powder
- 2 tbsp butter, melted
- 1/4 cup walnuts, chopped
- 6 tbsp erythritol
- 3/4 cup almond flour
- 2 tbsp unsweetened shredded coconut
- 1/2 tsp vanilla
- Pinch of salt

Directions:
1. In a large bowl, mix together almond flour, cloves, cinnamon, baking powder, shredded coconut, nuts, sweetener, and salt.
2. Stir in eggs, vanilla, butter, and shredded coconut until well combined.
3. Pour batter into the greased baking dish.
4. Select Bake mode.
5. Set time to 35 minutes and temperature 325 F then press START.
6. The air fryer display will prompt you to ADD FOOD once the temperature is reached then place the baking dish in the air fryer basket.
7. Slice and serve.

Nutritional Value (Amount per Serving):
Calories 51; Fat 4.6 g; Carbohydrates 1.5 g; Sugar 0.4 g; Protein 1.6 g; Cholesterol 24 mg

Chocolate Brownies

Preparation Time: 10 minutes; Cooking Time: 40 minutes; Serve: 12
Ingredients:
- 3 eggs
- 3/4 cup unsweetened cocoa powder
- 1 1/4 cups almond flour
- 1 cup coconut oil, melted
- 1 tsp vanilla
- 1/2 tsp vinegar
- 1/2 cup unsweetened almond milk
- 3/4 cup Swerve
- 1/2 cup walnuts, chopped
- 2 tbsp proteins collagen
- 1/4 tsp baking soda
- Pinch of salt

Directions:
1. Add eggs, vanilla, vinegar, milk, and swerve into the large bowl and blend with a hand mixer for 2-3 minutes.
2. In a separate bowl, whisk together coconut oil, protein collagen, baking soda, cocoa powder, almond flour, and salt until combined.
3. Add egg mixture and stir until well combined.
4. Add walnuts and fold well.
5. Pour batter into the greased 8*8-inch baking dish.
6. Select Bake mode.
7. Set time to 40 minutes and temperature 350 F then press START.
8. The air fryer display will prompt you to ADD FOOD once the temperature is reached then place the baking dish in the air fryer basket.
9. Slice and serve.

Nutritional Value (Amount per Serving):
Calories 241; Fat 24.7 g; Carbohydrates 4.4 g; Sugar 0.4 g; Protein 5.5 g; Cholesterol 41 mg

Walnut Muffins

Preparation Time: 10 minutes; Cooking Time: 15 minutes; Serve: 12
Ingredients:
- 4 eggs
- 1/2 cup walnuts, chopped
- 1 1/2 cups almond flour
- 1 tsp vanilla
- 1/4 cup unsweetened almond milk
- 2 tbsp butter, melted
- 1/2 cup Swerve
- 1 tsp psyllium husk
- 1/2 tsp ground cinnamon
- 2 tsp allspice
- 1 tbsp baking powder

Directions:
1. Beat eggs, almond milk, vanilla, sweetener, and butter in a bowl using a hand blender until smooth.
2. Add remaining ingredients and stir until well combined.
3. Pour batter into silicone muffin molds.
4. Select Bake mode.
5. Set time to 15 minutes and temperature 400 F then press START.
6. The air fryer display will prompt you to ADD FOOD once the temperature is reached then place muffin molds in the air fryer basket.
7. Serve and enjoy.

Nutritional Value (Amount per Serving):
Calories 97; Fat 8.3 g; Carbohydrates 3.4 g; Sugar 0.3 g; Protein 3.9 g; Cholesterol 60 mg

Cinnamon Strawberry Muffins

Preparation Time: 10 minutes; Cooking Time: 20 minutes; Serve: 12

Ingredients:
- 3 eggs
- 2/3 cup strawberries, diced
- 1 tsp cinnamon
- 2 tsp baking powder
- 2 1/2 cups almond flour
- 1/3 cup heavy cream
- 1 tsp vanilla
- 1/2 cup Swerve
- 5 tbsp butter, melted
- 1/4 tsp Himalayan salt

Directions:
1. In a bowl, beat together butter and swerve. Add eggs, cream, and vanilla and beat until frothy.
2. Sift together almond flour, cinnamon, baking powder, and salt.
3. Add almond flour mixture to the wet ingredients and mix until well combined. Add strawberries and fold well.
4. Pour batter into the silicone muffin molds.
5. Select Bake mode.
6. Set time to 20 minutes and temperature 350 F then press START.
7. The air fryer display will prompt you to ADD FOOD once the temperature is reached then place muffin molds in the air fryer basket.
8. Serve and enjoy.

Nutritional Value (Amount per Serving):
Calories 108; Fat 10.1 g; Carbohydrates 2.7 g; Sugar 0.7 g; Protein 2.8 g; Cholesterol 58 mg

Cream Cheese Cupcakes

Preparation Time: 10 minutes; Cooking Time: 20 minutes; Serve: 10

Ingredients:
- 2 eggs
- 8 oz cream cheese
- 1/2 tsp vanilla extract
- 1/2 cup Swerve

Directions:
1. In a bowl, mix together cream cheese, vanilla, Swerve, and eggs until soft.
2. Pour batter into the silicone muffin molds
3. Select Air Fry mode.
4. Set time to 20 minutes and temperature 350 F then press START.
5. The air fryer display will prompt you to ADD FOOD once the temperature is reached then place muffin molds in the air fryer basket.
6. Serve and enjoy.

Nutritional Value (Amount per Serving):
Calories 93; Fat 8.8 g; Carbohydrates 0.8 g; Sugar 0.2 g; Protein 2.8 g; Cholesterol 58 mg

Quick Brownie

Preparation Time: 10 minutes; Cooking Time: 10 minutes; Serve: 1

Ingredients:
- 1 scoop chocolate protein powder
- 1 tbsp unsweetened cocoa powder
- 1/2 tsp baking powder
- 1/4 cup unsweetened almond milk

Directions:
1. In a ramekin mix together baking powder, protein powder, and cocoa powder.
2. Add milk stir well.
3. Select Ai Fry mode.
4. Set time to 10 minutes and temperature 390 F then press START.

5. The air fryer display will prompt you to ADD FOOD once the temperature is reached then place the ramekin in the air fryer basket.
   6. Serve and enjoy.

Nutritional Value (Amount per Serving):
Calories 80; Fat 2.4 g; Carbohydrates 6.6 g; Sugar 1.1 g; Protein 11.3 g; Cholesterol 20 mg

Tasty Pumpkin Muffins

Preparation Time: 10 minutes; Cooking Time: 25 minutes; Serve: 10
Ingredients:
- 4 large eggs
- 1/2 cup pumpkin puree
- 1 tbsp pumpkin pie spice
- 1 tbsp gluten-free baking powder
- 2/3 cup Swerve
- 1 tsp vanilla extract
- 1/3 cup coconut oil, melted
- 1/2 cup almond flour
- 1/2 cup coconut flour
- 1/2 tsp sea salt

Directions:
1. In a large bowl, stir together coconut flour, pumpkin pie spice, baking powder, erythritol, almond flour, and sea salt.
2. Stir in eggs, vanilla, coconut oil, and pumpkin puree until well combined.
3. Pour batter into the silicone muffin molds.
4. Select Bake mode.
5. Set time to 25 minutes and temperature 350 F then press START.
6. The air fryer display will prompt you to ADD FOOD once the temperature is reached then place muffin molds in the air fryer basket.
7. Serve and enjoy.

Nutritional Value (Amount per Serving):
Calories 111; Fat 10.2 g; Carbohydrates 2.7 g; Sugar 0.7 g; Protein 3.1 g; Cholesterol 74 mg

Cappuccino Cupcakes

Preparation Time: 10 minutes; Cooking Time: 25 minutes; Serve: 12
Ingredients:
- 4 eggs
- 2 cups almond flour
- 1/2 tsp vanilla
- 1 tsp espresso powder
- 1/2 cup sour cream
- 1 tsp cinnamon
- 2 tsp baking powder
- 1/4 cup coconut flour
- 1/2 cup Swerve
- 1/4 tsp salt

Directions:
1. Add sour cream, vanilla, espresso powder, and eggs in a blender and blend until smooth.
2. Add almond flour, cinnamon, baking powder, coconut flour, sweetener, and salt. Blend again until smooth.
3. Pour mixture into the silicone muffin molds.
4. Select Bake mode.
5. Set time to 25 minutes and temperature 350 F then press START.
6. The air fryer display will prompt you to ADD FOOD once the temperature is reached then place muffin molds in the air fryer basket.
7. Serve and enjoy.

Nutritional Value (Amount per Serving):
Calories 71; Fat 5.8 g; Carbohydrates 2.3 g; Sugar 0.3 g; Protein 3.2 g; Cholesterol 59 mg

Lemon Blueberry Muffins

Preparation Time: 10 minutes; Cooking Time: 25 minutes; Serve: 12

Ingredients:
- 2 large eggs
- 1/2 cup fresh blueberries
- 1 tsp baking powder
- 5 drops stevia
- 1/4 cup butter, melted
- 1/4 tsp lemon zest
- 1/2 tsp lemon extract
- 1 cup heavy whipping cream
- 2 cups almond flour

Directions:
1. Add eggs to the mixing bowl and whisk until good mix.
2. Add remaining ingredients to the eggs and mix well to combine.
3. Pour batter into the silicone muffin molds.
4. Select Bake mode.
5. Set time to 25 minutes and temperature 350 F then press START.
6. The air fryer display will prompt you to ADD FOOD once the temperature is reached then place muffin molds in the air fryer basket.
7. Serve and enjoy.

Nutritional Value (Amount per Serving):
Calories 111; Fat 10.7 g; Carbohydrates 2.4 g; Sugar 0.9 g; Protein 2.4 g; Cholesterol 55 mg

Almond Butter Brownies

Preparation Time: 10 minutes; Cooking Time: 20 minutes; Serve: 4

Ingredients:
- 1 scoop vanilla protein powder
- 2 tbsp unsweetened cocoa powder
- 1 tsp vanilla
- 1/2 cup almond butter
- 1 cup ripe bananas

Directions:
1. Add all ingredients into the blender and blend until smooth.
2. Pour batter into the greased baking dish.
3. Select Bake mode.
4. Set time to 20 minutes and temperature 350 F then press START.
5. The air fryer display will prompt you to ADD FOOD once the temperature is reached then place the baking dish in the air fryer basket.
6. Slice and serve.

Nutritional Value (Amount per Serving):
Calories 83; Fat 1.6 g; Carbohydrates 10.7 g; Sugar 4.9 g; Protein 8.1 g; Cholesterol 0 mg

Choco Butter Brownie

Preparation Time: 10 minutes; Cooking Time: 20 minutes; Serve: 12

Ingredients:
- 2 eggs
- 1/2 tsp baking soda
- 2 tbsp unsweetened cocoa powder
- 1/4 cup Swerve
- 1/2 cup almond flour
- 1/2 cup peanut butter
- 2 tsp vanilla
- 1/3 cup coconut oil, melted

Directions:
1. In a bowl, mix together all dry ingredients.
2. Add remaining ingredients to the bowl and mix until well combined.
3. Pour batter into the greased 8*8-inch baking dish.
4. Select Bake mode.
5. Set time to 20 minutes and temperature 350 F then press START.
6. The air fryer display will prompt you to ADD FOOD once the temperature is reached then place the baking dish in the air fryer basket.

7. Serve and enjoy.

Nutritional Value (Amount per Serving):
Calories 137; Fat 12.9 g; Carbohydrates 3.1 g; Sugar 1.2 g; Protein 4 g; Cholesterol 27 mg

Almond Cake

Preparation Time: 10 minutes; Cooking Time: 40 minutes; Serve: 16

Ingredients:
- 4 eggs
- 1 tsp baking powder
- 1 1/2 cup almond flour
- 1/3 cup Erythritol
- 2 oz cream cheese, softened
- 2 tbsp butter
- 4 oz half and half
- 2 tsp vanilla
- Pinch of salt
- For topping:
- 1/3 cup Erythritol
- 6 tbsp butter, melted
- 1 cup almonds, toasted and sliced
- 1 cup almond flour

Directions:
1. Add all ingredients except topping ingredients into the large mixing bowl and mix with an electric mixer.
2. Pour batter into the greased 8-inch baking dish.
3. Mix together all topping ingredients.
4. Sprinkle topping mixture evenly on top of batter.
5. Select Bake mode.
6. Set time to 40 minutes and temperature 350 F then press START.
7. The air fryer display will prompt you to ADD FOOD once the temperature is reached then place the baking dish in the air fryer basket.
8. Slices and serve.

Nutritional Value (Amount per Serving):
Calories 149; Fat 14.1 g; Carbohydrates 2.9 g; Sugar 0.6 g; Protein 4.1 g; Cholesterol 63 mg

Ricotta Cake

Preparation Time: 10 minutes; Cooking Time: 55 minutes; Serve: 8

Ingredients:
- 4 eggs
- 1 fresh lemon zest
- 2 tbsp stevia
- 18 oz ricotta
- 1 fresh lemon juice

Directions:
1. In a large mixing bowl, whisk the ricotta with an electric mixer until smooth. Add egg one by one and whisk well.
2. Add lemon juice, lemon zest, and stevia and mix well.
3. Transfer mixture into the greased baking dish.
4. Select Bake mode.
5. Set time to 55 minutes and temperature 350 F then press START.
6. The air fryer display will prompt you to ADD FOOD once the temperature is reached then place the baking dish in the air fryer basket.
7. Place cake in the refrigerator for 1-2 hours.
8. Slice and serve.

Nutritional Value (Amount per Serving):
Calories 123; Fat 7.3 g; Carbohydrates 4.3 g; Sugar 0.7 g; Protein 10.2 g; Cholesterol 102 mg

Almond Brownie Bombs

Preparation Time: 10 minutes; Cooking Time: 20 minutes; Serve: 12

Ingredients:
- 3 eggs
- 3/4 cup Erythritol
- 1/2 cup almond flour
- 2 oz unsweetened chocolate
- 3/4 cup butter, softened
- 1/2 tsp baking powder
- 1/4 cup unsweetened cocoa powder

Directions:
1. Add dark chocolate and butter in a microwave-safe bowl and microwave for 30 seconds.
2. In a separate bowl, mix together almond flour, baking powder, cocoa powder, and swerve.
3. In a large bowl, beat eggs.
4. Slowly add chocolate and butter mixture and mix well.
5. Add dry ingredients mixture and mix until well combined.
6. Pour batter into the greased baking dish
7. Select Bake mode.
8. Set time to 20 minutes and temperature 350 F then press START.
9. The air fryer display will prompt you to ADD FOOD once the temperature is reached then place the baking dish in the air fryer basket.
10. Slice and serve.

Nutritional Value (Amount per Serving):
Calories 152; Fat 15.9 g; Carbohydrates 2.8 g; Sugar 0.2 g; Protein 2.7 g; Cholesterol 71 mg

Cinnamon Nut Muffins

Preparation Time: 10 minutes; Cooking Time: 15 minutes; Serve: 12

Ingredients:
- 4 eggs
- 1/4 cup walnuts, chopped
- 1/2 tsp ground cinnamon
- 2 tsp allspice
- 2 tbsp butter, melted
- 1/2 cup Swerve
- 1 tsp psyllium husk
- 1 tbsp baking powder
- 1 1/2 cups almond flour
- 1 tsp vanilla
- 1/4 cup unsweetened almond milk
- 1/4 cup pecans, chopped

Directions:
1. Beat eggs, almond milk, vanilla, sweetener, and butter in a mixing bowl using a hand mixer until smooth.
2. Add remaining ingredients and mix until well combined.
3. Pour batter into silicone muffin molds.
4. Select Bake mode.
5. Set time to 15 minutes and temperature 400 F then press START.
6. The air fryer display will prompt you to ADD FOOD once the temperature is reached then place muffin molds in the air fryer basket.
7. Serve and enjoy.

Nutritional Value (Amount per Serving):
Calories 95; Fat 8.3 g; Carbohydrates 3.4 g; Sugar 0.4 g; Protein 3.5 g; Cholesterol 60 mg

Easy Berry Muffins

Preparation Time: 10 minutes; Cooking Time: 30 minutes; Serve: 12

Ingredients:
- 4 eggs
- 1/2 cup cranberries
- 1/2 cup blueberries
- 2 tsp baking powder
- 1/2 cup sour cream
- 1/2 cup Swerve
- 3 cups almond flour
- 1 tsp vanilla
- 1/4 tsp salt

Directions:
1. Add eggs, vanilla, and sour cream into the blender and blend for 30 seconds.
2. Add baking powder, sweetener, and almond flour and blend until smooth.
3. Add berries and stir well.
4. Spoon mixture into the silicone muffin molds.
5. Select Bake mode.
6. Set time to 30 minutes and temperature 325 F then press START.
7. The air fryer display will prompt you to ADD FOOD once the temperature is reached then place muffin molds in the air fryer basket.
8. Serve and enjoy.

Nutritional Value (Amount per Serving):
Calories 89; Fat 7 g; Carbohydrates 3.8 g; Sugar 1.2 g; Protein 3.7 g; Cholesterol 59 mg

Chocolate Cheese Brownies

Preparation Time: 10 minutes; Cooking Time: 20 minutes; Serve: 12

Ingredients:
- 6 eggs
- 1/2 tsp baking powder
- 2/3 cup unsweetened cocoa powder
- 1 1/2 sticks butter, melted
- 4 tbsp Erythritol
- 4 oz cream cheese, softened
- 2 tsp vanilla

Directions:
1. Add all ingredients into the mixing bowl and beat until smooth.
2. Pour mixture into the greased square baking dish.
3. Select Bake mode.
4. Set time to 20 minutes and temperature 350 F then press START.
5. The air fryer display will prompt you to ADD FOOD once the temperature is reached then place the baking dish in the air fryer basket.
6. Slice and serve.

Nutritional Value (Amount per Serving):
Calories 179; Fat 17.6 g; Carbohydrates 3.2 g; Sugar 0.4 g; Protein 4.5 g; Cholesterol 123 mg

Chocolate Macaroon

Preparation Time: 10 minutes; Cooking Time: 20 minutes; Serve: 20

Ingredients:
- 2 eggs
- 1/4 cup unsweetened cocoa powder
- 3 tbsp coconut flour
- 1 cup almond flour
- 1/3 cup unsweetened coconut, shredded
- 1/3 cup Swerve
- 1 tsp vanilla
- 1/4 cup coconut oil
- 1/2 tsp baking powder
- Pinch of salt

Directions:
1. Add all ingredients into the mixing bowl and mix until well combined.
2. Make small balls from the mixture.
3. Place the cooking tray in the air fryer basket. Line air fryer basket with parchment paper.
4. Select Bake mode.
5. Set time to 20 minutes and temperature 350 F then press START.
6. The air fryer display will prompt you to ADD FOOD once the temperature is reached then place prepared balls onto the parchment paper in the air fryer basket.
7. Serve and enjoy.

Nutritional Value (Amount per Serving):

Calories 55; Fat 4.8 g; Carbohydrates 2.4 g; Sugar 0.4 g; Protein 1.4 g; Cholesterol 16 mg

Easy Chocolate Cake

Preparation Time: 10 minutes; Cooking Time: 30 minutes; Serve: 12
Ingredients:
- 6 eggs
- 10 oz butter, melted
- 10 oz unsweetened chocolate, melted
- 1 1/4 cup Swerve
- 1/2 cup almond flour
- Pinch of salt

Directions:
1. Add eggs into the large bowl and beat until foamy. Add sweetener and stir well.
2. Add melted butter, chocolate, almond flour, and salt and stir to combine.
3. Pour batter into the greased baking dish.
4. Select Bake mode.
5. Set time to 30 minutes and temperature 350 F then press START.
6. The air fryer display will prompt you to ADD FOOD once the temperature is reached then place the baking dish in the air fryer basket.
7. Slice and serve.

Nutritional Value (Amount per Serving):
Calories 326; Fat 34.3 g; Carbohydrates 7.7 g; Sugar 0.4 g; Protein 6.3 g; Cholesterol 133 mg

Cheesecake Muffins

Preparation Time: 10 minutes; Cooking Time: 20 minutes; Serve: 12
Ingredients:
- 2 eggs
- 1/2 cup Swerve
- 16 oz cream cheese
- 1/2 tsp vanilla
- 6 tbsp unsweetened cocoa powder

Directions:
1. In a bowl, beat cream cheese until smooth.
2. Add remaining ingredients and beat until well combined.
3. Spoon mixture into the silicone muffin molds.
4. Select Bake mode.
5. Set time to 20 minutes and temperature 350 F then press START.
6. The air fryer display will prompt you to ADD FOOD once the temperature is reached then place muffin molds in the air fryer basket.
7. Serve and enjoy.

Nutritional Value (Amount per Serving):
Calories 149; Fat 14.3 g; Carbohydrates 2.6 g; Sugar 0.2 g; Protein 4.3 g; Cholesterol 69 mg

Choco Protein Brownie

Preparation Time: 10 minutes; Cooking Time: 15 minutes; Serve: 8
Ingredients:
- 4 egg whites
- 2 scoops chocolate protein powder
- 3 tbsp unsweetened cocoa powder
- 1/4 cup Erythritol
- 1/4 cup almond flour
- 1/2 tsp vanilla
- 3 tbsp coconut butter, melted
- 1/4 tsp salt

Directions:
1. In a medium bowl, mix together dry ingredients.
2. Add egg whites, vanilla, and melted coconut butter into the mixing bowl and beat until smooth.
3. Add dry mixture into the egg white mixture and mix until well combined.

4. Pour batter into the greased baking dish.
5. Select Bake mode.
6. Set time to 15 minutes and temperature 300 F then press START.
7. The air fryer display will prompt you to ADD FOOD once the temperature is reached then place the baking dish in the air fryer basket.
8. Slice and serve.

Nutritional Value (Amount per Serving):
Calories 116; Fat 8.8 g; Carbohydrates 4.9 g; Sugar 1.2 g; Protein 5.6 g; Cholesterol 5 mg

Vanilla Butter Cookies

Preparation Time: 10 minutes; Cooking Time: 10 minutes; Serve: 10
Ingredients:
- 1 cup almond flour
- 3 tbsp butter, softened
- 1/2 tsp vanilla
- 1/4 cup Swerve

Directions:
1. Add all ingredients into the mixing bowl and mix until well combined.
2. Make 1-inch balls from the mixture.
3. Place the cooking tray in the air fryer basket. Line air fryer basket with parchment paper.
4. Select Bake mode.
5. Set time to 10 minutes and temperature 350 F then press START.
6. The air fryer display will prompt you to ADD FOOD once the temperature is reached then place cookies onto the parchment paper in the air fryer basket.
7. Serve and enjoy.

Nutritional Value (Amount per Serving):
Calories 47; Fat 4.9 g; Carbohydrates 0.7 g; Sugar 0.1 g; Protein 0.6 g; Cholesterol 9 mg

Sliced Apples

Preparation Time: 10 minutes; Cooking Time: 10 minutes; Serve: 6
Ingredients:
- 4 small apples, sliced
- 1/2 cup Swerve
- 2 tbsp coconut oil, melted
- 1 tsp apple pie spice

Directions:
1. Add apple slices in a bowl and sprinkle sweetener, apple pie spice, and coconut oil over apple and toss to coat.
2. Transfer apple slices in the baking dish.
3. Select Air Fry mode.
4. Set time to 10 minutes and temperature 350 F then press START.
5. The air fryer display will prompt you to ADD FOOD once the temperature is reached then place the baking dish in the air fryer basket.
6. Serve and enjoy.

Nutritional Value (Amount per Serving):
Calories 59; Fat 4.6 g; Carbohydrates 4.7 g; Sugar 3.1 g; Protein 0 g; Cholesterol 0 mg

Orange Muffins

Preparation Time: 10 minutes; Cooking Time: 15 minutes; Serve: 12
Ingredients:
- 4 eggs
- 1 orange zest
- 1 orange juice
- 3 cups almond flour
- 1 tsp baking soda
- 1/2 cup butter, melted

Directions:

1. Add all ingredients into the mixing bowl and mix until well combined.
2. Pour mixture into the silicone muffin molds.
3. Select Bake mode.
4. Set time to 20 minutes and temperature 350 F then press START.
5. The air fryer display will prompt you to ADD FOOD once the temperature is reached then place muffin molds in the air fryer basket.
6. Serve and enjoy.

Nutritional Value (Amount per Serving):
Calories 133; Fat 12.6 g; Carbohydrates 2.5 g; Sugar 1 g; Protein 3.5 g; Cholesterol 75 mg

Raspberry Cobbler

Preparation Time: 10 minutes; Cooking Time: 10 minutes; Serve: 6
Ingredients:
- 1 egg, lightly beaten
- 1 cup raspberries, sliced
- 1 tbsp butter, melted
- 1 cup almond flour
- 2 tsp swerve
- 1/2 tsp vanilla

Directions:
1. Add sliced raspberries into the air fryer baking dish. Sprinkle sweetener over berries.
2. Mix together almond flour, vanilla, and butter in the bowl.
3. Add egg in almond flour mixture and stir to combine.
4. Spread almond flour mixture over sliced berries. Cover dish with foil.
5. Select Bake mode.
6. Set time to 10 minutes and temperature 350 F then press START.
7. The air fryer display will prompt you to ADD FOOD once the temperature is reached then place the baking dish in the air fryer basket.
8. Serve and enjoy.

Nutritional Value (Amount per Serving):
Calories 67; Fat 5.1 g; Carbohydrates 4.2 g; Sugar 1.2 g; Protein 2.2 g; Cholesterol 32 mg

Brownie Bites

Preparation Time: 10 minutes; Cooking Time: 20 minutes; Serve: 12
Ingredients:
- 6 eggs
- 1/4 cup walnuts, chopped
- 4 tbsp Swerve
- 1/4 cup pecans, chopped
- 1/2 tsp baking powder
- 2 oz unsweetened cocoa powder
- 5 oz butter, melted
- 4 oz cream cheese
- 2 tsp vanilla

Directions:
1. Add all ingredients except nuts into the mixing bowl and beat until smooth.
2. Add nuts and stir well.
3. Pour batter into the greased baking dish.
4. Select Bake mode.
5. Set time to 20 minutes and temperature 350 F then press START.
6. The air fryer display will prompt you to ADD FOOD once the temperature is reached then place the baking dish in the air fryer basket.
7. Slice and serve.

Nutritional Value (Amount per Serving):
Calories 194; Fat 18.7 g; Carbohydrates 4.4 g; Sugar 0.5 g; Protein 5.4 g; Cholesterol 118 mg

Chapter 11: 30-Day Meal Plan

Day 1
Breakfast-Cheese Egg Quiche
Lunch-Healthy Chicken Tenders
Dinner-Pecan Dijon Pork Chops

Day 2
Breakfast-Savory Breakfast Casserole
Lunch-Healthy Roasted Vegetables
Dinner-Simple Baked Chicken Breast

Day 3
Breakfast-Egg Chorizo Casserole
Lunch-Sweet & Tangy Chicken
Dinner-Simple & Juicy Steak

Day 4
Breakfast-Zucchini Spinach Egg Casserole
Lunch-Garlic Herb Turkey Breast
Dinner-Moist & Juicy Baked Cod

Day 5
Breakfast-Sausage Egg Omelet
Lunch-Garlic Butter Fish Fillets
Dinner-Mayo Cheese Crust Salmon

Day 6
Breakfast-Ham Cheese Casserole
Lunch-Flavorful Tuna Steaks
Dinner-Baked Chicken Thighs

Day 7
Breakfast-Cheese Ham Egg Muffins
Lunch-Old Bay Cauliflower Florets
Dinner-Juicy Baked Halibut

Day 8
Breakfast-Crustless Cheese Egg Quiche
Lunch-Baked Tilapia
Dinner-Marinated Ribeye Steaks

Day 9
Breakfast-Perfect Baked Omelet
Lunch-Mushrooms Cauliflower Roast
Dinner-Italian Turkey Tenderloin

Day 10
Breakfast-Veggie Egg Casserole
Lunch-Baked Parmesan Tilapia
Dinner-Baked Mahi Mahi

Day 11
Breakfast-Broccoli Casserole
Lunch-Pecan Crusted Fish Fillets
Dinner-Baked Basa

Day 12
Breakfast-Delicious Zucchini Frittata
Lunch-Roasted Cauliflower Cherry Tomatoes
Dinner-Herb Pork Chops

Day 13
Breakfast-Cheesy Zucchini Quiche
Lunch-Cauliflower Chicken Casserole
Dinner-Pesto Parmesan Chicken

Day 14
Breakfast-Spinach Sausage Egg Muffins
Lunch-Bagel Crust Fish Fillets
Dinner-Old Bay Baked Cod

Day 15
Breakfast-Cheese Pepper Egg Bake
Lunch-Flavorful Greek Chicken
Dinner-Air Fried Pork Bites

Day 16
Breakfast-Simple & Easy Breakfast Quiche
Lunch-Parmesan Eggplant Zucchini
Dinner-Lemon Chicken Breasts

Day 17
Breakfast-Spinach Sausage Egg Muffins
Lunch-Bagel Crust Fish Fillets
Dinner-Air Fried Pork Bites
Day 18
Breakfast-Cheesy Zucchini Quiche
Lunch-Cauliflower Chicken Casserole
Dinner-Old Bay Baked Cod
Day 19
Breakfast-Delicious Zucchini Frittata
Lunch-Roasted Cauliflower Cherry Tomatoes
Dinner-Pesto Parmesan Chicken
Day 20
Breakfast-Broccoli Casserole
Lunch-Pecan Crusted Fish Fillets
Dinner-Herb Pork Chops
Day 21
Breakfast-Veggie Egg Casserole
Lunch-Baked Parmesan Tilapia
Dinner-Baked Basa
Day 22
Breakfast-Perfect Baked Omelet
Lunch-Mushrooms Cauliflower Roast
Dinner-Baked Mahi Mahi
Day 23
Breakfast-Crustless Cheese Egg Quiche
Lunch-Baked Tilapia
Dinner-Italian Turkey Tenderloin

Day 24
Breakfast-Cheese Ham Egg Muffins
Lunch-Old Bay Cauliflower Florets
Dinner-Marinated Ribeye Steaks
Day 25
Breakfast-Ham Cheese Casserole
Lunch-Flavorful Tuna Steaks
Dinner-Juicy Baked Halibut
Day 26
Breakfast-Sausage Egg Omelet
Lunch-Garlic Butter Fish Fillets
Dinner-Baked Chicken Thighs
Day 27
Breakfast-Zucchini Spinach Egg Casserole
Lunch-Garlic Herb Turkey Breast
Dinner-Mayo Cheese Crust Salmon
Day 28
Breakfast-Egg Chorizo Casserole
Lunch-Sweet & Tangy Chicken
Dinner-Moist & Juicy Baked Cod
Day 29
Breakfast-Savory Breakfast Casserole
Lunch-Healthy Roasted Vegetables
Dinner-Simple & Juicy Steak
Day 30
Breakfast-Cheese Egg Quiche
Lunch-Healthy Chicken Tenders
Dinner-Simple Baked Chicken Breast

Conclusion

In this book, I have introduced you with a healthy and nutritious diet plan is a combination of healthy air fryer cooking methods. The book contains information about the keto diet with healthier keto recipes. Keto is basically a low-carb high fat diet that allows a moderate amount of protein intake during the diet.

The book contains different types of healthy keto recipes from breakfast to desserts. All the recipes are made into instant vortex plus 6 in 1 air fryer. An instant vortex air fryer is equipped with advanced technology and comes with 6 built-in smart functions like Air fry, bake, broil. Roast, reheat and dehydrate, etc.

All the recipes written in this book are well balanced in a calorie which helps you to keep your carb level under control. All recipes written in this book comes with their exact nutritional values.

www.ingramcontent.com/pod-product-compliance
Lightning Source LLC
Chambersburg PA
CBHW081357070526
44583CB00020B/2579